Birnbaum's 94
Los Angeles

A BIRNBAUM TRAVEL GUIDE

Alexandra Mayes Birnbaum
EDITORIAL CONSULTANT

Lois Spritzer
Executive Editor

Laura L. Brengelman
Managing Editor

Mary Callahan
Senior Editor

Patricia Canole
Gene Gold
Jill Kadetsky
Susan McClung
Beth Schlau
Associate Editors

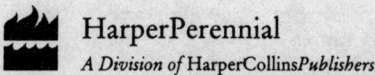

HarperPerennial
A Division of HarperCollinsPublishers

To Stephen, who merely made all this possible.

BIRNBAUM'S LOS ANGELES 94. Copyright © 1993 by HarperCollins Publishers. All rights reserved. Printed in the United States of America. No part of this book may be used or reproduced in any manner whatsoever without written permission except in the case of brief quotations embodied in critical articles and reviews. For information address HarperCollinsPublishers, 10 East 53rd Street, New York, NY 10022.

FIRST EDITION

ISSN 0749-2561 (Birnbaum Travel Guides)
ISSN 1056-4462 (Los Angeles)
ISBN 0-06-278135-9 (pbk.)

94 95 96 97 CC/CW 10 9 8 7 6 5 4 3 2 1

Cover design © Drenttel Doyle Partners
Cover photograph © Kathleen Campbell/AllStock

BIRNBAUM TRAVEL GUIDES

Bahamas, and Turks & Caicos
Berlin
Bermuda
Boston
Canada
Cancun, Cozumel & Isla Mujeres
Caribbean
Chicago
Disneyland
Eastern Europe
Europe
Europe for Business Travelers
France
Germany
Great Britain
Hawaii
Ireland
Italy
London
Los Angeles
Mexico
Miami & Ft. Lauderdale
Montreal & Quebec City
New Orleans
New York
Paris
Portugal
Rome
San Francisco
Santa Fe & Taos
South America
Spain
United States
USA for Business Travelers
Walt Disney World
Walt Disney World for Kids, By Kids
Washington, DC

Contributing Editors
Judith Krantz
Suzanne Lavenas
Patti Covello Pietschmann
Merrill Shindler
Tracy Smith
Melinda Tang

Maps
Mark Carlson
Susan Carlson

Contents

Foreword ... vii

How to Use This Guide ... 5

Getting Ready to Go

Practical information for planning your trip.

When to Go ... 9
Traveling by Plane ... 9
On Arrival ... 12
Package Tours ... 13
Insurance ... 15
Disabled Travelers ... 15
Single Travelers ... 18
Older Travelers ... 19
Money Matters ... 20
Time Zone ... 20
Business Hours ... 21
Mail ... 21
Telephone ... 21
Medical Aid ... 22
Legal Aid ... 23
For Further Information ... 23

The City

Thorough, qualitative guide to Los Angeles. Each section offers a comprehensive report on the city's most compelling attractions and amenities — highlighting our top choices in every category.

Specific Data About Los Angeles. ... 27

Diversions

A selective guide to a variety of unexpected pleasures, pinpointing the best places in which to pursue them.

Exceptional Experiences for the Mind and Body
Quintessential Los Angeles ... 91
Performing Arts ... 96

Audience Participation: Getting into the Act ... 98
Odditiеs, Insanities, and Just Plain Fun ... 100
Grave Matters ... 102
Spas ... 104
Best Beaches ... 107
Great Sailing and Cruising ... 109
Best Golf Outside the City ... 110
A Shutterbug's Los Angeles ... 110

Directions

Eight of the best tours in and around Los Angeles.

Introduction ... 117

Tour 1: Downtown ... 119
Tour 2: Melrose Avenue ... 125
Tour 3: Fairfax/Farmers' Market ... 131
Tour 4: Beverly Hills ... 135
Tour 5: Hollywood ... 141
Tour 6: Westwood ... 145
Tour 7: Beach Towns: South Bay Beaches — Manhattan, Hermosa, Redondo ... 149
Tour 8: Catalina ... 153

Index ... 157

Foreword

For dyed-in-the-wool New Yorkers like me, being mean to Los Angeles is almost a requirement, and the urge to growl about the nation's second city (sorry, Chicago) has grown over the last decade or so. New Yorkers of a certain age (me again) watched ungraciously as California overtook New York as the most populous state in the union, and seethed as expatriate East Coasters returned from new residences on the West Coast with reports of a lifestyle that's both stimulating and slush-free, albeit occasionally sociologically explosive. You could cut the envy with a knife!

Well, although it probably would be genetically impossible (something to do with a virulent strain of skyscraper syndrome) to actually consider Los Angeles as a potential residence, I'm forced to confess that the last few years have witnessed an exponential increase in the number of excuses I found to visit the City of Angels. To begin with, more and more friends have resettled beside the Pacific, so seeing them has required frequent hegiras to the warmth of Southern California. And once physically in the sway of the Pacific and the palm trees, it's hard to deny that the city has considerable appeal.

So this guide to Los Angeles is an attempt to demonstrate growing personal maturity and open-mindedness where Southern California is concerned. Just between us, it also provides a perfect excuse to spend a lot more time in LA.

Obviously, any guidebook to Los Angeles must keep pace with and answer the real needs of today's travelers. That's why we've tried to create a guide that's specifically organized, written, and edited for the more demanding modern traveler, one for whom qualitative information is infinitely more desirable than mere quantities of unappraised data. For years, dating back as far as Herr Baedeker, travel guides have tended to be encyclopedic, seemingly much more concerned with demonstrating expertise in geography and history than with a real analysis of the sorts of things that actually concern a typical modern tourist. Early on, we realized that giving up the encyclopedic approach precluded our listing every single route and restaurant, a realization that helped define our overall editorial focus. Similarly, when we discussed the possibility of presenting certain information in other than strict geographic order, we found that the new format enabled us to arrange data in a way that we feel best answers the questions travelers typically ask.

Travel guides are, understandably, reflections of personal taste, and putting one's name on a title page obviously puts one's preferences on the line. But I think I ought to amplify just what "personal" means. I don't believe in the sort of personal guidebook that's a palpable misrepresentation on its face. It is, for example, hardly possible for any single travel writer to visit thousands of restaurants (and nearly as many hotels) in any given year and provide accurate appraisals of each. And even if it were physically possible for one human being to survive such an itinerary, it would of necessity have to be done at a dead sprint, and the perceptions derived therefrom would probably be less valid than those of any other intelligent individual visiting the same establishments. It is, therefore, impossible (especially in a large, annually revised and updated guidebook *series* such as we offer) to have only one person provide all the data on the entire world.

I also happen to think that such individual orientation is of substantially less value to readers. Visiting a single hotel for just one night or eating one hasty meal in a random restaurant hardly equips anyone to provide appraisals that are of more than passing interest. We have, therefore, chosen what I like to describe as the "thee and me" approach to restaurant and hotel evaluation and, to a somewhat more limited degree, to the sites and sights we have included in the other sections of our text. What this really reflects is a personal sampling tempered by intelligent counsel from informed local sources, and these additional friends-of-the-editor are almost always residents of the city and/or area about which they are consulted.

In addition, very precise editing and tailoring keep our text fiercely subjective. So what follows is the gospel according to Birnbaum, and it represents as much of our own taste and instincts as we can manage. It is probable, therefore, that if you like your cities stylish and prefer small hotels with personality to huge high-rise anonymities, we're likely to have a long and meaningful relationship.

I also should point out something about the person to whom this guidebook is directed. Above all, he or she is a "visitor." This means that such elements as restaurants have been specifically picked to provide the visitor with a representative, enlightening, stimulating, and above all pleasant experience. Since so many extraneous considerations can affect the reception and service accorded a regular restaurant patron, our choices can in no way be construed as an exhaustive guide to resident dining. We think we've listed all the best places, in various price ranges, but they were chosen with a visitor's enjoyment in mind.

Other evidence of how we've tried to tailor our text to reflect modern travel habits is most apparent in the section we call DIVERSIONS. Where once it was common for travelers to spend an urban visit seeing only the obvious sights, the emphasis today is more likely to be directed toward pursuing some special interest. Therefore, we have collected these exceptional experiences so that it is no longer necessary to wade through a pound or two of superfluous prose just to find unexpected pleasures and treasures.

Finally, I also should point out that every good travel guide is a living enterprise; that is, no part of this text is carved in stone. In our annual revisions, we refine, expand, and further hone all our material to serve your travel needs better. To this end, no contribution is of greater value to us than your personal reaction to what we have written, as well as information reflecting your own experiences while using the book. Please write to us at 10 E. 53rd St., New York, NY 10022.

We sincerely hope to hear from you.

Alexandra Mayes Birnbaum

ALEXANDRA MAYES BIRNBAUM, editorial consultant to the *Birnbaum Travel Guides*, worked with her late husband Stephen Birnbaum as co-editor of the series. She has been a world traveler since childhood and is known for her lively travel reports on radio on what's hot and what's not.

Los Angeles

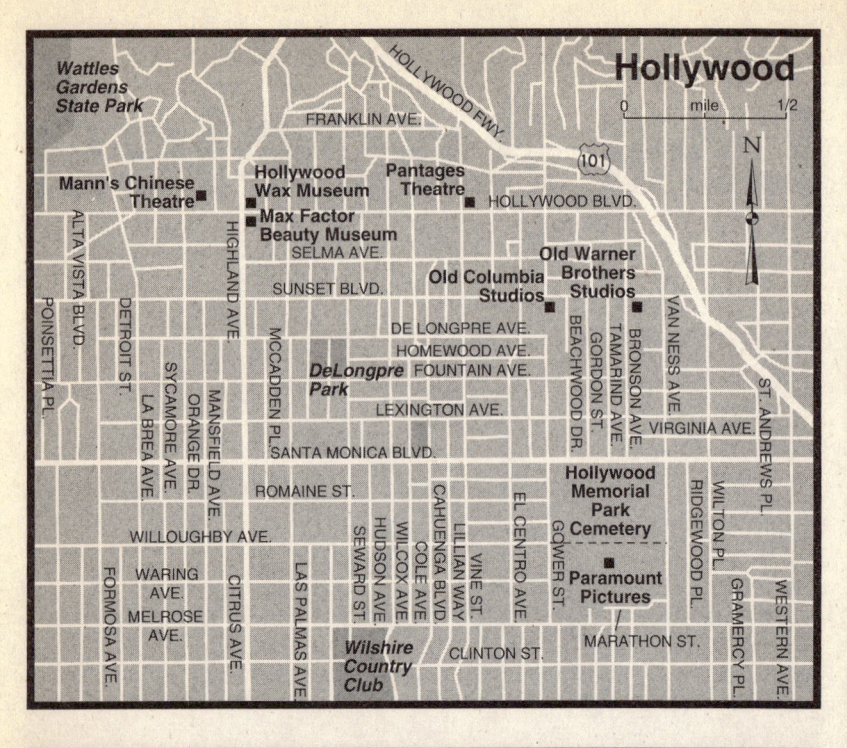

Hollywood

0 — mile — 1/2

- Wattles Gardens State Park
- HOLLYWOOD FWY.
- FRANKLIN AVE.
- 101
- Mann's Chinese Theatre
- Hollywood Wax Museum
- Pantages Theatre
- HOLLYWOOD BLVD.
- Max Factor Beauty Museum
- SELMA AVE.
- Old Columbia Studios
- Old Warner Brothers Studios
- SUNSET BLVD.
- DE LONGPRE AVE.
- HOMEWOOD AVE.
- DeLongpre Park
- FOUNTAIN AVE.
- LEXINGTON AVE.
- SANTA MONICA BLVD.
- ROMAINE ST.
- Hollywood Memorial Park Cemetery
- WILLOUGHBY AVE.
- WARING AVE.
- MELROSE AVE.
- Paramount Pictures
- CLINTON ST.
- MARATHON ST.
- Wilshire Country Club

Streets (Hollywood): ALTA VISTA BLVD., POINSETTIA PL., DETROIT ST., LA BREA AVE., SYCAMORE AVE., ORANGE DR., MANSFIELD AVE., HIGHLAND AVE., McCADDEN PL., LAS PALMAS AVE., CITRUS AVE., FORMOSA AVE., SEWARD ST., HUDSON AVE., WILCOX AVE., COLE AVE., CAHUENGA BLVD., LILLIAN WAY, VINE ST., EL CENTRO AVE., GOWER ST., BEACHWOOD DR., TAMARIND AVE., GORDON ST., BRONSON AVE., VAN NESS AVE., RIDGEWOOD PL., WILTON PL., VIRGINIA AVE., ST. ANDREWS PL., GRAMERCY PL., WESTERN AVE.

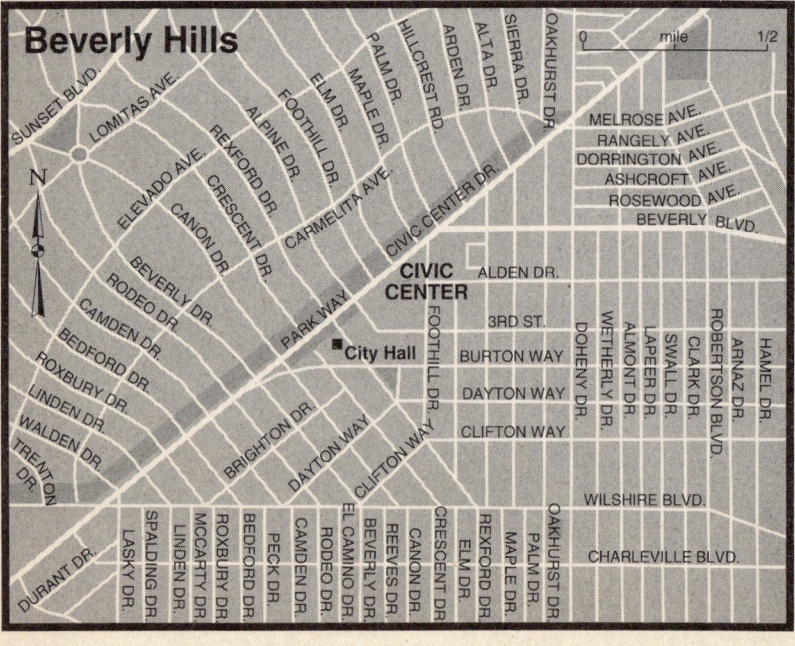

Beverly Hills

0 — mile — 1/2

- SUNSET BLVD.
- LOMITAS AVE.
- MELROSE AVE.
- RANGELY AVE.
- DORRINGTON AVE.
- ASHCROFT AVE.
- ROSEWOOD AVE.
- BEVERLY BLVD.
- CIVIC CENTER
- ALDEN DR.
- City Hall
- 3RD ST.
- BURTON WAY
- DAYTON WAY
- CLIFTON WAY
- PARK WAY
- CARMELITA AVE.
- CIVIC CENTER DR.
- WILSHIRE BLVD.
- CHARLEVILLE BLVD.

Streets (Beverly Hills): ELEVADO AVE., CANON DR., BEVERLY DR., RODEO DR., CAMDEN DR., BEDFORD DR., ROXBURY DR., LINDEN DR., WALDEN DR., TRENTON DR., CRESCENT DR., REXFORD DR., ALPINE DR., FOOTHILL DR., ELM DR., MAPLE DR., PALM DR., HILLCREST RD., ARDEN DR., ALTA DR., SIERRA DR., OAKHURST DR., DOHENY DR., WETHERLY DR., ALMONT DR., LAPEER DR., SWALL DR., CLARK DR., ROBERTSON BLVD., ARNAZ DR., HAMEL DR., BRIGHTON DR., DURANT DR., LASKY DR., SPALDING DR., McCARTY DR., ROXBURY DR., LINDEN DR., BEDFORD DR., PECK DR., CAMDEN DR., RODEO DR., EL CAMINO DR., BEVERLY DR., REEVES DR., CANON DR., CRESCENT DR., REXFORD DR., ELM DR., MAPLE DR., PALM DR., OAKHURST DR.

How to Use This Guide

A great deal of care has gone into the special organization of this guidebook, and we believe it represents a real breakthrough in the presentation of travel material.

Our text is divided into four basic sections in order to present information in the best way on every possible aspect of a vacation to Los Angeles. Our aim is to highlight what's where and to provide basic information — how, when, where, how much, and what's best — to assist you in making the most intelligent choices possible.

Here is a brief summary of what you can expect to find in each section. We believe that you will find both your travel planning and en route enjoyment enhanced by having this book at your side.

GETTING READY TO GO

A mini-encyclopedia of practical travel facts with all the precise data necessary to create a successful trip to Los Angeles. Here you will find how to get where you're going, plus selected resources — including useful publications, and companies and organizations specializing in discount and special-interest travel — providing a wealth of information and assistance useful both before and during your trip.

THE CITY

Our individual report on Los Angeles offers a short-stay guide, including an essay introducing the city as a historic entity and a contemporary place to visit; *At-a-Glance* material is actually a site-by-site survey of the most important, interesting, and sometimes most eclectic sights to see and things to do; *Sources and Resources* is a concise listing of pertinent tourist information, such as the address of the local tourist office, which sightseeing tours to take, where to find the best nightspot or hail a taxi, which are the shops which have the finest merchandise and/or the most irresistible bargains, and where the best museums and theaters are to be found. *Best in Town* lists our choices of the best places to eat and sleep on a variety of budgets.

DIVERSIONS

This section is designed to help travelers find the best places in which to engage in a variety of exceptional — and unexpected — experiences, without having to wade through endless pages of unrelated text.

In each case, our particular suggestions are intended to guide you to that special place where the quality of experience is likely to be highest.

DIRECTIONS

Here are eight tours that cover the city, along its main thoroughfares and side streets, past its most spectacular landmarks and most breathtaking sites, plus a tour of nearby Catalina Island.

To use this book to full advantage, take a few minutes to read the table of contents and random entries in each section to get a firsthand feel for how it all fits together. You will find that the sections of this book are building blocks designed to help you put together the best possible trip. Use them selectively as a tool, a source of ideas, a reference work for accurate facts, and a guidebook to the best buys, the most exciting sights, the most pleasant accommodations, the tastiest foods — *the best travel experience* that you can possibly have in Los Angeles.

Getting Ready to Go

When to Go

There isn't really a best time to visit Los Angeles, since it enjoys perpetual spring-like weather and sunshine in abundant supply. There are good reasons for visiting Los Angeles any time of the year. There are no real off-season periods when attractions are closed, and prices stay pretty much within the same range year-round. If anything, hotel room bargains are available on weekends, when business travel is slow, rather than during any particular season of the year.

The *Weather Channel* (2600 Cumberland Pkwy., Atlanta, GA 30339; phone: 404-434-6800) provides current weather forecasts — call 900-WEATHER from any touch-tone phone in the US; the 95¢ per-minute charge will appear on your phone bill.

Traveling by Plane

SCHEDULED FLIGHTS

Leading airlines offering flights to **Los Angeles International Airport (LAX)** include *America West, American, American Eagle, Continental, Delta, Delta Connection, Midwest Express, Northwest, Northwest Airlink, Southwest, TWA, United, USAir,* and *USAir Express.*

FARES The great variety of airfares can be reduced to the following basic categories: first class, business class, coach (also called economy or tourist class), excursion or discount, and standby, as well as various promotional fares. For information on applicable fares and restrictions, contact the airlines listed above or ask your travel agent. Most airfares are offered for a limited time period. Once you've found the lowest fare for which you can qualify, purchase your ticket as soon as possible.

RESERVATIONS Reconfirmation is not generally required on domestic flights, although it is wise to call ahead to make sure that the airline has your reservation and any special requests in its computer.

SEATING Airline seats usually are assigned on a first-come, first-served basis at check-in, although you may be able to reserve a seat when purchasing your ticket. Seating charts, which make choosing a seat easier, often are available from airlines and are included in the *Airline Seating Guide* (Carlson Publishing Co., PO Box 888, Los Alamitos, CA 90720; phone: 310-493-4877).

SMOKING US law prohibits smoking on flights scheduled for 6 hours or less within the US and its territories on both domestic and international carriers. A free wallet-size guide that describes the rights of nonsmokers is available from *ASH (Action on Smoking and Health;* DOT Card, 2013 H St. NW, Washington, DC 20006; phone: 202-659-4310).

SPECIAL MEALS When making your reservation, you can request one of the airline's alternate menu choices for no additional charge. Call to reconfirm your request 24 hours before departure.

BAGGAGE On a major airline, passengers usually are allowed to carry on board one bag that will fit under a seat or in an overhead bin. Passengers also can check two bags in the cargo hold, measuring 62 inches and 55 inches in combined dimensions (length, width, and depth) with a per-bag weight limit of 70 pounds. There may be charges for additional, oversize, or overweight luggage, and for special equipment or sporting gear. Note that baggage allowances may vary for children (depending on the percentage of full adult fare paid). Check that the tags the airline attaches are correctly coded for your destination.

CHARTER FLIGHTS

By booking a block of seats on a specially arranged flight, charter operators frequently offer travelers bargain airfares. If you do fly on a charter, however, read the contract's fine print carefully. Charter operators can cancel a flight or assess surcharges of 10% of the airfare up to 10 days before departure. You usually must book in advance (no changes are permitted, so invest in trip cancellation insurance); also make your check out to the company's escrow account. For further information, consult the publication *Jax Fax* (397 Post Rd., Darien, CT 06820; phone: 203-655-8746).

DISCOUNTS ON SCHEDULED FLIGHTS

COURIER TRAVEL In return for arranging to accompany some kind of freight, a traveler may pay only a portion of the total airfare and a small registration fee. One agency that matches up would-be couriers with courier companies is *Now Voyager* (74 Varick St., Suite 307, New York, NY 10013; phone: 212-431-1616).

Courier Companies

Courier Travel Service (530 Central Ave., Cedarhurst, NY 11516; phone: 516-763-6898).

Discount Travel International (169 W. 81st St., New York, NY 10024; phone: 212-362-3636; and 940 10th St., Suite 2, Miami Beach, FL 33139; phone: 305-538-1616).

Excaliber International Courier (c/o *Way to Go Travel,* 6679 Sunset Blvd., Hollywood, CA 90028; phone: 213-466-1126).

F.B. On Board Courier Services (10225 Ryan Ave., Suite 103, Dorval, Quebec H9P 1A2, Canada; phone: 514-633-0740).

Halbart Express (147-05 176th St., Jamaica, NY 11434; phone: 718-656-8279).

International Adventures (60 E. 42nd St., New York, NY 10165; phone: 212-599-0577).

Midnight Express (925 W. High Park Blvd., Inglewood, CA 90302; phone: 310-672-1100).

Publications
Insider's Guide to Air Courier Bargains, by Kelly Monaghan (The Intrepid Traveler; PO Box 438, New York, NY 10034; phone: 212-304-2207).
Travel Secrets (PO Box 2325, New York, NY 10108; phone: 212-245-8703).
Travel Unlimited (PO Box 1058, Allston, MA 02134-1058; no phone).
World Courier News (PO Box 77471, San Francisco, CA 94107; no phone).

CONSOLIDATORS AND BUCKET SHOPS These companies buy blocks of tickets from airlines and sell them at a discount to travel agents or to consumers. Since many bucket shops operate on a thin margin, before parting with any money check the company's record with the Better Business Bureau.

Bargain Air (655 Deep Valley Dr., Suite 355, Rolling Hills, CA 90274; phone: 800-347-2345).
Council Charter (205 E. 42nd St., New York, NY 10017; phone: 800-800-8222 or 212-661-0311).
International Adventures (60 E. 42nd St., New York, NY 10165; phone: 212-599-0577).
Travac Tours and Charters (989 Ave. of the Americas, New York, NY 10018; phone: 800-872-8800 or 212-563-3303).
Unitravel (1177 N. Warson Rd., St. Louis, MO 63132; phone: 800-325-2222 or 314-569-0900).

LAST-MINUTE TRAVEL CLUBS For an annual fee, members receive information on imminent trips and other bargain travel opportunities. Despite the names of these clubs, you don't have to wait until literally the last minute to make travel plans.

Discount Travel International (114 Forest Ave., Suite 203, Narberth, PA 19072; phone: 215-668-7184).
Last Minute Travel (1249 Boylston St., Boston, MA 02215; phone: 800-LAST-MIN or 617-267-9800).
Moment's Notice (425 Madison Ave., New York, NY 10017; phone: 212-486-0500, -0501, -0502, or -0503).
Spur-of-the-Moment Cruises (411 N. Harbor Blvd., Suite 302, San Pedro, CA 90731; phone: 800-4-CRUISES in California; 800-343-1991 elsewhere in the US; or 310-521-1070).
Traveler's Advantage (3033 S. Parker Rd., Suite 900, Aurora, CO 80014; phone: 800-548-1116 or 800-835-8747).
Vacations to Go (1502 Augusta, Suite 415, Houston, TX 77057; phone: 713-974-2121 in Texas; 800-338-4962 elsewhere in the US).

Worldwide Discount Travel Club (1674 Meridian Ave., Miami Beach, FL 33139; phone: 305-534-2082).

GENERIC AIR TRAVEL These organizations operate much like an ordinary airline standby service, except that they offer seats on not one but several scheduled and charter airlines. One pioneer of generic flights is *Airhitch* (2790 Broadway, Suite 100, New York, NY 10025; phone: 212-864-2000).

BARTERED TRAVEL SOURCES Barter is a common means of exchange between travel suppliers. Bartered travel clubs such as *Travel World Leisure Club* (225 W. 34th St., Suite 909, New York, NY 10122; phone: 800-444-TWLC or 212-239-4855) offer discounts to members for an annual fee.

CONSUMER PROTECTION

Passengers with complaints who are not satisfied with the airline's response can contact the US Department of Transportation (DOT; Consumer Affairs Division, 400 7th St. SW, Room 10405, Washington, DC 20590; phone: 202-366-2220). Also see *Fly Rights* (Publication #050-000-00513-5; US Government Printing Office, PO Box 371954, Pittsburgh, PA 15250-7954; phone: 202-783-3238).

On Arrival

FROM THE AIRPORT TO THE CITY

The drive downtown from **Los Angeles International Airport (LAX)** takes from 30 minutes to an hour, depending on traffic. Taxi fares run between $25 and $30.

The *Southern California Rapid Transit District* (phone: 310-273-0910) links LAX to downtown Los Angeles at Broadway and 6th Street; the trip takes about an hour and costs $1.10 ($1 bills accepted). Scheduled buses running to other parts of the city require one or more transfers; for information, call the *Metropolitan Transit Agency (MTA)* (phone: 310-273-0910 in Beverly Hills/west Los Angeles; 310-626-4455 in Hollywood/central Los Angeles; and 818-781-5890 in the San Fernando Valley).

A more efficient alternative is to use private transport companies, which can be called from the courtesy phones at the airport and are listed in the yellow pages. For instance, *Supershuttle* (phone: 213-775-6600 or 310-338-1111) offers van service between LAX and downtown hotels for $12 (more for Beverly Hills).

RENTING A CAR

You can rent a car through a travel agent or national rental firm before leaving home, or from a regional or local company once in Los Angeles. Reserve in advance.

Most car rental companies require a credit card, although some will accept a substantial cash deposit. The minimum age to rent a car is set by the company; some impose special conditions on drivers above a certain age. Electing to pay for collision damage waiver (CDW) protection will add to the cost of renting a car, but releases you from financial liability for the vehicle. Additional costs include drop-off charges or one-way service fees.

Car Rental Companies
Ace Rent-A-Car (phone: 800-230-2230).
Agency Rent-A-Car (phone: 800-321-1972).
Airways Rent-A-Car (phone: 800-952-9200).
Ajax Rent-A-Car (phone: 213-386-3363 or 310-278-0601).
Alamo (phone: 800-327-9633).
Avis (phone: 800-331-1084).
Bob Leech's Auto Rental (phone: 800-635-1240 or 310-673-2727).
Budget (phone: 800-472-3325).
Dollar Rent A Car (phone: 800-800-4000).
Enterprise Rent-A-Car (phone: 800-325-8007).
Hertz (phone: 800-654-3001).
National (phone: 800-227-3876).
Payless Car Rental (phone: 800-PAYLESS).
Rocket Rent-A-Car (phone: 213-380-4866 or 310-674-1820).
Sears Rent-A-Car (phone: 800-527-0770).
Thrifty Rent-A-Car (phone: 800-367-2277).

NOTE *Rent-A-Wreck* (phone: 310-478-0676) rents cars that are well worn but (presumably) mechanically sound. *LuxuryLine-Rent-A-Car* (phone: 800-826-7805 or 310-659-5555) and *Regency Exotic Car Rental* (phone: 310-337-7827) rent luxury models. For larger vehicles, try *MPG Car Van Truck Rental* (phone: 213-746-2421) and *El Monte RV Center* (phone: 800-367-3687 or 818-443-6158).

Package Tours

A package is a collection of travel services that can be purchased in a single transaction. Its principal advantages are convenience and economy — the cost is usually lower than that of the same services bought separately. Tour programs generally can be divided into two categories: escorted or locally hosted (with a set itinerary) and independent (usually more flexible).

When considering a package tour, read the brochure *carefully* to determine what is included and other conditions. Check the company's record with the Better Business Bureau. The *United States Tour Operators Association (USTOA;* 211 E. 51st St., Suite 12B, New York, NY 10022; phone: 212-944-5727) also can be helpful in determining a package tour operator's reliability. As with charter flights, always make your check out to the company's escrow account.

Many tour operators offer packages focused on special interests such as the arts, nature study, sports, and other recreations. *All Adventure Travel* (PO Box 4307, Boulder, CO 80306; phone: 800-537-4025 or 303-499-1981) represents such specialized packagers; some also are listed in the *Specialty Travel Index* (305 San Anselmo Ave., Suite 313, San Anselmo, CA 94960; phone: 415-459-4900 in California; 800-442-4922 elsewhere in the US). If you would like to add some additional organized touring, note that a number of companies offer 1-day (or shorter) guided tours of the city.

Package Tour Operators

Adventure Tours (9819 Liberty Rd., Randallstown, MD 21133; phone: 410-922-7000 in Baltimore; 800-638-9040 elsewhere in the US).

American Airlines FlyAAway Vacations (phone: 800-321-2121).

American Express Vacations (offices throughout the US; phone: 800-241-1700 or 404-368-5100).

Cartan Tours (2809 Butterfield Rd., Suite 350, Oak Brook, IL 60521; phone: 800-422-7826 or 708-571-1400).

Continental Grand Destinations (phone: 800-634-5555).

Dailey-Thorp (330 W. 58th St., New York, NY 10019-1817; phone: 212-307-1555).

Delta's Dream Vacations (phone: 800-872-7786).

Domenico Tours (751 Broadway, Bayonne, NJ 07002; phone: 800-544-8687 or 201-823-8687).

Funway Holidays Funjet (PO Box 1460, Milwaukee, WI 53201-1460; phone: 800-558-3050).

GoGo Tours (69 Spring St., Ramsey, NJ 07446-0507; phone: 201-934-3500).

Marathon Tours (108 Main St., Charlestown, MA 02129; phone: 800-783-0024 or 617-242-7845).

Mayflower (1225 Warren Ave., Downers Grove, IL 60515; phone: 800-323-7604 or 708-960-3430).

New England Vacation Tours (PO Box 560, West Dover, VT 05356; phone: 800-742-7669 or 802-464-2076).

Northwest World Vacations (phone: 800-727-1111).

Sunmakers (15375 SE 30th Pl., Suite 350, Bellevue, WA 98007; phone: 800-841-4321 or 206-643-8180).

SuperCities (11330 Blondo St., Omaha, NE 68164; phone: 800-333-1234 or 402-498-8234).

Tauck Tours (PO Box 5027, Westport, CT 06881; phone: 800-468-2825 for continental US; 203-226-6911 elsewhere).

Travel Tours International (250 W. 49th St., Suite 600, New York, NY 10019; phone: 800-767-8777 or 212-262-0700).

TWA Getaway Vacations (phone: 800-GETAWAY).

Companies Offering Shorter Tours

Casablanca Tours (*Hollywood Roosevelt Hotel,* 7000 Hollywood Blvd., Cabaña 4, Hollywood, CA 90028; phone: 213-461-0156).

Heli USA Helicopters (3200 Airport Ave., Suite 6, Santa Monica, CA 90405; phone: 310-553-4354).
Hollywood Fantasy Tours (6773 Hollywood Blvd., Hollywood, CA 90028; phone: 213-469-8184).
Los Angeles Conservancy Tours (727 W. 7th St., Suite 955, Los Angeles, CA 90017; phone: 213-623-2489).
Los Angeles Harbor Cruise (Village Boat House, Berth 78, Ports O' Call Village, San Pedro, CA 90731; phone: 310-831-0996).
Los Angeles Sightseeing Tours (2101 E. Washington Blvd., Los Angeles, CA 90021; phone: 213-748-3415).
Magic Line Sightseeing Tours (5322 Wilshire Blvd., Suite 710, Los Angeles, CA 90036; phone: 213-653-1090).
Starline/Gray Line Tours (6541 Hollywood Blvd., Los Angeles, CA 90028; phone: 213-856-5900).

Insurance

The first person with whom you should discuss travel insurance is your own insurance broker. You may discover that the insurance you already carry protects you adequately while traveling and that you need little additional coverage. If you charge travel services, the credit card company also may provide some insurance coverage (and other safeguards).

Types of Travel Insurance

Baggage and personal effects insurance: Protects your bags and their contents in case of damage or theft anytime during your travels.

Personal accident and sickness insurance: Covers cases of illness, injury, or death in an accident while traveling.

Trip cancellation and interruption insurance: Guarantees a refund if you must cancel a trip; may reimburse you for the extra travel costs incurred for catching up with a tour or traveling home early.

Default and/or bankruptcy insurance: Provides coverage in the event of default and/or bankruptcy on the part of the tour operator, airline, or other travel supplier.

Flight insurance: Covers accidental injury or death while flying.

Automobile insurance: Provides collision, theft, property damage, and personal liability protection while driving your own or a rented car.

Combination policies: Include any or all of the above.

Disabled Travelers

Make travel arrangements well in advance. Specify to all services involved the nature of your disability to determine if there are accommodations and facilities that meet your needs. For detailed information on accessibility, contact the *Junior League of Los Angeles* (at *Farmers' Market,* Third and Fairfax, Los Angeles, CA 90036; phone: 213-937-5566), which publishes *Around the Town with Ease.*

Organizations

ACCENT on Living (PO Box 700, Bloomington, IL 61702; phone: 309-378-2961).

Access: The Foundation for Accessibility by the Disabled (PO Box 356, Malverne, NY 11565; phone: 516-887-5798).

American Foundation for the Blind (15 W. 16th St., New York, NY 10011; phone: 800-232-5463 or 212-620-2147).

Information Center for Individuals with Disabilities (Ft. Point Pl., 1st Floor, 27-43 Wormwood St., Boston, MA 02210; phone: 800-462-5015 in Massachusetts; 617-727-5540 or 617-727-5541 elsewhere in the US; TDD: 617-345-9743).

Mobility International USA (*MIUSA;* PO Box 3551, Eugene, OR 97403; phone: 503-343-1284, both voice and TDD; main office: 228 Borough High St., London SE1 1JX, England; phone: 44-71-403-5688).

National Rehabilitation Information Center (8455 Colesville Rd., Suite 935, Silver Spring, MD 20910; phone: 301-588-9284).

Paralyzed Veterans of America (*PVA;* PVA/ATTS Program, 801 18th St. NW, Washington, DC 20006; phone: 202-872-1300 in Washington, DC; 800-424-8200 elsewhere in the US).

Partners of the Americas (1424 K St. NW, Suite 700, Washington, DC 20005; phone: 800-322-7844 or 202-628-3300).

Royal Association for Disability and Rehabilitation (*RADAR;* 25 Mortimer St., London W1N 8AB, England; phone: 44-71-637-5400).

Society for the Advancement of Travel for the Handicapped (*SATH;* 347 Fifth Ave., Suite 610, New York, NY 10016; phone: 212-447-7284).

Travel Information Service (MossRehab Hospital, 1200 W. Tabor Rd., Philadelphia, PA 19141-3099; phone: 215-456-9600; TDD: 215-456-9602).

Publications

Access Travel: A Guide to the Accessibility of Airport Terminals (Consumer Information Center, Dept. 578Z, Pueblo, CO 81009; phone: 719-948-3334).

Air Transportation of Handicapped Persons (Publication #AC-120-32; US Department of Transportation, Distribution Unit, Publications Section, M-443-2, 400 7th St. SW, Washington, DC 20590).

The Diabetic Traveler (PO Box 8223 RW, Stamford, CT 06905; phone: 203-327-5832).

Directory of Travel Agencies for the Disabled and *Travel for the Disabled,* both by Helen Hecker (Twin Peaks Press, PO Box 129, Vancouver, WA 98666; phone: 800-637-CALM or 206-694-2462).

Guide to Traveling with Arthritis (Upjohn Company, PO Box 989, Dearborn, MI 48121).

The Handicapped Driver's Mobility Guide (American Automobile Association, 1000 AAA Dr., Heathrow, FL 32746; phone: 407-444-7000).

Handicapped Travel Newsletter (PO Box 269, Athens, TX 75751; phone: 903-677-1260).

Handi-Travel: A Resource Book for Disabled and Elderly Travellers, by Cinnie Noble (*Canadian Rehabilitation Council for the Disabled,* 45 Sheppard Ave. E., Suite 801, Toronto, Ontario M2N 5W9, Canada; phone: 416-250-7490, both voice and TDD).

Incapacitated Passengers Air Travel Guide (*International Air Transport Association,* Publications Sales Department, 2000 Peel St., Montreal, Quebec H3A 2R4, Canada; phone: 514-844-6311).

Ticket to Safe Travel (*American Diabetes Association,* 1660 Duke St., Alexandria, VA 22314; phone: 800-232-3472 or 703-549-1500).

Travel for the Patient with Chronic Obstructive Pulmonary Disease (Dr. Harold Silver, 1601 18th St. NW, Washington, DC 20009; phone: 202-667-0134).

Travel Tips for Hearing-Impaired People (*American Academy of Otolaryngology,* 1 Prince St., Alexandria, VA 22314; phone: 703-836-4444).

Travel Tips for People with Arthritis (*Arthritis Foundation,* 1314 Spring St. NW, Atlanta, GA 30309; phone: 800-283-7800 or 404-872-7100).

Traveling Like Everybody Else: A Practical Guide for Disabled Travelers, by Jacqueline Freedman and Susan Gersten (Modan Publishing, PO Box 1202, Bellmore, NY 11710; phone: 516-679-1380).

The Wheelchair Traveler, by Douglass R. Annand (123 Ball Hill Rd., Milford, NH 03055; phone: 603-673-4539).

Package Tour Operators

Accessible Journeys (35 W. Sellers Ave., Ridley Park, PA 19078; phone: 215-521-0339).

Accessible Tours/Directions Unlimited (Lois Bonnani, 720 N. Bedford Rd., Bedford Hills, NY 10507; phone: 800-533-5343 or 914-241-1700).

Beehive Business and Leisure Travel (1130 W. Center St., N. Salt Lake, UT 84054; phone: 800-777-5727 or 801-292-4445).

Classic Travel Service (8 W. 40th St., New York, NY 10018; phone: 212-869-2560 in New York State; 800-247-0909 elsewhere in the US).

Evergreen Travel Service (4114 198th St. SW, Suite 13, Lynnwood, WA 98036-6742; phone: 800-435-2288 or 206-776-1184).

Flying Wheels Travel (143 W. Bridge St., PO Box 382, Owatonna, MN 55060; phone: 800-535-6790 or 507-451-5005).

Good Neighbor Travel Service (124 S. Main St., Viroqua, WI 54665; phone: 608-637-2128).

The Guided Tour (7900 Old York Rd., Suite 114B, Elkins Park, PA 19117-2339; phone: 800-783-5841 or 215-782-1370).

Hinsdale Travel (201 E. Ogden Ave., Hinsdale, IL 60521; phone: 708-325-1335 or 708-469-7349).

MedEscort International (ABE International Airport, PO Box 8766, Allentown, PA 18105; phone: 800-255-7182 or 215-791-3111).

Prestige World Travel (5710-X High Point Rd., Greensboro, NC 27407; phone: 800-476-7737 or 919-292-6690).
Sprout (893 Amsterdam Ave., New York, NY 10025; phone: 212-222-9575).
Weston Travel Agency (134 N. Cass Ave., PO Box 1050, Westmont, IL 60559; phone: 708-968-2513 in Illinois; 800-633-3725 elsewhere in the US).

NOTE **Wheelchair Getaways (24252 Tahoe Court, Laguna Niguel, CA 92656; phone: 800-659-1972 or 714-831-1972) rents vans designed to accommodate wheelchairs.**

Single Travelers

The travel industry is not very fair to people who vacation by themselves—they often end up paying more than those traveling in pairs. Services catering to singles match travel companions, offer travel arrangements with shared accommodations, and provide useful information and discounts. Also consult publications such as *Going Solo* (Doerfer Communications, PO Box 123, Apalachicola, FL 32329; phone: 904-653-8848) and *Traveling on Your Own,* by Eleanor Berman (Random House, Order Dept., 400 Hahn Rd., Westminster, MD 21157; phone: 800-733-3000).

Organizations and Companies

Gallivanting (515 E. 79th St., Suite 20F, New York, NY 10021; phone: 800-933-9699 or 212-988-0617).
Jane's International and Sophisticated Women Travelers (2603 Bath Ave., Brooklyn, NY 11214; phone: 718-266-2045).
Marion Smith Singles (611 Prescott Pl., N. Woodmere, NY 11581; phone: 516-791-4852, 516-791-4865, or 212-944-2112).
Partners-in-Travel (11660 Chenault St., Suite 119, Los Angeles, CA 90049; phone: 310-476-4869).
Singles in Motion (545 W. 236th St., Riverdale, NY 10463; phone: 718-884-4464).
Singleworld (401 Theodore Fremd Ave., Rye, NY 10580; phone: 800-223-6490 or 914-967-3334).
Solo Flights (63 High Noon Rd., Weston, CT 06883; phone: 203-226-9993).
Suddenly Singles Tours (161 Dreiser Loop, Bronx, NY 10475; phone: 718-379-8800 in New York City; 800-859-8396 elsewhere in the US).
Travel Companion Exchange (PO Box 833, Amityville, NY 11701; phone: 516-454-0880).
Travel Companions (Atrium Financial Center, 1515 N. Federal Hwy., Suite 300, Boca Raton, FL 33432; phone: 800-383-7211 or 407-393-6448).

Travel in Two's (239 N. Broadway, Suite 3, N. Tarrytown, NY 10591; phone: 914-631-8301 in New York State; 800-692-5252 elsewhere in the US).

Older Travelers

Special discounts and more free time are just two factors that have given older travelers a chance to see the world at affordable prices. Many travel suppliers offer senior discounts — sometimes only to members of certain senior citizen organizations, which provide other benefits. Prepare your itinerary with one eye on your own physical condition and the other on a map, and remember that it's easy to overdo when traveling.

Publications

The Mature Traveler (GEM Publishing Group, PO Box 50820, Reno, NV 89513-0820; phone: 702-786-7419).

The Senior Citizen's Guide to Budget Travel in the US and Canada, by Paige Palmer (Pilot Books, 103 Cooper St., Babylon, NY 11702; phone: 516-422-2225).

Take a Camel to Lunch and Other Adventures for Mature Travelers, by Nancy O'Connell (Bristol Publishing Enterprises, PO Box 1737, San Leandro, CA 94577; phone: 510-895-4461 in California; 800-346-4889 elsewhere in the US).

Travel Tips for Older Americans (Publication #044-000-02270-2; Superintendent of Documents, US Government Printing Office, PO Box 371954, Pittsburgh, PA 15250-7954; phone: 202-783-3238).

Unbelievably Good Deals & Great Adventures That You Absolutely Can't Get Unless You're Over 50, by Joan Rattner Heilman (Contemporary Books, 180 N. Michigan Ave., Chicago, IL 60601; phone: 312-782-9181).

Organizations

American Association of Retired Persons (*AARP;* 601 E St. NW, Washington, DC 20049; phone: 202-434-2277).

Golden Companions (PO Box 754, Pullman, WA 99163-0754; phone: 208-858-2183).

Mature Outlook (Customer Service Center, 6001 N. Clark St., Chicago, IL 60660; phone: 800-336-6330).

National Council of Senior Citizens (1331 F St. NW, Washington, DC 20004; phone: 202-347-8800).

Package Tour Operators

Elderhostel (PO Box 1959, Wakefield, MA 01880-5959; phone: 617-426-7788).

Evergreen Travel Service (4114 198th St. SW, Suite 13, Lynnwood, WA 98036-6742; phone: 800-435-2288 or 206-776-1184).

Gadabout Tours (700 E. Tahquitz Canyon Way, Palm Springs, CA 92262; phone: 800-952-5068 or 619-325-5556).

Grand Circle Travel (347 Congress St., Boston, MA 02210; phone: 800-221-2610 or 617-350-7500).

Grandtravel (6900 Wisconsin Ave., Suite 706, Chevy Chase, MD 20815; phone: 800-247-7651 or 301-986-0790).

Interhostel (UNH Division of Continuing Education, 6 Garrison Ave., Durham, NH 03824; phone: 800-733-9753 or 603-862-1147).

OmniTours (104 Wilmont Rd., Deerfield, IL 60015; phone: 800-962-0060 or 708-374-0088).

Saga International Holidays (222 Berkeley St., Boston, MA 02116; phone: 800-343-0273 or 617-262-2262).

Money Matters

TRAVELER'S CHECKS AND CREDIT CARDS

It's wise to carry traveler's checks while on the road, since they are replaceable if stolen or lost. You can buy traveler's checks at banks and some are available by mail or phone. Although most major credit cards enjoy wide domestic and international acceptance, not every hotel, restaurant, or shop in Los Angeles accepts all (or in some cases any) credit cards. Keep a separate list of all traveler's checks (noting those that you have cashed) and the names and numbers of your credit cards. Both traveler's check and credit card companies have international numbers to call for information or in the event of loss or theft.

CASH MACHINES

Automated teller machines (ATMs) are increasingly common worldwide. Most banks participate in one of the international ATM networks; cardholders can withdraw cash from any machine in the same network using either a "bank" card or, in some cases, a credit card. At the time of this writing, most ATMs belong to the *CIRRUS* (phone: 800-4-CIRRUS) or *PLUS* (phone: 800-THE-PLUS) network. For further information, ask at your bank branch.

SENDING MONEY

Should the need arise, it is possible to have money sent to you via the services provided by *American Express* (*MoneyGram;* phone: 800-926-9400 or 800-666-3997 for information; 800-866-8800 for money transfers) or *Western Union Financial Services* (phone: 800-325-4176).

Time Zone

Los Angeles is in the pacific time zone. Daylight saving time is observed from the first Sunday in April until the last Sunday in October.

Business Hours

Los Angeles maintains business hours that are fairly standard throughout the US: 9 AM to 5 PM on weekdays. Banks generally are open weekdays from 9 AM to 3 PM. Retail stores usually are open Mondays through Saturdays from 10 AM to 6 PM; many also are open on Sundays from noon until 5 PM. Some retail stores remain open on weekdays until 9 PM.

Mail

Los Angeles' main post office is downtown at 7101 S. Central Ave. (phone: 213-586-1723). It is open weekdays from 7 AM to 7 PM and Saturdays from 7 AM to 3 PM. In Beverly Hills, there is a branch at 469 N. Crescent Dr. (phone: 213-276-3161); near LAX, the *World Way* post office (5800 Century Blvd.; phone: 310-337-8885) has a self-service area open 24 hours.

For other post office branches, call the main office or check the yellow pages. Stamps also are available at most hotel desks and from public vending machines. For rapid, overnight delivery to other cities, use *Express Mail* (available at post offices), *Federal Express* (phone: 800-238-5355), or *DHL Worldwide Express* (phone: 800-225-5345).

You can have mail sent to you care of your hotel (marked "Guest Mail, Hold for Arrival") or to a post office ("c/o General Delivery, Hold for 30 Days"). *American Express* offices will hold mail for customers ("c/o Client Letter Service"); information on this service is provided in their pamphlet *Travelers' Companion*. Members of the *American Automobile Association (AAA;* 1000 AAA Dr., Heathrow, FL 32746-5063; phone: 407-444-8544) also can have mail (marked "Hold for Arrival") held at *AAA* branch offices.

Telephone

The area code for central Los Angeles is 213; Hollywood is divided between the 213 and 310 area codes. Beverly Hills, Malibu, Santa Monica, Venice, West Hollywood, and other coastal areas are in the 310 area code. The 818 area code covers the San Fernando Valley and the upper half of the San Gabriel Valley, the 805 area code the Ventura/Santa Barbara area, and the 714 area code Orange County.

To make a long-distance call, dial 1 + the area code + the local number. The nationwide number for information is 555-1212; if you need a number in another area code, dial 1 + the area code + 555-1212. (If you don't know the area code, dial 0 for an operator.)

Although you can use a telephone company calling card number on any phone, pay phones that take major credit cards (*American Express, MasterCard, Visa,* and so on) are increasingly common. Also available are combined telephone calling cards/bank credit cards, such as *AT&T Univer-*

sal (phone: 800-662-7759), *Executive Telecard International* (phone: 800-950-3800), and *Sprint* (phone: 800-877-4646). *MCI VisaPhone* (phone: 800-866-0099) can add phone card privileges to your existing *Visa* card.

Long-distance telephone services that help you avoid the surcharges that hotels routinely add to phone bills are provided by *American Telephone and Telegraph* (*AT&T Communications,* International Information Service, 635 Grant St., Pittsburgh, PA 15219; phone: 800-874-4000), *MCI* (323 3rd St. SE, Cedar Rapids, IA 52401; phone: 800-444-3333), *Metromedia Communications Corp.* (1 International Center, 100 NE Loop 410, San Antonio, TX 78216; phone: 800-275-0200), and *Sprint* (offices throughout the US; phone: 800-877-4000). Some hotels still may charge a fee for line usage.

Also useful are the *AT&T 800 Travel Directory* (available at *AT&T Phone Centers* or by calling 800-426-8686), the *Toll-Free Travel & Vacation Information Directory* (Pilot Books, 103 Cooper St., Babylon, NY 11702; phone: 516-422-2225), and *The Phone Booklet* (*Scott American Corporation,* PO Box 88, W. Redding, CT 06896; phone: 203-938-2955).

Medical Aid

In an emergency: Dial 911 for assistance, "0" for an operator, or go directly to the emergency room of the nearest hospital.

Hospitals
California Medical Center (1401 S. Hope St.; phone: 213-748-2411).
Cedars Sinai Medical Center (8700 Alden Dr.; phone: 310-855-5000).
University of Southern California Medical Center (1200 N. State St.; phone: 213-226-2622).

Pharmacies
Cadillac Pharmacy (*Kaiser Hospital*; 6041 Cadillac Ave. and La Cienega Blvd.; phone: 213-857-2151). Open 24 hours daily.
Savon (6360 W. 3rd St.; phone: 213-937-3030). Open 24 hours daily.

Additional Resources
International Association of Medical Assistance to Travelers (*IAMAT;* 417 Center St., Lewiston, NY 14092; phone: 716-754-4883).
International Health Care Service (440 E. 69th St., New York, NY 10021; phone: 212-746-1601).
International SOS Assistance (PO Box 11568, Philadelphia, PA 19116; phone: 800-523-8930 or 215-244-1500).
Medic Alert Foundation (2323 Colorado Ave., Turlock, CA 95380; phone: 800-ID-ALERT or 209-668-3333).
TravMed (PO Box 10623, Baltimore, MD 21285-0623; phone: 800-732-5309 or 410-296-5225).

Legal Aid

If you don't have, or cannot reach, your own attorney, most cities offer legal referral services maintained by county bar associations. These services ensure that anyone in need of legal representation gets it and can match you with a local attorney. In Los Angeles, contact the *Los Angeles County Bar Association Lawyer Referral and Information Service* (617 S. Olive St.; phone: 213-622-6700). If you must appear in court, you are entitled to court-appointed representation if you can't obtain a lawyer or can't afford one.

For Further Information

The **Los Angeles Convention & Visitors Bureau** is at 633 W. 5th St., Suite 6000, Los Angeles, CA 90071 (phone: 213-689-8822). The **Office of Tourism of the California Department of Commerce** is at 801 K St., Suite 1600, Sacramento, CA 95814 (phone: 800-TO-CALIF or 916-322-0972). For other local tourist information see *Sources and Resources* in THE CITY.

The City

Los Angeles

Whatever you have heard — or think you know — about Los Angeles is probably wrong. Or misleading. Or hyperbole. This is a city that leads the league in misconceptions. To set the record straight on a few points:

- Despite the palm trees, Los Angeles is not tropical.
- Los Angeles is not a clutch of countless suburbs in search of a city, but rather it's a vast metropolis encompassing the City of Los Angeles, plus a sprawl of municipalities and unincorporated areas.
- One cannot swim comfortably in the Pacific during the winter, when cold Alaskan currents often drop the water temperature into the 50s.
- Debilitating smog is rare, most often occurs in summer, and usually is confined to a small area.
- It is possible to visit Los Angeles happily without spending every minute inside a car.
- The arts — music, theater, dance — can be readily enjoyed, are flourishing, and have made Los Angeles a leading cultural city.
- The city has more people than swimming pools.
- Gang violence and other street crime continue to plague the inner city, just as in most other major metropolises.
- Sunglasses are not issued to residents at birth.

Los Angeles, like it or not, is a city of dreams, myths, and misunderstandings. It is our nation's Olympus, where certain of our gods live and cavort and where both good and bad are inflated to larger-than-life proportions. Rarely have a city's virtues, excesses, shortcomings, and sins been exaggerated with such glee and small regard for current fact. Yes, certainly, there is glitter and foolishness and often much about which to chuckle. Yes, admittedly, there are the curses of snarled traffic and eye-tearing smog.

But much of the rest can be sublime.

To begin with, the 8.6 million people who call the LA metropolitan area home care little about the City of Angels' skewed — and skewered — reputation. They are there, for the most part, not for the glitz and hijinks but for the quality of life.

There is no doubt that Los Angeles is one of the most beautifully situated and climate-blessed (except for the smog) of the world's metropolises. The mile-high San Gabriel Mountains skirt Los Angeles to the north and the Santa Monica Mountains bisect it, thus allowing Angelenos to enjoy magnificent vistas and offering the unusual opportunity for secluded hillside living in the midst of a vast metropolis. These lofty ranges also mean that this is one of the few places on the globe where it is possible in the same day both to ski and to surf (though you'd better wear a wetsuit while surfing in winter to avoid freezing).

On the other hand, many visitors are stunned to learn that Los Angeles isn't always favored with blue skies and perpetual sunshine. Late summer and early fall usually are the hottest times of year, when the dusty, dry Santa Ana winds blow out of the nearby eastern desert to elevate temperatures into the 90s — and sometimes 100s — and escalate temperaments into the danger zone. This is the time, wrote LA crime novelist Raymond Chandler, that wives finger the sharp edges of knives and study the contour of their husbands' necks. Oddly enough, spring and early summer can bring the dullest weather of the year — chill fog and overcast skies. Winter is the rainy season and can be glorious or awful — and normally is both, in spurts. Rainfalls can be quick and violent, giving way to clear warm days and cool nights. Although the city has experienced occasional severe floods in recent years, there is little danger of it being transformed into swampland.

Despite these vicissitudes, it is virtually inevitable that *New Year's Day* will dawn bright and sunny, with temperatures in the 80s, and that the achingly beautiful panoramas seen by the tens of millions watching the *Rose Bowl* game on television only will reinforce the LA legend.

Los Angeles traces its origins to a dusty little settlement founded in 1781 by order of a Spanish colonial governor. The settlers gave it the monumental name of El Pueblo de Nuestra Señora la Reina de los Angeles de Porciuncula. By 1850, after California was ceded to the United States (following the Mexican-American War), it had a population of only 1,610, and at the turn of the century, it was the home of only a few more than 100,000 residents.

Still largely citrus groves and bean fields, Los Angeles retained much of the character of its Spanish and Mexican roots — and remained that way until the massive American migration to the West Coast began in the 1920s. California was the country's last frontier, a chance to start a new life and make one's fortune, and the city, along with the state, boomed. In the 1930s, the area attracted those rendered homeless and near hopeless by the Great Depression; in the 1940s, servicemen on their way home from World War II stopped here to put the past behind them. The 1950s and 1960s saw LA develop into a center for new industries — the technological and aerospace industries of the future.

The film industry also had begun to develop in the 1920s, with the arrival of the early movie moguls who were drawn from New York by the sun, which permitted outdoor filming year-round. Later, the city attracted the television and music businesses as well. To much of the rest of the nation, however, Los Angeles was still "the Coast," a place dismissed laughingly and almost automatically as provincial and self-absorbed.

Meanwhile, Los Angeles began an effort to shed its second class mantle. The archaic ordinance that limited downtown buildings to the height of City Hall (presumably for earthquake protection) was scrapped, and a skyline began to rise. Major league sports arrived in 1946 with the NFL

Rams from Cleveland, followed by professional teams in the top ranks of baseball, basketball, and hockey. Finally, in 1964, the city proudly opened the ambitious, multi-theater complex called the *Music Center.*

Today's LA is a sophisticated city boasting the kinds of hotels, restaurants, shopping, nightlife, museums, and cultural events that befit the second-largest city in the nation.

Over the years, Los Angeles also has become a favorite vacation destination and now welcomes more than 60 million visitors annually from all over the world, making Los Angeles International Airport the fourth-busiest in the country. They are lured to LA not only by its salubrious weather and the chance of glimpsing a movie or TV personality but also by its theaters, symphony orchestras, opera and light opera companies, dance companies, museums, and scores of top professional and college sporting events. Specific areas of Los Angeles have become attractions in themselves: Hollywood and its *Mann's Chinese Theatre,* with its footprints and handprints of the stars embedded in cement; Beverly Hills and its expensive shops and Rolls-Royce lifestyle; Westwood, with its footloose university-town ambience; the casual but wealthy beach communities stretching from Malibu to the Palos Verdes Peninsula. The more traditional tourist sites and activities — *Disneyland, Universal Studios, Movieland, Knott's Berry Farm, Marineland,* and so on — continue to draw many visitors to Los Angeles and its surrounding areas as well.

More of a sophisticated lady now, Los Angeles is all spruced up with ultramodern hotels, world class restaurants, and even a state-of-the-art regional commuter rail service (*Metrolink*) that connects downtown with a host of cities from north to south between Ventura and Oceanside and west to east to San Bernadino. In addition, 1993 ushered in the advent of a subway with the opening of the first leg of the *Metro Red Line* — a 4.4-mile segment between Union Station and MacArthur Park. The underground train will eventually cover 22.7 miles of the city. The $5.3-billion project was designed to ease the city's traffic congestion; and tax-paying Angelenos surely hope it does. Even the *Visitors and Convention Bureau* sports a spiffy new look thanks to a $485-million expansion that added 2.5 million square feet of space to the downtown facility, making it the largest on the West Coast. Improvements include 685,000 square feet of exhibit hall space, two 400-seat restaurants, food courts, a picturesque plaza landscaped with palm trees, and two 150-foot-high glass lobby pavilions.

Los Angeles still has its critics. Its vast size (the city itself is almost half as big as the entire state of Rhode Island) may make it seem uncomfortably spread out and sometimes difficult to negotiate. But most people find LA a pleasant and easy city in which to live and to visit. Beneath the official municipal veneer, away from the sunshine, and removed from the artificial glitter of show biz, Los Angeles has an essentially solid, all-American soul. Add the fascination of the ethnic mix — European, African, and Mexican stock, plus Chinese, Japanese, Korean, Vietnamese,

Russian, and Thai — as well as its environmental meld of sea, mountain, and desert, and Los Angeles affirms its logical position as one of the great cities of the world.

Los Angeles At-a-Glance

SEEING THE CITY

There are at least three great places to go for a fantastic view of Los Angeles. The most famous is Mulholland Drive, a twisting road that winds through the Hollywood Hills. Another is the top of Mt. Olympus, in Laurel Canyon, north of Sunset Boulevard. Then there's the 27-story, 454-foot City Hall Tower with its sweeping view of downtown, the mountains, and the Pacific Ocean. Open weekdays. City Hall, near the south end of *Los Angeles Mall* (phone: 213-485-2891).

SPECIAL PLACES

A walk along Hollywood Boulevard from Vine Street to Highland Avenue will delight anyone who loves the era of those great movies that made Hollywood famous. No longer the physical center of film production, however, Hollywood's glamour is, sadly, long gone. X-rated movies now seem to outnumber the kinds of films that made the area world-renowned. Hollywood Boulevard usually bustles with tourists and a smattering of locals night and day. There is a lot to enjoy here, much of it at little or no cost. For more information see *Tour 5: Hollywood* in DIRECTIONS.

OLD HOLLYWOOD: MEMORIES AND EMPTY BUILDINGS

MANN'S CHINESE THEATRE Known to movie fans around the world as *Grauman's Chinese Theatre,* this is probably the most visited site in Hollywood. If you wander down Hollywood Boulevard toward Highland Avenue looking for the *Grauman's* sign, you'll never find it, though. Several years ago, Ted Mann took over the theater, added it to his movie chain, and took down the sign that had made Syd Grauman famous, replacing it with his own. The *Chinese Theatre* forecourt is world-famous for its celebrity footprints and handprints immortalized in cement. If you join the crowd of visitors outside the box office, you'll probably find imprints of your favorite stars from the 1920s to the present. If you buy a ticket to get in, you'll be treated to one of the world's most impressive and elaborate movie palaces. The ornate carvings, high, decorative ceiling, traditionally plush seats, heavy curtains that whoosh closed when the film ends, and the enormous screen itself are all part of a Hollywood that no longer exists. The less opulent *Chinese Twin* next door also shows films. 6925 Hollywood Blvd. (phone: 213-464-8111).

HOLLYWOOD WAX MUSEUM If the *Chinese Theatre* makes you nostalgic for the faces belonging to celluloid souls, stop in at the *Hollywood Wax Museum.*

Here images of many of the immortals of the film industry are captured both in and out of character — in wax. Marilyn Monroe, Jean Harlow, Paul Newman, Raquel Welch, Michael Jackson, Madonna, Sylvester Stallone as Rambo, and many more fill the star-studded display cases. There's also the Academy Award film library, a horror chamber, and a re-creation of the Last Supper. Open daily; weekdays to midnight, Fridays and Saturdays to 2 AM. Admission charge; no charge for children under 6. 6767 Hollywood Blvd. (phone: 213-462-8860; information: 213-462-5991).

HOLLYWOOD STUDIO MUSEUM If nostalgia is what you seek, you also can find it at the largest single historic movie artifact in existence. Called the De Mille Barn, it was the production site of the first feature-length film made in Hollywood — Cecil B. De Mille's *The Squaw Man*. Designated a California Cultural Landmark in 1956, it was moved by Paramount Studios to the *Hollywood Bowl* parking lot and turned it into the *Hollywood Studio Museum* in 1979. Inside are a replica of De Mille's office and stills from silent motion pictures. The outside of the building is interesting, too: When it was on the back lot of Paramount Studios, it often was used in Westerns and, for many years, was seen as the railroad station in the "Bonanza" TV series. In addition, there's a gift shop, filled with old autographs, books, and pictures. Open only Saturdays and Sundays, 10 AM to 4 PM. Admission charge (no charge for children under 6). 2100 N. Highland, across from the *Hollywood Bowl* (phone: 213-874-2276).

PARAMOUNT PICTURES At one time, RKO studios adjoined the Paramount lot. After RKO folded in 1956, its studio became the home of television's Desilu Productions, which in turn sold its property to next-door Paramount. Close to the Bronson Avenue intersection with Melrose is the famous Paramount Gate, the highly decorative studio entrance that many people will remember from the film *Sunset Boulevard*. The Gower Street side of today's Paramount was the old front entrance to RKO. At what used to be 780 Gower Street, you now will find simply an unimpressive back door to Paramount, painted in that dull, flat beige many studios use to protect their exterior walls. The door no longer bears its old marquee with distinctive Art Deco neon letters spelling out RKO, the numbers have been torn from the front steps, and the Art Deco front doors are gone. RKO is just a memory now. Paramount extends from Melrose Avenue on the south to Gower Street on the west, Van Ness Avenue on the east, and Willoughby Avenue on the north (phone: 213-956-5000).

GOWER STREET This was once the center for so many small film studios that it became known in the biz as Gower Gulch. It was also nicknamed Poverty Row, since so many of its independent producers were perpetually strapped for production money. Poverty Row's most famous studio was Columbia Pictures, which ultimately grew healthy enough to acquire most of the smaller parcels of studio real estate in the neighborhood. Columbia's old studios still stand at Gower Street and Sunset Boulevard, although Columbia moved out several years ago. It found a new home in Burbank at the Warner Brothers Studio, which was then renamed The Burbank Studios (TBS). Today the two film companies operate TBS — not to be confused with the Turner Broadcasting System (TBS) television network — as a rental facility for film and TV production.

WARNER BROTHERS During the late 1920s, when Warner's was introducing "talkies" to America, its pictures were filmed here. It also was the home of Warner's radio station at the time, KFWB. Today the old studio is the headquarters for KTLA-TV and KMPC radio. The stately Southern mansion that served as Warner's administration building still stands on Sunset Boulevard. Sunset Blvd. and Van Ness Ave.

MAX FACTOR BEAUTY MUSEUM The only museum in the world devoted to makeup is housed in the famous Max Factor Building, just off Hollywood Boulevard, where (since the 1930s) the stars came to have their faces painted, their hair styled, and to be fitted for wigs or toupees. There are exhibits of beauty techniques used in the early days of Hollywood, and some outlandish makeup tools invented by Max Factor. One of the most unusual is a collection of special head blocks of famous stars, used to create wigs and toupees without the actors and actresses having to spend hours being fitted and styled. There is also "The Scroll of Fame," one of the most extensive collections of movie star autographs around. Open 10 AM to 4 PM, Mondays through Saturdays. No admission charge. Free parking. 1666 N. Highland Ave. (phone: 213-463-6668).

"HOLLYWOOD": ALIVE AND WELL

"Hollywood," meaning the film business, is no longer geographically in the district bearing that name. If your nostalgic walking tour of Old Hollywood has made you curious about modern production methods, we suggest a tour of one of the following Los Angeles studios:

UNIVERSAL STUDIOS HOLLYWOOD Only during a trip to Universal Studios can one encounter a 30-foot, 6.5-ton King Kong, beam up to the starship *Enterprise,* experience 15 minutes in the life of a "Miami Vice" cop, and get caught in an earthquake measuring 8.3 on the Richter scale. The combination movie studio tour and theme park has been attracting more than 5 million people a year. The Universal Studios Hollywood experience includes a guided tram tour through the 420 studio acres. Other highlights are a look at some of the 34 sound stages and other production facilities; the house used in Alfred Hitchcock's *Psycho;* re-created sets from such movies as *All Quiet on the Western Front, Jaws,* and *The Sting;* a burning house; a collapsing bridge; a multimedia special-effects show; the parting of the Red Sea; the Doomed Glacier Expedition, where you get to plunge down an alpine avalanche; and an earthquake simulation called "The Big

One." If this isn't enough, there are other tricks and treats: *An American Tale,* a musical production; *The Riot Act,* a western stunt show; *Backdraft,* a vivid re-creation of the burning warehouse from the movie; and *Back to the Future,* which reveals how the special effects were created for that movie series. You can also travel through time on Universal's newest attraction, Back to the Future: The Ride. Fans of the late Lucille Ball will enjoy "Tribute to Lucy," a dazzling display of memorabilia and highlights of the comedienne's TV and movie career. If you're ready for all that, visit Universal Studios any day of the week. Admission charge; no charge for children under 3. Hollywood Fwy. to Lankershim exit, Universal City (phone: 818-508-9600).

WARNER BROTHERS STUDIOS To take a look at real production rather than the Universal extravaganza, try these studios in Burbank — home of Warner Brothers as well as many independent production companies. Nothing on the tour is staged, so visitors watch whatever is happening on that particular day. Not only do you get to see some actual shooting whenever possible, you also see a lot of behind-the-scenes action — scenery construction, sound recording, and prop departments. Since tours are limited to 12 people (with children under 10 not permitted), reservations are required a week in advance. Open Mondays through Saturdays, tours at 10 AM and 2 PM. Admission charge. 4000 Warner Blvd. (phone: 818-954-1744).

UNIVERSAL CITYWALK If the studio tours aren't enough to keep you entertained, stroll over to this $100-million shopping and entertainment extravaganza — a 4-block stretch of retail shops, restaurants, theaters, and offices created by the folks at MCA Development Company, owners of Universal Studios. It's worth the trip if only for an affordable pizza at *Wolfgang Puck's Pizzeria,* where the Italian pies cost a fraction of their higher priced cousins at *Spago,* or for the show at the *Wizardz Magic Theater,* where the world's top magicians strut their illusionary stuff. You can even walk down a replica of Olvera Street and grab a bite of authentic Mexican fare at *Camacho's Cantina.* Then enjoy a cup of coffee with a good book at *Upstart Cow,* a coffee bar/bookstore. And if you're too queasy for a real roller coaster ride, you can get your thrills vicariously at the Dynamic Motion Simulator, which lets you experience the sensation through visual effects. The facility also houses the recently transplanted *Museum of Neon Art, Gladstone's 4 Fish* restaurant, and a 14-classroom UCLA Extension Center. *CityWalk* is located in the center of Universal City and is accessible from the Universal off ramps of the Hollywood (101) Fwy. via Lankershim, Cahuenga, or Barham Blvd. entrances; Universal Center Dr.

BEVERLY HILLS After a hard day on the lot, movie stars still living in Beverly Hills return to their mansions for a good night's sleep. Even during the sunshiny daylight hours, Beverly Hills is remarkably tranquil, with nary a person walking on the residential streets. Without a doubt the most affluent and elegant neighborhood in Southern California, Beverly Hills is a must-see. If you want to window-shop or purchase high-fashion clothing, stroll along Rodeo Drive between Santa Monica and Wilshire Boulevards. If you want to make sure you don't succumb to an impulse to buy anything, go during the evening or on Sundays, when many stores are closed. *Gray Line* is one of several companies offering van and limousine tours of the area (phone: 213-856-5900). During summer, an old-fashioned trolley, which departs from in front of the *Chanel* boutique on Rodeo Drive tours Beverly Hills (cost is $1). For more information see *Tour 4: Beverly Hills* in DIRECTIONS.

DOWNTOWN LOS ANGELES

To see a Los Angeles that most people don't know about, take a walking tour downtown (for more information see *Tour 1: Downtown* in DIRECTIONS).

THE PLAZA If you ever wondered what the place looked like before shopping centers were created, step across the Plaza and marvel. The Plaza, a wide square, is the scene of monthly fiestas. The Old Plaza Church, which dates to 1822, has a curious financial history: It was partially paid for by the sale of seven barrels of brandy. The city's first firehouse is here, too; closed Mondays. Colorful local anecdotes are retold during a narrated walking tour of the Plaza, offered Tuesdays through Saturdays, 10 AM to noon. For information, contact El Pueblo de los Angeles State Historic Park on the Plaza, 845 N. Alameda St. (phone: 213-628-1274).

OLVERA STREET Music from the Plaza fiesta spills into Olvera Street, a block-long pedestrian alley filled with colorful Mexican shops, restaurants, and spicy food stalls. The oldest house in Los Angeles is here — the 1818 adobe Avila House; closed Mondays. The first brick house also is here, but now it's home to *La Golondrina* restaurant. There is a visitors' center in the 1887 Sepulveda House (closed Sundays), and a free 18-minute film on the history of Los Angeles (phone: 213-628-1274).

LOS ANGELES CIVIC CENTER AND MALL An unusually quiet, well-landscaped city mall, with tropical plants, gentle splashing fountains, and sculpture half hidden among the lush greenery. It's the first mall of shops and restaurants to be built on City Hall property (at Main and Los Angeles Sts.). Stop in the rotunda to see a rotating art show. Make sure you get to the top of City Hall Tower at the south end of the mall for one of the best views of the city. Mall open daily (phone: 213-485-2891 and 213-485-2121).

THIRD AND BROADWAY Several places in this area are worth noting. First is the skylit, 5-story indoor court of the Bradbury Building, now a registered historic landmark. Open Mondays through Fridays, 8 AM to 5 PM. You can ride an old hydraulic elevator to the top balcony and walk down a magnificent staircase guaranteed to evoke visions of bygone splendors. Across the corner from the Bradbury Building is the *Million Dollar Theater* — Syd Grauman's first; it's currently a Spanish-language picture palace inside, but it has a fascinating exterior. Just south of the theater is the entrance to the *Grand Central Public Market,* a conglomeration of stalls selling food from all over the world amid the sounds and smells of a Mexican *mercado.*

LITTLE TOKYO This is the social, economic, cultural, and religious center of the largest Japanese-American community in the US. There are four specialty shopping centers here, as well as the Japanese Cultural Center and many fine restaurants. 1st and San Pedro Sts. (phone: 213-620-8861).

MUSIC CENTER The best time to visit the *Music Center* is during a concert or performance, but it's worth seeing anytime. The *Ahmanson Theater* is the base for a branch of the *Center Theater Group* and hosts classical dramas, comedies, and international premieres with big-name stars. The *Mark Taper Forum,* a small, award-winning theater, houses the branch of the *Center Theater Group* that specializes in new works and experimental material. The glittering *Dorothy Chandler Pavilion,* a 3,200-seat auditorium, is the home of the *Los Angeles Philharmonic* and the *Los Angeles Master Chorale.* It's also the setting for most of the season of the *Los Angeles Opera Company.* The orchestra season runs from October through May; musical theater is presented generally in summer, when the orchestra moves to the *Hollywood Bowl.* Take the free guided tour of the theaters. A plus is a sneak preview of the *Walt Disney Concert Hall* — a megamillion-dollar, 2,380-seat, Frank Gehry–designed facility; scheduled to open in 1997, it will house the *Los Angeles Philharmonic.* Made possible by a $50-million grant from Lillian B. Disney in memory of her late husband, Walt, the hall will contain four theaters and an outdoor park and gardens. Also see *Performing Arts* in DIVERSIONS. 1st and Grand Sts. (phone: 213-972-7483 for tour information; 213-972-7211 for general information).

CHINATOWN Chinatown has the usual assortment of restaurants, vegetable stores, and weird little shops selling ivory chess sets and acupuncture charts. The 900 block of N. Broadway.

MUSEUM OF CONTEMPORARY ART This is one museum in two buildings: the *MOCA* at California Plaza, designed by Arata Isozaki, a modern-art exhibit in itself, and the *Temporary Contemporary,* a renovated warehouse about 10 blocks away, on Bunker Hill downtown. Both house artworks from the 1940s to the present. Also, in *MOCA's Ahmanson Auditorium,* there is a Media and Performing Arts Program, which looks at performance — contemporary dance, theater, film, and video — as an art form.

There's also a gift shop, as well as a pleasant café. Closed Mondays. Admission charge (except Thursdays from 5 to 8 PM). One ticket covers admission to both buildings on the same day. *MOCA:* 250 S. Grand Ave. at California Plaza (phone: 213-621-2766); *Temporary Contemporary:* 152 N. Central Ave. (phone: 213-626-6222).

MIDTOWN

FARMERS' MARKET Yossarian, the hero of *Catch-22* (book by Joseph Heller, movie by Mike Nichols) used to say "eat your liver" all the time, and at the *Farmers' Market* you can do just that. It's also possible to eat anything else within the realm of gastronomic imagination. There are more than 160 stalls of American, Mexican, Italian, Chinese, and vegetarian food and any number of exquisite bakeries and fruit and candy shops. If you don't like to eat standing up, there are tables set among the aisles of this indoor, covered market. It's a great place to be hungry. Open daily. 6333 W. 3rd St. at Fairfax (phone: 213-933-9211). For more information see *Tour 3: Fairfax/Farmers' Market* in DIRECTIONS.

LA BREA TAR PITS A midtown green space, the gift of an early oil magnate, G. Allen Hancock. The *Los Angeles Museum of Art* keeps building over remaining deposits where Hancock's oil pumps once bobbed. With five buildings surrounding a spacious central court, it is one of the top museums in the country and the largest in the West. The permanent collection features paintings, sculpture, graphic arts, photography, costumes, textiles, and decorative arts from a wide range of cultures and periods from prehistoric times to the present. The museum's holdings include American and European painting, sculpture, and decorative arts; 20th-century arts; pre-Columbian Mexican art; a unique assemblage of glass from Roman times to the 19th century; the renowned Gilbert collection of mosaics and monumental silver; and Indian and Islamic art. Major traveling loan exhibitions also are presented, along with lectures, films, concerts, and other educational events in the 600-seat *Leo S. Bing Theater.* The Pavilion for Japanese Art houses the internationally renowned Shin'enkan collection of Japanese paintings and a collection of Japanese ceramics, sculpture, lacquerware, screens, scrolls, and prints. Closed Mondays. Admission charge. 5905 Wilshire Blvd. (phone: 213-857-6000).

The colorful *George C. Page Museum of La Brea Discoveries,* also in La Brea Tar Pits, has in excess of 1 million fossils from the ice age, as well as entire skeletons of prehistoric animals trapped in the tar pits. Over 500,000 specimens of plants, reptiles, insects, birds, and mammals have been recovered. One of the museum's more unusual exhibits is the open paleontological laboratory, where one may observe the cleaning and identification of fossils found in the tar pits. Also of interest are two films, the *La Brea Story* and *Dinosaurs, the Terrible Lizards,* that are shown when enough of a crowd gathers. Closed Mondays. Admission charge (combination *Mu-*

seum of *Art/Page Museum* tickets available). 5801 Wilshire Blvd. (phone: 213-936-2230).

FARTHER AFIELD

GRIFFITH PARK The largest municipal park in the country, Griffith has three golf courses, a wilderness area and bird sanctuary, tennis courts, three miniature railroads, a carousel, pony rides, and picnic areas within its 4,043 acres. Not only that — this is where you'll find the famous Los Angeles Zoo, home to more than 1,500 mammals, birds, and reptiles. Open daily, except *Christmas*. Admission charge except for children under 2 (5333 Zoo Dr.; phone: 213-666-4650). If you like railroads, you'll love *Travel Town*, a unique outdoor museum of old railroad engines, cars, railroad equipment, and fire trucks. The *Griffith Observatory* (2800 E. Observatory Rd.; phone: 213-664-1191) near Mt. Hollywood houses a 500-seat planetarium theater, a twin-refracting telescope, and the Hall of Science. Admission charge for planetarium shows. Most park facilities are open daily (phone: 213-665-5188).

SIX FLAGS MAGIC MOUNTAIN A 260-acre family theme park, featuring 100-plus rides, shows, and other attractions, this is the home of Bugs Bunny and his Looney Tunes friends in Bugs Bunny World. In addition to the mighty Colossus (a huge, wooden roller coaster) and the spine-tingling Revolution (a 360-degree vertical loop coaster), there's also the challenge of Roaring Rapids (a whitewater rafting experience), the Z Force mock starship ride, and a magic show run by the wily rabbit himself. Ninja, the West Coast's only suspended roller coaster, promises a delightfully terrifying trip. Other attractions include the 6-coaster Psyclone, a replica of Coney Island's Cyclone, and Flashback, a thrilling roller coaster that shoots through six 180° dives, fast switchbacks, and a startling 540° spiral. The Viper is one of the world's largest — and LA's scariest — multiple-looped roller coasters. The dolphin show and a children's village and petting zoo also are worthwhile. Open daily from *Memorial Day* through *Labor Day*, weekends the rest of the year. Admission charge except for children under 3. Twenty-five minutes north of Hollywood on the Golden State Fwy., Magic Mountain exit in Valencia (phone: 818-367-2271 or 805-255-4100; for recorded information, 805-255-4111 or 818-367-5965).

PORTS O' CALL VILLAGE Some 60 specialty shops here feature merchandise from around the world. You can relax by taking a boat or helicopter tour of Los Angeles Harbor and dining in your choice of 25 restaurants and snack shops. Open daily. Berths 76–79 at the foot of the Harbor Fwy., San Pedro (phone: 310-831-0287).

REDONDO BEACH MARINA A delightful waterfront recreation showplace, the marina offers boat cruises and sport fishing. Open daily. 181 N. Harbor Dr., Redondo Beach. Take the Harbor Fwy. to the Torrance Blvd. exit and proceed west to the ocean (phone: 310-374-3481). For more information see *Tour 7: Beach Towns* in DIRECTIONS.

FOREST LAWN MEMORIAL PARK A major tourist attraction, Forest Lawn is a huge cemetery calling itself a memorial park; it advertises on huge billboards overlooking the freeways. Humphrey Bogart, Walt Disney, W. C. Fields, Clark Gable, and Bette Davis are buried here, among others. The cemetery contains a major collection of art treasures and marble sculptures including the largest religious painting in the world, Jan Styka's 195-by-45-foot *The Crucifixion*. And don't be surprised if you also find a real live bride and groom — some people like to get married here. Open daily. Donations appreciated. 1712 S. Glendale Ave., Glendale (phone: 818-241-4151). For more information, see *Grave Matters* in DIVERSIONS.

QUEEN MARY You can explore the 81,000-ton ship, now permanently docked in Long Beach, from stem to stern, either on your own or with one of the daily guided tours; you even can spend the night — nearly 400 converted staterooms now make up the *Queen Mary* hotel. When she was launched in 1936, the *Queen* was the ultimate transatlantic travel experience of its time. In 1971, after retiring from a long career on the high seas, she was "relaunched" in this picturesque harbor by the Disney Company. After Disney pulled out in late 1992, the behemoth boat closed down for several months before being bought and reopened by a local entrepreneur. Open daily. Admission charge. Long Beach Fwy. to *Queen Mary* exit (phone: 310-435-3511).

CATALINA ISLAND It's 1 hour by boat from Long Beach or 1½ hours from San Pedro to Catalina Island, where you can spend the day wandering around the flower-filled hills, swimming, sightseeing, playing golf, or riding horses. There are places to stay overnight, but be sure to reserve in advance during the summer. Boats to Catalina leave daily from Catalina Landing (320 Golden Shore Blvd., Long Beach), and from the Catalina Terminal Building (foot of Harbor Fwy., Berths 95 and 96, San Pedro). Boats are operated by *Catalina Cruises* (phone: 213-514-3838) and the super-fast *Catalina Channel Express* (phone: 310-519-1212 or 310-519-7957); they depart from the Queen Mary terminal. For more information see *Tour 8: Catalina* in DIRECTIONS.

J. PAUL GETTY MUSEUM The home of Vincent van Gogh's masterpiece, *Irises*. There is also an extensive collection of Greek and Roman antiquities; pre-20th-century Western European paintings, drawings, sculpture, illuminated manuscripts, and decorative arts; and 19th- and 20th-century American and European photographs. The museum building is patterned after a 1st-century Roman country villa that was buried at Herculaneum in AD 79 by the eruption of Mt. Vesuvius. Closed Mondays. No admission charge. Parking is by advance reservation only. 17985 Pacific Coast Hwy. (phone: 310-458-2003).

ORANGE COUNTY

DISNEYLAND For many people, this is the most compelling magnet in all of Southern California — and the inspired creation that forever changed the image of theme and amusement parks. More than 50 attractions delight visitors of all ages including the ever-popular Pirates of the Caribbean, the intergalactic thriller Star Tours, Main Street, a re-creation of a typical 1890s American street, and Fantasmic!, a dazzling display of streaking lasers and wild pyrotechnics between Frontierland and Tom Sawyer's Island, featuring Mickey Mouse as master of ceremonies. *Birnbaum's Disneyland* can provide complete details about this still-expanding wonderland. 40 minutes from downtown LA, *Disneyland* is open daily. Admission charge. 1313 Harbor Blvd., Anaheim (phone: 714-999-4565). Also see *Quintessential Los Angeles* in DIVERSIONS.

MOVIELAND WAX MUSEUM About a 10-minute drive from *Disneyland,* with more than 250 movie and television stars preserved in wax, molded into stances from their most famous roles. Newer arrivals include Bette Davis, Marlon Brando, and Clint Eastwood. The original props and sets from many films are here, too. At the Chamber of Horrors, 15 sets with wax figures re-create the special effects that made movies such as *Psycho* and *The Exorcist* famous. Open daily. Admission charge. 7711 Beach Blvd., Buena Park (phone: 714-522-1154).

MEDIEVAL TIMES Across the street from the *Movieland Wax Museum* is a castle-like structure that houses an arena. It's an evening of 11th-century entertainment during which colorfully attired knights on horseback compete in medieval games, jousting, and sword fighting. The show comes with dinner (whole roasted chicken, spareribs, herb-basted potatoes, and various other finger foods, since people in those days didn't use forks). Open daily. Admission charge. 7662 Beach Blvd., Buena Park (phone: 714-521-4740 or 800-899-6600).

KNOTT'S BERRY FARM The theme is the Old West. Scattered throughout two of the five sections (Fiesta Village, a Roaring Twenties area, a Ghost Town, an early-California-Spanish area, and Camp Snoopy, a children's park) are old finds, antiques. Here and there you'll spot an old wagon wheel, some airplane parts, narrow-gauge locomotives, or an antique carousel. An old-fashioned stagecoach and authentic steam coach will take you around the grounds, past rides called the Whirlpool, Mountain Log Ride, Sky Jump, XK-1, Tumbler, Slammer, and Slingshot, as well as bumper cars. There also are a mine train, Montezooma's Revenge, the multiple-looped Boomerang roller coaster, Camp Snoopy, and the exciting Kingdom of the Dinosaurs. *Knott's Berry Farm* has top country-and-western artists performing frequently, as well as cancan dancers, marionettes, and a great ice show at *Christmastime.* There are delightful aquatic attractions in the Pacific Pavilion, and you can play games in the largest arcade west of the Mississippi. And there's plenty of good eating right on the grounds: Sicilian pizza, extra-juicy hot dogs, and barbecued ribs, as well as *Mrs. Knott's Chicken Dinner Restaurant,* which is older than the park. Open daily. Admission charge. 10 minutes from *Disneyland* at 8039 Beach Blvd., Buena Park (phone: 714-827-1776 or, for recorded information, 714-220-5200).

EXTRA SPECIAL For one of the most spectacular drives in California, follow the Pacific Coast Highway (Route 1) north about 95 miles from LA to Santa Barbara, a picturesque California mission town facing the Pacific, where bright bougainvillea burst with purple and magenta against classic white adobe, Mediterranean-style architecture. A "red tile" walking tour zigzags through the historic district and runs along downtown State Street — a truly Spanish experience down to the last tile-enclosed trash bin and mailbox. The Spanish-Moorish courthouse is worth a visit for its opulent interior and the incomparable panorama from the tower. The city center owes its harmonious look to the strict architectural guidelines for reconstruction that were imposed after the devastating earthquake of 1925. Overnighters can opt for a hacienda-style hostelry, such as the *Four Seasons Biltmore* (phone: 805-969-2261); Charlie Chaplin's favorite hotel, the *Montecito Inn* (phone: 805-969-7854); an exclusive hideaway, such as the *San Ysidro Ranch,* with its excellent French *StoneHouse* restaurant (phone: 805-969-5046; see *Checking In*); the Victorian *Upham* hotel, with *Louie's,* its highly regarded restaurant serving California fare (phone: 805-962-0058); or one of many period bed and breakfast establishments. The *Cold Spring Tavern* (5995 Stagecoach Rd.; phone: 805-967-0066), about 10 miles northwest of Santa Barbara on Route 154, goes back to the old stagecoach days. Chili is popular at lunch. At dinner, the menu tends more toward chicken, steaks, and game. Open daily.

Sources and Resources

TOURIST INFORMATION

For free information, brochures, and maps, contact the Greater Los Angeles Visitors and Convention Bureau (633 West 5th St., Suite 6000, Los Angeles, CA 90071; phone: 213-624-7300). For all the latest information on events and happenings, call the Visitors and Convention Bureau *Events Hotline* (phone: 213-689-8822); the service is available 24 hours a day in English, plus Spanish, French, Japanese, and German. For the best (albeit most expensive) maps of the Los Angeles area as well as travel books, try *Thomas Bros. Maps & Books* (603 W. 7th St.; phone: 213-627-4018). Contact the California state hotline (800-TO-CALIF) for maps, calendars of events, health updates, and travel advisories. Also, *West Hollywood Marketing Corporation* offers free brochures, maps, and information (phone: 310-274-7294).

To really get a handle on this massive metropolis, pick up a copy of *50 Maps of LA* (H.M. Gousha, $9.95). This whimsical yet informative tome — a compilation of hot spots from artists, movie stars, and critics in map form — includes such gems as where Nancy Reagan gets her facials and a diagram of celebrity seating at *Laker* games. An even more unusual guide is *Permanent Californians: An Illustrated Guide to the Cemeteries of California*, by Judi Culbertson and Tom Randall (Chelsea Publishing Co., $16.95), which describes the final resting places of many famous Californians and provides some interesting biographical notes. For more information see *Grave Matters* in DIVERSIONS.

LOCAL COVERAGE *Los Angeles Times*, morning daily; *Daily News*, published in the San Fernando Valley, morning daily; *Los Angeles* magazine, monthly; *LA Style* magazine, monthly; *Angeles Magazine*, monthly; *LA Weekly* and *LA Reader*, free newspapers with local listings of events about town.

TELEVISION STATIONS KCBS Channel 2–CBS; KNBC Channel 4–NBC; KABC Channel 7–ABC; KTTV Channel 11–Fox; KCET Channel 28–PBS.

RADIO STATIONS AM: KFWB 980 (all news); KNX 1070 (all news); KLAC 570 (country); KABC 790 (talk). FM: KCRW 89.9 (public); KUSC 91.5 (public); KCBS 93.1 (oldies); KPWR 105.5 (Top 40); KRTH 100.1 (oldies); KQLZ 100.3 (hard rock); KBIG 104.3 (adult contemporary).

FOOD To keep absolutely up-to-date, check the restaurant listings in *Los Angeles* magazine or consult the concierge at your hotel. Other good resources are the magazine and "Calendar" sections of the Sunday *LA Times*.

TELEPHONE The area code for central Los Angeles is 213. To reach Santa Monica, Inglewood, Beverly Hills, West Los Angeles, and Long Beach, the area code is 310. The 818 area code covers the San Fernando Valley and the upper half of the San Gabriel Valley. The 805 area code covers the Ventura–Santa Barbara area; the 714 area code, Orange County.

SALES TAX The sales tax is 8.25%; there also is a 12.5% hotel tax.

GETTING AROUND It's always more convenient to have a car for exploring Los Angeles; however, there are buses, taxis, and tour operators. In addition, the *Metrolink* rail service is scheduled to be completed this year.

BUS For route information on scheduled city buses, call the *Metropolitan Transit Agency (MTA)* (phone: 310-273-0910 in the Beverly Hills/West LA area; 626-4455 in Hollywood/central LA; and 818-781-5890 in the San Fernando Valley). There's also the *DASH* minibuses, whose routes travel through downtown's most scenic areas — from the Civic Center district to

California Plaza, Broadway, or Pershing Square — 24 hours a day, Mondays through Saturdays. The fare is a mere 25¢.

CAR RENTAL For information on renting a car, see GETTING READY TO GO.

SUBWAY Yes, we said subway — LA's first! A $5.3-billion underground rail running between Union Station (Alameda St. at Sunset Blvd.) and MacArthur Park, from 5 AM to 7 PM daily with stops at the Civic Center (1st and Hill Sts.), Pershing Square (5th and Hill Sts.), 7th Street, and Westlake-MacArthur Park. Tokens and tickets are available from vending machines at each station and cost $1.10 each.

TAXI Cabs *don't* cruise the streets in LA. Check at your hotel desk; different firms serve different areas. A few companies to try: *Bell Cab* (phone: 213-221-1112), *United Independent Taxi* (phone: 213-653-5050), and *LA Taxi* (phone: 213-627-7000).

TOURS *Star Line/Gray Line* (541 Hollywood Blvd., Hollywood; phone: 213-856-5900) is one of many companies offering tours of downtown LA (*Music Center,* Chinatown, Little Tokyo, Olvera St., and more) and of the Hollywood–Beverly Hills area, as well as *Disneyland, Knott's Berry Farm,* and *Universal Studios Hollywood.* There are tours that offer more than the usual sights, including tasteful trips through Southern California wine country, and the ghoulish *Graveline Tours,* which visits scenes of scandals, crimes, and misdemeanors in a renovated hearse (PO Box 931694, Hollywood, CA 90093; phone: 213-876-4286). *Insider's Tours* (phone: 310-392-4435) offers "Marilyn Monroe's Los Angeles," a visit to more than 50 sites frequented by the legendary blonde bombshell.

LOCAL SERVICES

AUDIOVISUAL EQUIPMENT *Ametron Rents* (phone: 213-466-4321).

BABY-SITTING *Weston's Babysitters Guild* (phone: 213-658-8792); *Community Job Shop* (phone: 818-345-2950).

BUSINESS SERVICES *Century Secretarial Service,* 2040 Ave. of the Stars, Suite 400, Century City (phone: 310-277-3329).

DRY CLEANER/TAILOR *Top Hat Cleaners* (8122 Santa Monica Blvd., W. Hollywood; phone: 213-654-5595); *The Cleaning Baron,* free pickup and delivery service (510 Washington Blvd.; phone: 310-823-8003).

LIMOUSINE *Brentwood Limousine* (phone: 800-296-5466 or 310-395-0932); *Carey Limousine* (phone: 310-275-4153 or 310-272-0081); *Classic Fleet Limousine Service* (phone: 213-753-4384).

MECHANIC *Bliss & Bothwell Auto Service,* 2110 Kotner Ave. (phone: 310-475-8651).

MEDICAL EMERGENCY For information on area hospitals and pharmacies, see GETTING READY TO GO.

MESSENGER SERVICES *Jet Delivery Inc.* (phone: 213-749-0123). Many hotels also can make arrangements.

PHOTOCOPIES *Barbara's Place,* 24-hour service Mondays through Thursdays; Fridays until 10 PM; and Saturdays from 10 AM to 4 PM (7925 Santa Monica Blvd., W. Hollywood; phone: 213-654-5902); *Copy Print,* 24-hour service, pickup and delivery (404 S. Figueroa Ave., in the *Bonaventure* hotel; phone: 213-620-6279).

PROFESSIONAL PHOTOGRAPHER *Vanguard Photography* (phone: 213-467-0552); *Atkinson Business Photography* (phone: 213-624-5950).

SECRETARY/STENOGRAPHER *Century Secretarial Service* (phone: 310-277-3329); *HQ Headquarters Company,* word processing, telex, fax, conference rooms (phone: 310-277-6660 and 310-551-6666).

TELECONFERENCE FACILITIES With the exception of the *Bel-Air* and the *Beverly Hilton,* all hotels listed in the very expensive and expensive categories under *Best in Town* have teleconferencing facilities.

TRANSLATOR *Berlitz* (phone: 213-380-1144).

WESTERN UNION/TELEX Many offices are located around the city (phone: 800-325-6000).

OTHER *Word Shop,* for word processing, is one of the many agencies in the area catering to business executives (phone: 213-381-3801); many hotels also can make arrangements.

SPECIAL EVENTS

Los Angeles is bustling with activity all year long. No matter what time of year you arrive, some not-to-be-missed festival or event will probably be taking place. For complete listings, check the local publications listed above or call the Greater Los Angeles Visitors and Convention Bureau (phone: 213-624-7300).

Here are a few of our favorite fetes.

CINCO DE MAYO! CINCO DE MAYO!

One of Mexico's most popular holidays is celebrated May 5 at the El Pueblo de Los Angeles Historic Park with puppet shows, mariachi music, and folkloric dancing. No admission charge. Downtown (phone: 213-625-5045).

STRAWBERRY FESTIVAL

Every year strawberry lovers gather to celebrate their favorite fruit. Included in the 2-day festivities in mid-May are chocolate dipping, a strawberry blonde contest, and much more. Admission charge. Oxnard (phone: 805-485-8833).

LOTUS FESTIVAL

A celebration of Asian Pacific cultures with dragon boat races, festive flower shows, art exhibits, and ethnic foods. Held every July in Echo Park. Take the Hollywood Freeway to the Echo Park Avenue exit. Downtown LA (phone: 213-485-8746).

INTERNATIONAL SURF FESTIVAL

At Manhattan, Hermosa, Torrance, and Redondo beaches, this event has no surfboarding competitions, but does have many other events — such as paddleboard races, a pier-to-pier swim, a sand-castle-making contest, and a body-surfing contest. Late July or August. Contact the Chamber of Commerce, 325 15th St., PO Box 3007, Manhattan Beach, CA 90266 (phone: 310-545-5313).

FESTIVAL OF THE ARTS AND PAGEANT OF THE MASTERS

Hundreds of artworks are displayed at the festival, held in August in scenic Laguna Beach, while the pageant features re-creations of great works of art using live models (phone: 714-494-1145).

NISEI JAPANESE FESTIVAL

This extraordinary week-long display of cultural pride and beauty features food, music, and dancing, plus a parade of locals dressed in native costume and a carnival. The festival is held in mid-August; in recent years, the crowds often have been surprised by celebrity appearances. No admission charge. Little Tokyo (phone: 714-620-0570).

AFRICAN MARKETPLACE & CULTURAL FAIR

An annual event that showcases arts and crafts from 23 different African cultures along with "tastes of Africa," a culinary sampling from local restaurants. The festival also features jazz, reggae, and *igbo irji new yam* (music native to the Nigerian culture). Held during the months of August and September at Rancho Cienega Park, 5001 Rodeo Blvd., near La Brea and Santa Monica Fwy. (phone: 213-734-1164).

LOS ANGELES COUNTY FAIR

The world's largest annual county fair, running a full 18 days from mid-September to early October, has something for everyone: Music, dancing, shows, rides, horse races, and contests of every sort all are part of the celebration. For information, contact the Los Angeles County Fair Association, Box 2250, Pomona, CA 91769 (phone: 714-623-3111).

LOS ANGELES BACH FESTIVAL

Now in its 59th year, this classical music fete features the works of Bach and other legendary composers including Handel and Vivaldi. The popular program is presented annually in October at the First Congregational Church at 540 S. Commonwealth St. (phone: 213-385-1345).

INTERNATIONAL FESTIVAL OF MASKS

A "fashion show" celebrating the city's great diversity, it features ethnic dance performances representing the Sudanese, Middle Eastern, Hawaiian, Guatemalan, and Greek cultures — all done in authentic native costumes, too. The fun begins late in October at Hancock Park (Wilshire Blvd. at Cloverdale). Downtown LA (phone: 213-937-5544).

Other annual events include the *Tournament of Roses Parade* and *Rose Bowl*, the traditional *New Year's Day* gridiron spectacle; *Los Angeles Open Golf Tournament*, Pacific Palisades, in February; *Los Angeles Marathon*, in March; *Long Beach Grand Prix Formula One Auto Racing*, in April; *Disneyland's Easter Parade*, UCLA's *Mardi Gras*, and *Manhattan Beach Art Festival*, in May; the *Playboy Jazz Festival*, at the *Hollywood Bowl*, in June; this year on June 18, 19, 22, and 26, and July 3, 13, 16, and 17, the *FIFA World Cup* soccer matches will be played at Pasadena's *Rose Bowl*; Fourth of July fireworks go off at *Anaheim Stadium* and Pasadena's *Rose Bowl*, as well as at the *Hollywood Bowl* and Burton Chase Park in Marina del Rey; *All-Star Shrine Football Game*, usually held in Pasadena's *Rose Bowl*, in July; *SeaFest*, Long Beach, in August; *Hollywood Christmas Parade* and the irreverent *DooDah Parade*, Pasadena, in November; and the *Christmas Boat Parade*, Marina del Rey, in December.

MUSEUMS

In addition to those described in *Special Places*, other fine museums in LA are the following:

ARMAND HAMMER MUSEUM OF ART Rembrandts, van Goghs, Cézannes, and Goyas are among the masterpieces that the late industrialist collected during his lifetime. Open daily. Admission charge. 10899 Wilshire Blvd. (phone: 310-443-7000).

GENE AUTRY WESTERN HERITAGE MUSEUM Featuring art and artifacts from the Wild West, this nonprofit collection, sponsored and run by the legendary Western singer–film star's Autry Foundation, spans the years from the late 17th century to the present. Fun for the whole family; many of the hands-on displays were created by the Walt Disney Imagineering design firm.

Open Tuesdays through Sundays, 10 AM to 5 PM. Admission charge. 4700 Western Heritage Way, Hollywood (phone: 213-667-2000).

HOLLYWOOD MOVIE COSTUME MUSEUM Original costumes of Tinseltown's greatest stars from 6 decades of moviemaking. Open Sundays through Thursdays, 10 AM to 8 PM. Admission charge. 6630 Hollywood Blvd., Hollywood (phone: 213-962-6892).

JAPANESE AMERICAN NATIONAL MUSEUM Dedicated to preserving the history of Japanese-Americans, this museum is housed in poignant and appropriate quarters. The building, erected in 1925 as a Buddhist temple, was used as a warehouse for the possessions of Japanese-Americans when they were herded into internment camps during World War II. The exhibits, which change quarterly, include photographs, moving images, letters, tools, clothing, works of art and personal possessions that have been passed from generation to generation. Closed Mondays. Admission charge. 369 E. 1st St. (phone: 213-625-0414).

LOS ANGELES CHILDREN'S MUSEUM There are 18 hands-on exhibits and special workshops for children of all ages. Open daily. No admission charge for children under 2. 310 N. Main St. (phone: 213-687-8800).

MUSEUM OF FLYING A collection of vintage flying machines along with a model plane shop, restoration hangar, and a theater showing various films on topics related to air travel, such as old airplanes and the history of flight technology. Open Wednesdays through Sundays, 10 AM to 5 PM. Admission charge. 2772 Donald Douglas Loop N., Santa Monica (phone: 310-392-8822).

MUSEUM OF NEON ART Calling this "art" is debatable, but still you're bound to get a charge out of this whimsical collection of neon and electric signs, including sculpture and classic theater marquees. Open Tuesdays through Saturdays. Admission charge. 1000 Universal Center Dr., No. 154 *CityWalk* (phone: 213-617-0274).

MUSEUM OF SCIENCE AND INDUSTRY Hands-on science, mathematics, aerospace, energy, and health exhibits encourage children to take an active role in their own education. One of the newer additions to the museum's permanent exhibitions is Our Urban Environment, an innovative ecological exploration. Also be sure to check out the Space Garden, with a DC-8 and a real Apollo space capsule on display — a treat for children and adults alike. Open daily. No admission charge, except for IMAX theater (phone: 213-744-2014). 700 S. State, Exposition Park (phone: 213-744-7400).

NATURAL HISTORY MUSEUM If you only have time to visit one museum, make it this one. With exhibits illustrating the cultural and technological changes of the past 100 years, it has a wing devoted to American history, a dazzling hall of gems and minerals, the Ralph W. Schreiber Hall of Birds, a large taxidermy collection of North American and African mammals imaginatively posed in picturesque display cases, and ever-changing, traveling exhibitions. The Ralph M. Parsons Discovery Center is entertaining and educational. Learning is easy with hands-on exhibits that are as much fun for adults as they are for children. Closed Mondays. Admission charge, except the first Tuesday of each month. 900 Exposition Blvd. (phone: 213-744-3466).

NORTON SIMON MUSEUM OF ART The rich industrialist's multimillion-dollar collection. Five centuries of European art from the Renaissance to the 20th century. You'll find Rembrandts, such as *The Bearded Man in the Wide Brimmed Hat, Self Portait,* and *Titus;* a sizable collection of Picasso's paintings, sketches, and sculptures, highlighted by his famous *Woman with Book;* and a Degas gallery, featuring *Waiting,* one of Degas's many masterpieces. The museum's collection of Impressionist art (van Gogh, Monet, Renoir) and its selections of early Renaissance and baroque art also are impressive. In addition, there's Asian sculpture spanning a period of 2,000 years. The only thing the museum lacks is a place to eat. Open Thursdays through Sundays. Admission charge. 411 W. Colorado Blvd., Pasadena (phone: 818-449-6840).

RICHARD NIXON LIBRARY & BIRTHPLACE Opened in 1990, it includes a 52,000-square-foot, Spanish-style library with exhibits chronicling the former president's life and career, plus the modest frame house in which Nixon was born in 1913. Open daily. Admission charge. 18001 Yorba Linda Blvd., Yorba Linda (phone: 714-993-3393).

ROY ROGERS & DALE EVANS MUSEUM An exact replica of a frontier fort, featuring highlights of the lives of this famed Wild West celluloid couple, who trotted their way through dozens of motion pictures, as well as a tribute to Roy's Trigger and Dale's faithful steed, Buttermilk — the horses themselves are preserved and mounted on pedestals. Open daily. Admission charge. 15650 Seneca Rd., Victorville (phone: 619-243-4547).

SIMON WEISENTHAL CENTER BEIT HASHOAH MUSEUM OF TOLERANCE Quite a name for this $50-million, 165,000-square-foot museum and educational center, founded in 1993 to "challenge visitors to confront bigotry and racism and understand the Holocaust in both historical and contemporary contexts." Besides a permanent exhibition level, the center features a multimedia learning facility with 30 workstations from which visitors can access extensive historical and informational data; an extensive archival collection; and the dramatic Tower of Witness, which showcases more than 2,000 photographs of victims of Auschwitz-Birkenau. The 8-level complex also features a theater, an auditorium, a memorial plaza, and a temporary exhibit area. Closed Saturdays. Admission charge. 9786 W. Pico Blvd. (phone: 310-553-9036).

SOUTHWEST MUSEUM Devoted to the anthropology of the Southwest, this museum contains some of the finest examples of Native American art and artifacts in the US. Be sure to ask about the featured exhibit, as periodically there are special displays, all dealing with Indian culture and lore. Closed Mondays. Admission charge. 234 Museum Dr., near *Dodger Stadium* (phone: 213-221-2163).

MAJOR COLLEGES AND UNIVERSITIES

There are many major university campuses spread throughout the LA area, in addition to dozens of colleges and junior colleges. The University of California, Los Angeles (UCLA) is among the top-ranked universities in the nation and is known to college football and basketball fans for its *Bruins* teams (main campus at 405 Hilgard Ave.; phone: 310-825-4321). The University of Southern California (USC) also is a major institution and, with teams like the *Trojans,* is UCLA's archrival in sports (Exposition Blvd. and Figueroa St.; phone: 213-740-2311). California Institute of Technology, which excels in science and engineering, counts more than 20 Nobel laureates among its alumni and past and present faculty (main campus at 1201 E. California Blvd., Pasadena; phone: 818-356-6326).

SHOPPING

No single street on this planet so typifies consumer excess as Rodeo Drive in Beverly Hills. Few mortals will be able to afford the prices, but window shopping along this avenue for the affluent makes for as much fun as studying the boutiques along Paris's Rue du Faubourg-St.-Honoré, London's Bond Street, or New York's Fifth Avenue. In fact, many of the shop names are the same. Only a few are homegrown, such as *Fred Hayman.* This supposed model for the title store of Judith Krantz's steamy novel *Scruples* sold its name and wildly successful fragrance to Avon. Don't miss *Two Rodeo,* a charming enclave of pricey shops and boutiques set on Italianate cobblestone lanes that surround a piazza, travertine fountains, and an elaborate staircase similar to the Spanish Steps in Rome. The retail newcomers who have settled here represent the crème-de-la-crème in high fashion and jewelry. Here is a list of the top emporia along Rodeo and environs:

BALLY OF SWITZERLAND High-style shoes for men (340 N. Rodeo Dr.; phone: 310-271-0666); and for women (409 N. Rodeo Dr.; phone: 310-275-0962).

BIJAN Where the rich and famous shop for men's clothing; by appointment only. 420 N. Rodeo Dr. (phone: 310-273-6544).

BULGARI The century-old purveyor of fine jewelry known for its exquisitely designed bangles and baubles. 201 N. Rodeo Dr., in the *Two Rodeo* complex (phone: 310-858-9216).

CARROLL & CO. Ivy League clothing for men. 466 N. Rodeo Dr. (phone: 310-273-9060).

CARTIER Internationally renowned jewelers since 1847, with two locations on Rodeo. 370 N. Rodeo Dr. (phone: 310-275-4272); and 220 N. Rodeo Dr. (phone: 310-275-4855).

CHANEL Clothes, scents, and accessories from the famous fashion house. 301 N. Rodeo Dr. (phone: 310-278-5500).

CHARLES JOURDAN Clothes, shoes, and accessories from the French firm. 201 N. Rodeo Dr., in the *Two Rodeo* complex (phone: 310-273-3507).

CHRISTIAN DIOR In the spiffy *Two Rodeo Drive* complex, this is a replica of the Paris flagship store, with Louis XVI furnishings, and features women's ready-to-wear, cosmetics, men's and women's accessories, jewelry, and watches. 230 N. Rodeo Dr. (phone: 310-859-4700).

DAVID ORGELL Crystal, china, antique and modern silver, and jewelry. 320 N. Rodeo Dr. (phone: 310-273-6660).

DYANSEN GALLERIES Fine art. 339 N. Rodeo Dr. (phone: 310-275-0165).

ELLIOTT KATT'S BOOKS ON THE PERFORMING ARTS Crammed with a tremendous selection of rare books pertaining to the performing arts, this amazingly informative shop is frequented by professionals in the movie and theater industry, as well as celebrities, who thumb through the vast casting and agency directories. Owner Katt stocks biographies of actors and directors, books on film, scores from famous Broadway musicals, as well as how-to books on everything from writing for television to getting a job in the music industry. 8568 Melrose Ave. (phone: 310-652-5178).

FERRAGAMO A large selection of the famous Ferragamo shoes and leather goods, women's ready-to-wear and men's furnishings — ties, dress shirts, polo shirts, silk robes. Jason Robards and Ricardo Montalban shop here. 357 N. Rodeo Dr. (phone: 310-273-9990).

FRANCES KLEIN Antique jewelry. 310 N. Rodeo Dr. (phone: 310-273-0155).

FRED HAYMAN Beverly Hills' legendary landmark store. Home of the "273" Exceptional Fragrance collection, FHBH signature leather goods and evening bags, and collections from hot, young designers such as Eva Chun, Zang Toi, Christian Francis Roth, and C.D. Greene, to name a few. It has a stand-up bar and complimentary drinks for shoppers in what used to be *Giorgio*. 273 N. Rodeo Dr. (phone: 310-271-3000).

FRED JOAILLIER Expensive jewelry, leather goods, and gifts. 401 N. Rodeo Dr. (phone: 310-278-3733).

GIORGIO ARMANI BOUTIQUE The designer's coveted clothes for men and women. 436 N. Rodeo Dr. (phone: 310-271-5555).

GUCCI Italian leather goods, jewelry, clothing, and accessories. 347 N. Rodeo Dr. (phone: 310-278-3451).

HARRY WINSTON Exquisite, expensive jewelry. 371 N. Rodeo Dr. (phone: 310-271-8554).

HERMÈS Classic signature scarves, famous perfumes (including Caléche, Parfum d'Hermès, Amazone, and Equipage), and sumptuous leather goods from France. 343 N. Rodeo Dr. (phone: 310-278-6440).

JURGENSEN'S Fine and fancy foods. 316 N. Beverly Dr. (phone: 310-858-7814).

KRIZIA The Italian designer's boutique. 410 N. Rodeo Dr. (phone: 310-276-5411).

LOUIS VUITTON Famous French handbags, accessories, and luggage. 307 N. Rodeo Dr. (phone: 310-859-0457).

NEIMAN MARCUS The specialty store from Dallas for those who have almost everything. 9700 Wilshire Blvd. (phone: 310-550-5900).

POLO/RALPH LAUREN Every Lauren item you ever wanted and then some. Goldie Hawn, Tom Selleck, and Sally Field are among the regulars. 444 N. Rodeo Dr. (phone: 310-281-7200).

THE RODEO COLLECTION A posh half-block mall, representing *Gianni Versace, Sonia Rykiel, Merletto, Fogal,* and *Furla,* among others. 421 N. Rodeo Dr. (phone: 310-858-7580).

SAMUEL FRENCH This West Coast outlet for the oldest play publishers in the world (since 1833) has an extensive collection of drama books, biographies of film directors and stars, and a tremendous selection of plays. 7623 Sunset Blvd. (phone: 310-876-0570).

SCRIPTORIUM This gallery sells the autographs of a wide variety of famous people — mostly historical figures such as Jimmy Carter, Abraham Lincoln, Lillian Gish, and Andy Warhol, although there are a few signatures of contemporary celebrities as well. Closed Mondays. 427 N. Canon Dr. (phone: 310-275-6060).

SHARPER IMAGE The very latest in high-tech toys. 9550 Santa Monica Blvd. (phone: 310-271-0515).

SUPERIOR STAMP & COIN Gold coins and rare stamps. 9478 W. Olympic Blvd. (phone: 310-278-9740).

TIFFANY & CO. Fine jewelry in the famous blue boxes. 210 N. Rodeo Dr. (phone: 310-273-8880).

WILLIAMS-SONOMA Dining-table and kitchen outfitters. 317 N. Beverly Dr. (phone: 310-274-9127).

For specialty shopping with more native character, browse in several burgeoning areas, such as the following:

MELROSE AVENUE It runs an eastward gamut from upscale to funky to weird, with Gallery Row found roughly between Doheny Drive and Fairfax Avenue. *LA Impressions* (8318 Melrose Ave.; phone: 310-659-3336) specializes in Mexican art. At *Gemini Gel* (8365 Melrose Ave.; phone 213-651-0513), a superb maker and exhibitor of limited-edition prints, customers watch the printing process through upstairs gallery windows. At *A Star Is Worn* (7303 Melrose Ave.; phone: 213-939-4922) celebrity clothes, from the dress Barbra Streisand wore to the 1968 Academy Awards to Cher's more casual togs, even Richard Gere's tie, are for sale. For an offbeat souvenir, try *Wild Blue* (7220 Melrose Ave.; phone: 213-939-8434) where the ceramics and crockery seem to have a sense of humor.

Finals (7374½ Melrose Ave.; phone: 213-653-8292) is filled with unique leather jackets, denim shirts, and such. For those who never left the 1960s behind, *Retail Slut* (7264 Melrose Ave.; phone: 213-934-1339) is a must for its collection of campy shoes, clothing, and tacky accessories. With an authentic 1944 AT-6 attack plane dangling from the ceiling, *The Cockpit* (9609 Santa Monica Blvd., Beverly Hills; phone: 310-274-7525) carries everything aviation-related, from bomber jackets, jeans, and glasses to the very chic white "Red Baron" silk scarf. Antiques and gift shops, fashion boutiques, restaurants, and small theaters prosper all the way to La Brea Boulevard. Also see *Quintessential Los Angeles* in DIVERSIONS.

WEST THIRD STREET Due to the rising rents on Melrose Avenue, many merchants have relocated to West Third Street and other blocks nearby. *Craft and Folk Art Museum Gift Shop* (5800 Wilshire Blvd.; phone: 213-937-9099) features outstanding handcrafts by American artisans. *Freehand* (8413 W. Third St.; phone: 213-655-2607) boasts three rooms of beautiful ceramics, handloomed, raw-silk clothing, and imaginative jewelry. Next door, *New Stone Age* (8407 W. Third St.; phone: 213-658-5969) features one-of-a-kind, artist-designed goods that have to be seen to be believed. Baskets woven out of telephone wire, reconditioned radios painted Day-Glo colors, ceramics, vases, and jewelry made out of God-knows-what.

For city slickers who dream of owning a ranch in the hills (Hollywood, that is) *Paris Go* (8432 Sunset Blvd., W. Hollywood; phone: 213-650-8395) has everything for the well-dressed cowpoke — hats, neckerchiefs, belt buckles, leather boots, and other Western–style paraphernalia. *Sonrisa* (7609 Beverly Blvd., phone: 213-935-8438), a Taos transplant, is the place to go for unique crafts from New Mexico and Mexico. Located in the decorator showroom district, *Tesoro* (319 S. Robertson Blvd.; phone: 310-273-9890) showcases functional and wearable art. Pick out a sculpted bowl for a wedding gift, have dinnerware made to match your decor, or buy jewelry that looks like sugar candy.

MONTANA AVENUE This cornucopia of small shops has sprung up between 7th and 17th Streets along this Santa Monica thoroughfare and has become a window shopper's delight. Among the pricey and super-specialized boutiques, there's silk lingerie at *Lisa Norman* (1134 Montana Ave.; phone: 310-854-4422); *Where's My Conga!* for funky, retro clothing (900 Montana Ave.; phone: 310-451-1879); *Private Stock* features unusual men's apparel (1609-B Montana Ave.; phone: 310-451-9431); be sure to browse through *Nonesuch Art & Antiques* (1211 Montana Ave.; phone: 310-393-1245). Afterward quench your thirst with a brew at *Father's Office,* an authentic English-style pub (1018 Montana Ave.; phone: 213-393-BEER). Then mosey on up to *Yippie-ei-o,* purveyors of trendy cowboy collectibles (1308 Montana Ave.; phone: 310-451-2520). Pick up a Gene Autry coffee mug or just enjoy a free cup of "joe."

Lest anyone forgo the rather overwhelming experience of shopping in a mall, LA offers some of the finest, as well as some of the most eclectic, merchandise marts in the country. Among the largest shopping complexes are *Beverly Center* (8500 Beverly Blvd.; phone: 310-854-0070); *Century City Shopping Center* (10250 Santa Monica Blvd.; phone: 310-277-3898); *Del Amo Shopping Center* (Hawthorne Blvd. and Carson St.; phone: 310-542-8525); *Glendale Galleria* (2148 *Glendale Galleria;* phone: 818-240-9481); *South Coast Plaza* (3333 Bristol St.; phone: 714-435-2000); *One Colorado* (24 E. Union St. Pasadena; phone: 818-564-1066); *Sherman Oaks Galleria* (15301 Ventura Blvd.; phone: 818-884-7090); *Westside Pavilion* (10800 W. Pico Blvd.; phone: 310-474-5940); and *Woodland Hills Promenade* (50 *Promenade Mall;* phone: 818-884-7090).

DISCOUNT STORES

From the sublime to the funky — and now to the ridiculously inexpensive. Should you need some help in planning your shopping spree, *Geri Cook's Tours* (14755 Ventura Blvd., Sherman Oaks; phone: 818-907-6111) offers five discount shopping tours in greater Los Angeles: Downtown Garment District; LA's Chic Westside; San Fernando Valley Treasures; Pasadena Roundup; and the Barstow Factory Outlets. The price ($30 per person) includes a fancy box lunch (except on the Barstow tour), prizes, and surprises. The tours are run for groups, but individual shoppers can join if there's space. Custom-tailored tours and a newsletter, *Best Bargains,* are also available. *Outlet Shopping Tours* (2629 Manhattan Ave., Hermosa Beach; phone: 310-372-9930) features excursions to Barstow priced at $24 per person. The tours usually are run for groups, but individual shoppers can tag along if there's room.

Here are some real LA bargains.

THE ADDRESS A resale boutique offering designer duds by Adolfo, Chanel, Armani, and Valentino from some star-studded closets. 1116 Wilshire Blvd., Santa Monica (phone: 310-394-1406).

ALANDALE'S Armani for the masses. These men's suits, of the finest Italian fabrics, come from the same factory that makes Giorgio Armani's upscale line, only without the label — and about half the price. 10500 W. Pico Blvd. (phone: 310-838-8100).

ALMOST (AND) PERFECT ENGLISH CHINA This is in the Valley and well worth a trip. Top-quality English china at discount prices. 14519 Ventura Blvd., Sherman Oaks (phone: 818-905-6650).

AVERY Just about everything that goes into a kitchen — from wire whisks to stockpots. Also some fun items like movie-theater popcorn machines and hot-fudge dispensers. 905 E. Second St. (phone: 213-624-7832).

BLACK & WHITE A great place with rock-bottom prices. Most of the merchandise costs twice as much in other stores; mainly carries the Karen Kane label. 1250 S. Broadway (phone: 213-746-5841).

CHIC CONSPIRACY Another snazzy resale shop selling designer clothes, shoes, and accessories at great prices. 10955 W. Pico Blvd., West Los Angeles (phone: 310-475-5542).

CITADEL OUTLET COLLECTION Housed in an incredibly beautiful, restored Assyrian temple, it features 44 outlet stores that sell goods from fashion to home furnishings at 30% to 75% off. Big-name stores include *AnnTaylor, Adolfo II, The Gap, Eddie Bauer, Linen Club, Perry Ellis Shoes* — *The Citadel* has it all, minutes from downtown LA. 5675 E. Telegraph Rd., City of Commerce (phone: 213-888-1220).

COOPER BUILDING Located in the heart of the Garment District, this is an entire building of clothing manufacturers' outlet shops. Check out the building directory if you know what you're looking for; if not, just start at the top and work your way down. Designer clothes for women can be had for 50% off, and popular, casual clothes for men can be scooped up at savings of from 33% to 50%. 860 S. Los Angeles St. (phone: 213-622-1139).

DESIGNER LABELS FOR LESS A shopper's wonderland of women's and men's designer fashion for 40% to 80% below department store prices. 1924 S. Main St., Downtown LA (phone: 213-746-2347).

DUTY FREE PERFUMERY INC. Over 2,000 domestic and French fragrances offered at 40% discount. 9636 Brighton Way, Beverly Hills (phone: 310-273-1969).

DUTY FREE SHOPPER WEST Savings on everything from fine apparel for men and women to liquor and tobacco products. 420 E. Third St., Downtown LA (phone: 213-615-1039).

FACTORY MERCHANTS OUTLET PLAZA More than 50 outlets such as *Lenox China, Anne Klein, Evan-Picone, Ralph Lauren, Levi's,* and *London Fog.* There's something for everyone at rock-bottom prices, 20% to 70% off normal retail. This outlet is referred to by its location — "Barstow." (Barstow is about a 2-hour drive from Los Angeles, halfway to Las Vegas. Take the No. 15 Freeway north and exit at Lenwood Road, just south of Barstow, and follow the signs to the *Plaza* — it's visible from the freeway. If you're a committed shopper, the trip is well worth it.) To avoid the hassle of driving, consider an escorted shopping tour (see above). 2837 Lenwood Rd., Barstow (phone: 619-253-7342 or 619-253-7354).

FOR KIDS ONLY Some of the finest names in children's togs, at 30% to 60% off. An incredible collection of European imports — shoes, too! 746 N. Fairfax Ave., Los Angeles (phone: 213-650-4885).

FREEPORT INTERNATIONAL This is a wholesale perfume distributor with the genuine article: top-name scents at top savings. No watered-down formulas here. 1058 S. Main St., Downtown LA (phone: 213-745-3000).

JEAN'S STAR APPAREL Savvy women shoppers descend upon this place for designer wear at a fraction of its original price. Chanel, Adolfo, Armani are just a few of the names represented here. 1536 Ventura Blvd., Sherman Oaks (phone: 818-789-3710).

MAX FACTOR COSMETICS OUTLET Located in the beauty museum, this store offers huge discounts on Max Factor, Cover Girl, and Clarion products. Also look for special premiums such as tote bags, T-shirts, and sweatshirts. 1666 N. Highland Ave., Hollywood (phone: 213-463-6164).

THE PLACE AND COMPANY A first-rate resale boutique for designer casual and evening wear. 8820 S. Sepulveda Blvd., Los Angeles (phone: 213-645-1539).

ROBERTS INTERIORS Tucked away in an industrial complex, this is actually a catalogue operation with a large in-house inventory. All styles of furnishing and accessories at 40% discount. 4935 McConnell Ave., No. 10, Los Angeles (phone: 310-822-3028).

ROCK STAR Strictly for rock 'n' roll wannabes, this place features all sorts of spandex, Madonna-like bustiers, and vibrantly hued leather apparel. 7280 Melrose Ave., Los Angeles (phone: 213-939-STAR).

SILK FACTORY This is the place for affordable silks, linen, and quality cotton garments in women's larger sizes. 3100 Wilshire Blvd., Los Angeles (phone: 213-487-0087).

STEVEN CRAIG WHOLESALE CLOTHIERS Open to the public Wednesdays through Saturdays only, this place offers fine contemporary men's apparel at 50% off. A no-frills operation, but their selection and prices can't be beat. 19365 Business Center Dr., No. 9, Northridge (phone: 818-701-7473).

SUSIE'S DEALS The latest in hip, happening junior sportswear at discount prices. 1408 Vine St., Hollywood (phone: 213-466-3081).

VINTAGE SHOPPING It doesn't get any hipper or more happening than *American Rag,* an Art Deco complex of five affiliated shops showcasing a mixed bag of high-ticket haute couture, outrageous accessories, and budget-friendly fashions. You could spend an entire day just browsing here. The complex is set along one city block on the east side of La Brea Avenue. Its shops sport a French countryside motif with high, vaulted ceilings and funky flooring. *American Rag,* the main store, proffers new and vintage fashions from designer jeans to outlandish leather jackets priced as high as $8,000. Happily, most of the clothes are more affordable (150 S. La Brea Ave.; phone: 213-935-3154). *Maison et Café,* next door and accessible through an inside passageway, is a perky sidewalk café and curio shop rolled into one. Enjoy a cappuccino and baguette or browse among unique bric-a-brac and artifacts. For collectors, there are antique Pernod bottles and rare books, marvelous mosaic tile tables, and handpicked European dinnerware (148 S. La Brea Ave.; phone: 213-935-3157). A short walk away is *Shoes,* a Moroccan-style bootery featuring French and Italian footwear along with tennis shoes (144 S. La Brea Ave.; phone: 213-931-6903). *Colours,* a super-hip bargain outlet, is popular with rock and rap stars; nothing here costs more than $30 (124 S. La Brea Ave.; phone: 213-931-6903). Next door is *Youth,* a stylish kid's shop with unusual togs, accessories, and playthings (136 S. La Brea Ave.; phone: 213-965-1404). Even if you're not in a shopping mood, this complex is worth a stroll if only to see Margot Werts's riveting window displays of life-like mannequins posed to depict the retro-contemporary and vintage-trendy theme of each individual shop.

SPORTS AND FITNESS

There is no question that Southern California is a paradise for sports lovers.

BASEBALL The Los Angeles *Dodgers, Dodger Stadium* (1000 Elysian Park Ave.; phone: 213-224-1500); California *Angels, Anaheim Stadium* (2000 State College Blvd., Anaheim; phone: 213-625-1123 or 714-937-6700).

BASKETBALL The NBA *Lakers* play at the *Great Western Forum* (3900 Manchester Blvd., Inglewood; phone: 310-419-3100 or 310-419-3182 for tickets). The *Clippers* play at the *LA Memorial Coliseum and Sports Arena* (3939 S. Figueroa; phone: 213-748-6131).

BICYCLING Biking is great around the Westwood UCLA campus, Griffith Park, and on the oceanside, where there is a 19-mile bike path between the city of Torrance and Pacific Palisades.

FISHING Power and sailing boats can be rented from *Rent-A-Sail* (13719 Fiji Way, Marina del Rey; phone: 310-822-1868). Fishermen catch halibut, bonito, and bass off the LA shores. Sportfishing boats leave daily from San Pedro, 22 minutes from downtown Los Angeles, site of the LA port, and from the Redondo Beach Marina in Redondo Beach.

FITNESS CENTERS *The Sports Connection* (8612 Santa Monica Blvd., West Hollywood; 310-652-7440) caters to starlets, models, and movie industry types. This branch of a Southern California chain is equipped with Nautilus machines, weight rooms, steamrooms, sauna, pool, and Jacuzzi as well as a full schedule of exercise classes. *Sports Club LA* (1835 Sepulveda Blvd.; 310-473-1447), a $22-million fitness center complete with state-of-the-art amenities, is where the city's "power" players work out. It's not uncommon to catch a glimpse of celebrities such as Madonna, Debra Winger, or Brooke Shields. *Nautilus and Aerobics Plus,* on the ground floor of the International Tower Building (888 Figueroa St.; phone: 213-488-0095), offers aerobics classes and has a Jacuzzi and sauna. It also has branches all over the metropolitan area. Many hotels have their own health clubs, too (see *Checking In*).

FOOTBALL Champions of the Big 10 and Pacific 10 college conferences meet in the *Pasadena Rose Bowl* every *New Year's Day.* UCLA plays its home games at the *Rose Bowl,* and USC plays at the *Coliseum* (3939 S. Figueroa; phone: 213-747-7111). The NFL *Rams* play at *Anaheim Stadium* (phone: 213-625-1123 or 714-937-6767). The NFL *Raiders* kick off at the *Coliseum.*

GOLF The *Industry Hills Golf Club* (One Industry Hills Pkwy., City of Industry; phone: 818-810-HILL) boasts two 18-hole golf courses, designed by William Bell, with 160 sand bunkers, 8 lakes, and miles of astoundingly long fairways. Greens fees are $42 weekdays, $60 on weekends. There are also an ultramodern, lighted driving range and four practice putting greens. For more information on golf courses in the Los Angeles area, see *Best Golf Outside the City* in DIVERSIONS. Golf enthusiasts gather to watch the *Los Angeles Open,* which attracts some of the world's top golfers. Held in February at the *Riviera Country Club,* Pacific Palisades (phone: 310-454-6591).

HOCKEY The *Kings* make their home at the *Great Western Forum,* 3900 Manchester Blvd., Inglewood (phone: 310-673-1300 or 310-480-3282 for tickets).

HORSE RACING If you like to spend your nights at the track, make tracks for *Los Alamitos.* There's harness, quarterhorse, and thoroughbred racing year-round, and it's especially festive during the *Orange County Fair Meet.* Take Freeway 605 south to Katella Avenue exit in Orange County (phone: 310-431-1361 or 714-995-1234). If you prefer daytime action, try *Hollywood Park* between mid-April and late July and from early November to *Christmas Eve* (near Los Angeles International Airport between Manchester and Century Blvds.; phone: 310-419-1500). There's also thoroughbred racing at *Santa Anita Park,* home of this year's *Breeder's Cup* (Huntington

Dr. and Baldwin Ave., Arcadia; phone: 818-574-7223), from late December to mid-April and in October and November.

JOGGING Downtown, run around Echo Park Lake (a little less than a mile) during the day only; get there by going up Sunset and taking a right onto Glendale. In Griffith Park, run in the woodsy Ferndale area near the Vermont Avenue entrance; get to the park via the Golden State Freeway and watch for the sign to turn off. In Westwood, UCLA has a hilly 4-mile perimeter course and a quarter-mile track. Four blocks from Century City, Cheviot Hills Park (at 2551 Motor Ave.) has a runners' course. And in Beverly Hills, jog in Roxbury Park (entrance at 471 S. Roxbury Dr. and Olympic) or along the 1½-mile stretch of Santa Monica Boulevard between Doheny and Wilshire. Jogging also is popular along the oceanside bike path between Marina del Rey and the Palos Verdes Peninsula, in Santa Monica's Palisades Park on Ocean Avenue, and along San Vicente Boulevard from Brentwood to Ocean Avenue.

POLO Will Rogers State Park (14253 Sunset Blvd., Pacific Palasades; phone: 310-454-8212) offers free matches to spectators on weekends year-round. Matches are played on Saturdays and Sundays, 10 AM to 12:30 PM and 2 to 4 PM. At the 4,000-seat *Equidome* in Griffith Park, games run twice a month from July to December, 7 to 8 PM. For information, contact *Polo America,* LA Equestrian Center, 480 Riverside Dr., Burbank (phone: 818-842-4827). The *Santa Barbara Polo Club* is open to the public on Sundays from April to October. Matches are scheduled at 1 and 3 PM; there is a reasonable admission charge.

SWIMMING AND SURFING The best beaches for swimming: El Porto Beach in Manhattan Beach, Will Rogers State Beach in Pacific Palisades, and Zuma Beach, north of Malibu. For surfing, Malibu Surfrider Beach, Hermosa Beach, El Porto Beach, and Zuma Beach are tops. For more information see *Best Beaches* in DIVERSIONS.

TENNIS *Griffith Park* (Riverside and Los Feliz; phone: 213-664-1191), one of the top 25 municipal tennis facilities in the US according to *Tennis* magazine, boasts 12 outdoor courts, all lighted for night play. Reservations can be made through the city of Los Angeles for a small fee. At the *Racquet Centre* (10933 Ventura Blvd., Studio City; phone: 818-760-2302), there are 20 lighted courts, a tennis shop, and a locker room and showers. If you're pressed for time, go to the *Tennis Place* (5880 West Third St.; phone: 213-931-1715). With a prime LA location, it has 16 lighted, hard-surface courts; lessons and practice sessions with a ball machine are also available. Top-seeded players on the pro circuit generally show up for the *Volvo/Los Angeles Pro Tournament* held in July at UCLA (phone: 310-208-0730).

VOLLEYBALL If volleyball is your game, you won't have any trouble having a hands-on or a spectator's experience. There are nets up on most beaches in Los Angeles County, and both amateur and professional tournaments take place year-round. At Manhattan and Hermosa beaches, 26 professional competitions are held during March and September. For a schedule of the competitions, contact the *Association of Volleyball Professionals* (phone: 310-337-4842). Indoor volleyball is also popular and played regularly by local leagues at most of the area's 150 public parks. For more information, contact the *Southern California Volleyball Association* (phone: 310-320-9440) or the *Valley Municipal Sports Office* (phone: 818-989-8070).

SOCCER SPECIAL International soccer's premier event, the *FIFA World Cup*, will be hosted for the first time by the US this year. The 52 games of the quadrennial event, the world's largest single-sport competition, take place from June 17 through July 17 in nine venues, including the *Rose Bowl* in Pasadena, CA. The games in the Los Angeles region are set for June 18, 19, 22, and 26; and July 3, 13, 16, and 17. The schedule includes a semifinal game on July 13, a third place match on July 16, and the World Cup final on July 17. Tickets are available in groups of five games; prices for the games at the *Rose Bowl* range from $140 to $355 per group. Tickets for individual games will be available in February. For further information, call the *World Cup USA Hotline* at 310-277-9494.

THEATER

There is no shortage of stages in LA, despite the overshadowing presence of the film industry. The *Center Theater Group* performs at the *Music Center*'s *Ahmanson Theater* and *Mark Taper Forum*. For information about either, call 213-972-7211. Also downtown is the *Los Angeles Theatre Center* (514 S. Spring St.; phone: 213-627-5599). The revived *State Theatre of California* is at the *Pasadena Playhouse* (39 S. El Molina Ave.; phone: 818-356-7529). Other Los Angeles theaters include the *Doolittle Theatre* (1615 N. Vine St., Hollywood; phone: 213-462-6666); the *Shubert Theatre* (in the ABC Entertainment Center, 2020 Ave. of the Stars, Century City; for information and credit card reservations, call 800-233-3123); the *Odyssey Theatre Ensemble* in three small theaters (all at 2055 S. Sepulveda; phone: 310-477-2055); and the *Pantages Theatre* (6233 Hollywood Blvd.; phone: 310-410-1062). Tickets for all major events can be ordered over the telephone through *Ticketmaster* (phone: 213-480-3232). For more information, see *Performing Arts* in DIVERSIONS.

MUSIC

All kinds of music can be heard in LA's concert halls and clubs. The *Los Angeles Philharmonic* plays at the *Dorothy Chandler Pavilion, Music Cen-*

ter (phone: 213-972-7211). The *Hollywood Bowl* (2301 N. Highland Ave., Hollywood; phone: 213-850-2000) is a 17,630-seat hillside amphitheater that features famous guest entertainers and is the summer home of the *Philharmonic*. Leading popular performers in a wide range of musical styles play year-round at the *Universal Amphitheatre* (Hollywood Fwy. at Lankershim Blvd.; phone: 818-980-9421). The *Greek Theatre* (2700 N. Vermont Ave.; phone: 310-410-1062) is a 6,200-seat indoor theater with concerts by top names. The *Roxy Theatre* (9009 Sunset Blvd.; phone: 310-276-2222) is also good for concerts. For country music, check out the *Palomino Club* (6907 Lankershim Blvd., N. Hollywood; phone: 818-983-1321). Rock and jazz buffs should try the *Palace* (1735 N. Vine, near Hollywood and Vine; phone: 213-462-3000), where the rock theater–dance club downstairs often has live shows as well as dancing. Upstairs, the *Palace Court* has live jazz on weekends. Other choices include the *Hollywood Roosevelt* hotel's *Cinegrille* (7000 Hollywood Blvd., Hollywood; phone: 213-466-7000), an Art Deco cabaret with blues, jazz, and Broadway show performances; *Kingston 12* (814 Pico Blvd., Santa Monica; phone: 310-451-4423) for reggae; *The Music Machine* (12220 Pico Blvd., W. Los Angeles; phone: 310-820-5150), featuring a mixed bag of musical styles. For more information, see *Performing Arts* in DIVERSIONS.

NIGHTCLUBS AND NIGHTLIFE

Anything goes in LA, especially after dark. Swinging nightspots open and close quickly, since the restless search for what's "in" keeps people on the move. *Doug Weston's Troubador Club* has pioneered a number of top rock music acts (9081 Santa Monica Blvd., West Hollywood; phone: 310-276-6168). Another place that seems to be able to hold its own is *Whisky A Go-Go* (8901 Sunset Blvd.; phone: 310-652-4202). With Movietown's pool of talent, comedy clubs are a better bet than elsewhere. Among the options: *Improvisation,* the grandparent of them all (8162 Melrose Ave.; phone: 213-651-2583, and at 321 Santa Monica Blvd., Santa Monica; phone: 310-394-8664); and the *Comedy Store,* another survivor (8433 Sunset Blvd.; phone: 213-480-3232). If you want to get into the act, head over to *All That Glitz* (1911 Sunset Blvd.; phone: 310-278-7712), where musical comedy comes with a twist when cast members "roast" certain folks in the audience. Comedy is king at the *Groundling Theater* (7307 Melrose Ave., W. Hollywood; phone: 213-934-9700), LA's answer to Chicago's *Second City* and the launching pad for *Saturday Night Live* funny man Phil Hartman. *Roxbury's* (8225 Sunset, W. Hollywood; phone: 213-656-1750) is the "in" place for celebrities and the wannabe crowd. There are 3 levels for entertainment, a good restaurant, and an exclusive VIP room. Other nightspots include *Club Lingerie* (6507 Sunset Blvd., Hollywood; phone: 213-466-8557), a hip, happening rock club; *Club Lux* (2800 Donald Douglas Loop N., Santa Monica; phone: 310-399-1577), where you can boogie to the latest beat on an elevated "boxing ring" dance floor; *Gazzarri's*

(9039 Sunset Blvd., W. Hollywood; phone: 310-273-6606) for hard-core rockers; *Hollywood Athletic Club* (6525 Sunset Blvd.; phone: 213-962-6600), with pool tables plus the latest rock groups; and *Café Largo* (432 Fairfax, Hollywood; phone: 213-852-1073), a modern cabaret with a mix of rock 'n' roll, folk, country, and oldies. Jazz fans will appreciate *My Place* (1026 Wilshire Blvd., Santa Monica; phone: 310-451-8596), and blues aficionados, *Mint* (6010 W. Pico Blvd.; phone: 213-937-9630), a neighborhood bar. In downtown LA, step out at the hip *Mayan* (1038 Hill St.; phone: 213-746-4287) or *Vertigo* (333 S. Boylston; phone: 213-747-4849), where a well-heeled crowd gathers on weekend nights to dine and dance until 4 AM. If you want to mingle with LA's trendiest, try to make the scene at the *Olive* (119 S. Fairfax Ave.; phone: 213-939-2001); admission here depends on who you are, who you know, and how you're dressed. Since it's not often easy to get in the door at these hot spots, *LA Nighthawks* (phone: 310-392-1500) has club-hopping tours conducted in stretch limousines that travel to your choice of 250 popular nighttime nooks. Prices vary depending on destination and include cover charge and a bottle of French champagne.

Best in Town
CHECKING IN

Los Angeles is the city where mere mortals stand the best chance of checking in alongside a movie star, although, obviously, it costs more for the possible privilege of rubbing shoulders with cinematic royalty. (Note: The *Beverly Hills* hotel, one of the most popular with members of the film industry, has temporarily closed while it undergoes a complete renovation; it's scheduled to reopen next year.) If you're looking for someplace simply to shower and sleep, you'll be happier at one of the smaller hotels or motels sprinkled throughout the area. Generally speaking, accommodations are less expensive in the San Fernando and San Gabriel valleys than in Hollywood or downtown. Expect to pay $245 and way up for a double room at those places we've bracketed as very expensive; between $140 and $240 at those places listed as expensive; between $80 and $140, moderate; and under $80, inexpensive. (Be sure to ask about special "commercial" rates and inexpensive "weekend" package deals.) For statewide B&B accommodations, contact *Eye Openers Bed & Breakfast* (PO Box 694, Altadena, CA 91001; phone: 213-684-4428 or 818-797-2055) or *California Houseguests International* (605 Lindley Ave., Suite 6, Tarzana, CA 91356; phone: 818-344-7878). Twenty-four-hour room service is the norm, unless otherwise noted.

Note: All telephone numbers below include their area codes.

For an unforgettable experience in Los Angeles, we begin with our favorites, followed by our recommendations of cost and quality choices of accommodations, listed by price category.

GRAND HOTELS AND SPECIAL HAVENS

Bel-Air In the fashionable Bel-Air district of Los Angeles, this member of the prestigious Relais & Châteaux group has been a favorite hideaway of Gary Cooper, Howard Hughes, Grace Kelly, Sophia Loren, Marilyn Monroe, and other celebs since it opened during the 1920s. The hotel's perfectly appointed 92 rooms (39 of which are suites) are in 1- and 2-story mission-style buildings and bungalows scattered amid 11.5 exquisitely landscaped acres; privacy prevails. Executive chef Gary Clausen caters to the sophisticated tastes of patrons with "back to basics" culinary artistry: Meats are lightly marinated rather than doused in rich sauces, and herbs are grown on the premises. Meeting rooms accommodate up to 200, and other business services include secretarial assistance, photocopiers, and A/V equipment. There's also a very gracious and helpful concierge desk. 701 Stone Canyon Rd. (phone: 310-472-1211 or 800-648-4097 outside California; fax: 310-476-5890; telex: 674151).

Four Seasons Located in a residential area referred to as "Beverly Hills adjacent," this elegant place is reminiscent of a grand European manor house. But instead of making guests feel self-conscious, the attentive service puts one at ease. The 285 rooms are more than ample and luxuriously appointed. The decor is pleasantly subdued, with an emphasis on comfort, yet there are all the services you would expect in a world class hotel, and then some: Instead of providing the usual little in-room sewing kits, the hotel offers an on-premises seamstress — on duty 24 hours a day. On the fourth-floor rooftop terrace is a heated pool/spa area surrounded by palm trees and lounge chairs, with a small exercise area nearby. The *Gardens* restaurant, bright, cheery, and casually elegant, is a delight for lunch, dinner, or a lavish Sunday buffet brunch. The menu features the second-best club sandwich available in this country. All rooms have computer modems. Other conveniences include a concierge, meeting rooms for up to 500, secretarial services, A/V equipment, photocopiers, and express checkout. 300 S. Doheny Dr. (phone: 310-273-2222 or 800-332-3442; fax: 310-859-3824; telex: 00194364).

Peninsula Beverly Hills A luxury property with 200 rooms, suites, and villas, its intimate scale, residential location (complete with lavish gardens and winding gravel pathways), antique furnishings, and fine artworks give it the feel of a private palazzo. An additional 16 rooms and suites are located in 5 villas, some of which offer private terraces and fireplaces. The wonderful rooftop deck has its own lush garden — it even boasts a manicured lawn and Moroccan–style cabañas! A health spa features a weight room, lap pool, whirlpool bath, steam/sauna sun deck, and masseuses. *The Living Room,* a lobby lounge, serves traditional afternoon tea, and the *Belvedere* restaurant, with its handsome bar, is one of the most popular (and priciest) dining spots in town. If you have to stay in touch with the office, suites are equipped with individual fax machines, and the business center provides A/V equipment, photocopiers, computers, and secretarial service. Express checkout is available. There is also a room attendant on each floor around the clock. 9882 Santa Monica Blvd., Beverly Hills (phone: 310-273-4888 or 800-462-7899; fax: 310-213-858-666).

Regent Beverly Wilshire Built in 1928, this Beaux Arts jewel — a favorite spot among celebrities and visiting royalty — sits at the foot of Rodeo Drive. In the tower wing, all the rooms are done in different color schemes, furniture styles, and themes. The Wilshire Wing (our favorite) has 147 units, as well as 3 restaurants (the *Dining Room* is the best) and bars. There are 459 rooms in all, and the marble bathrooms are particularly plush. With the addition of a health spa, heated pool, hot tubs, and sauna, who could ask for more? Meeting rooms hold up to 850. Other services include a concierge desk, secretarial assistance, photocopiers, A/V equipment, computers, and express checkout. 9500 Wilshire Blvd., Beverly Hills (phone: 310-275-5200 or 800-545-4000; fax: 310-274-3709; telex: 69822).

St. James's Club The first American branch of this international hotel group — with branches in London, Paris, and Antigua — its West Coast outpost is located smack-dab in the middle of the Sunset Strip, in the lovingly restored 1931 Art Deco Sunset Tower building. To rub shoulders with celebrities (Joan Collins, Quincy Jones, and David Bowie to name just a few), check into one of the 18 rooms and 44 suites or have dinner at the *St. James* restaurant (formerly the *Members Room*). For the business traveler, there are meeting rooms accommodating up to 200 people, secretarial services, A/V equipment, photocopiers, and express checkout. 8358 Sunset Blvd., W. Hollywood (phone: 213-654-7100 or 800-225-2637; fax: 213-654-9287; telex: 4979817).

EXTRA SPECIAL Originally owned by the Franciscan Missions, the 540-acre San Ysidro Ranch near Santa Barbara, which opened in 1893, enjoyed a long season as the choice vacation spot of the rich and the famous: Laurence Olivier and Vivien Leigh were married here; John F. Kennedy honeymooned here with Jackie; John Galsworthy, Aldous Huxley, Sinclair Lewis, Winston Churchill, Somerset Maugham, Bing Crosby, Jack Benny, and many others stayed here; and Ronald Colman owned the place from the mid-1930s until his death in 1958. But during the 1960s, the legend began to fade, and the inn was well down the road to total ruin when a former president of New York's great *Plaza* hotel put up the money to clean up, fix up, and paint up. Today the 45 cottages, 2 tennis courts, stables, restaurant, and swimming pool all are as spiffy as they were when Galsworthy revised his *Forsyte Saga* here (if not more so: 10 of the guest cottages have their own Jacuzzis). Mix with fellow guests in the *Plow & Angel* bar, or the *Stonehouse* restaurant, where chef

Gerard Tompson creates fine regional American fare. Special meals grace the tables on holidays. The ranch is one of only 21 American hostelries to be made a member of the prestigious Relais & Châteaux group. 900 San Ysidro La., Montecito (phone: 805-969-5046 or 800-368-6788).

VERY EXPENSIVE

Bel Age This hotel's European tone is similar to *L'Ermitage* (below), its former sister. Its 198 suites are gracefully decorated with hand-carved rosewood and pecan wood furnishings complemented by pastel color schemes. *La Brasserie* is the hotel's casual café; *Diaghilev,* its more formal dining room, serves Franco-Russe cuisine. Also available is a heated rooftop pool. Meeting rooms can accommodate up to 500, and there's a concierge, secretarial services, A/V equipment, and photocopiers. 1020 N. San Vicente Blvd., W. Hollywood (phone: 310-854-1111 or 800-424-4443; fax: 310-854-0926; telex: 49555516LEGG).

Century Plaza The 750-room hotel and the 322-room tower (which boasts spectacular views from spacious rooms and private balconies) are run separately but share many facilities. This is a favorite spot for conventiongoers; the hotel has a full-service business center. There are plenty of shops in which to browse and several fine restaurants on the premises, including the casual seafood bar and grill, *Waters Edge,* and the California-continental *La Chaumière* (see *Eating Out*). In Century City, near the ABC Entertainment Center, it offers complimentary town car service for trips within a 5-mile radius. Meeting rooms accommodate up to 2,000, and additional business services include a concierge desk, secretarial services, A/V equipment, photocopiers, computers, and express checkout. 2025 Ave. of the Stars, Century City (phone: 310-277-2000; fax: 310-551-3355; telex: 215554).

Checkers Kempinski Geared to the needs of the business traveler, this 190-room property in the center of Los Angeles's financial district has conference rooms, fax machines, A/V equipment, photocopiers, 24-hour room service, secretarial and courier services, and interpreters. To ease the stress of the work day, this elegant hostelry offers a guest library and a rooftop spa with sauna, steamroom, and exercise equipment. And for mixing business with pleasure, *Checkers* restaurant, open for "power" breakfasts and lunches, as well as dinners, serves sophisticated American fare. A complimentary limo is available to downtown business locations. Six complimentary newspapers are available each day. Additional conveniences include modems for computers and fax outlets in all the rooms. There's also a concierge desk. 535 S. Grand Ave. (phone: 213-624-0000 or 800-628-4900; fax: 213-626-9906; telex: 403525CHECKERS).

Doubletree Across the road from Marina del Rey — the world's largest man-made small-craft harbor — this 338-room seaside resort, with ocean and mountain views, is a short ride (by free shuttle) from the airport. Sailing, jogging, swimming, and bicycling are among the relaxing amenities. Two restaurants are on the property. Meeting rooms can accommodate up to 700, and there is a concierge, plus secretarial services, photocopiers, A/V equipment, and express checkout. 4100 Admiralty Way, Marina del Rey (phone: 310-301-3000 or 800-528-0444; fax: 310-213-301-6890; telex: 183365).

L'Ermitage This hostelry has a European ambience, 112 suites with kitchens, sunken living rooms, and large marble bathrooms with whirlpool baths, plus a rooftop Jacuzzi and pool, a piano lounge, and its own fine dining room, *The Club*. It is very well run and blissfully low-key. Parking is available. Business amenities include a concierge desk, secretarial services, A/V equipment, and photocopiers. 9291 Burton Way, Beverly Hills (phone: 310-278-3344 or 800-800-2113; fax: 310-278-8247; telex: 4955516LEGG).

J. W. Marriott On spacious grounds in Century City, this is Marriott's West Coast luxury flagship, in fashionable château style. The lobby is opulent yet intimate, with art objects and a resident live cockatoo. The hotel features 375 rooms, of which more than half are suites, and indoor and outdoor pools. Among the extra-special touches here are loofahs and natural sponges on tub edges. There's a concierge desk and express checkout. Meeting rooms can accommodate up to 300; and secretarial services, A/V equipment, photocopiers, and computers all are on call. 2151 Ave. of the Stars (phone: 310-277-2777 or 800-228-9290; fax: 310-785-9240).

Marina del Rey Casual and California-style, this property is practically a peninsula, for it is surrounded by boats on three sides. The 160 pastel-decorated rooms and suites all have patios and balconies. Request a "Main Channel" room for the best views. There are 2 restaurants, a pool, and complimentary airport shuttle service. Meeting rooms seat up to 120. Other business conveniences include a concierge, secretarial services, A/V equipment, photocopiers, and express checkout. 13534 Bali Way, Marina del Rey (phone: 310-301-1000; 800-8-MARINA within California; 800-882-4000 elsewhere in the US; fax: 310-301-8167).

Marina International Don't be misled by the less-than-grand exterior, for the meandering tile walkways eventually lead to spacious accommodations in wooden, shingled buildings. There are 135 rooms, but request one of the 25 bungalows decorated in soothing pastels. Although there is no restaurant on the premises, there are plenty within walking distance, and a continental breakfast and light fare are available in the downstairs coffee shop. There are a pool and a Jacuzzi as well as complimentary airport shuttle service. The meeting rooms offer space for 110, and there are secretarial services, A/V equipment, and photocopiers available for guests' use. 4200 Admiralty Way, Marina del Rey (phone: 310-822-1010; 800-421-

8145 or 800-8-MARINA within California; 800-882-4000 elsewhere in the US; fax: 310-301-6687).

Ritz-Carlton Marina del Rey This Los Angeles outpost borders the world's largest pleasure-craft harbor. There are sailboats for rent and a shore promenade, as well as tennis courts, a pool and fitness center, and 306 rooms with traditional decor. The club-like *Grill* serves dinner; all meals are provided in *The Café*, which has both indoor and outdoor seating with marina views. Afternoon tea and after-dinner cordials are served in the handsome library and lounge. Transportation to and from LAX is complimentary. Business conveniences include meeting rooms accommodating up to 800, secretarial services, a concierge, A/V equipment, photocopiers, computers, and express checkout. 4375 Admiralty Way, Marina del Rey (phone: 310-823-1700 or 800-241-3333; fax: 310-823-2403).

Sheraton Grande Pampering on a grand scale — the only hotel in town with personal butler service on every floor and other amenities beyond the call of duty. The 469 spacious rooms are tastefully decorated. Conference and entertainment space is all first class and includes a ballroom, meeting rooms, teleconferencing, and, during the day, use of a 4-movie-theater complex in the building. There's a pool (but no health club), and each guest receives a complimentary membership to the *YMCA*, right across the street via a pedestrian bridge. Meeting rooms can accommodate up to 600, and there are secretarial and concierge services, A/V equipment, photocopiers, computer modems in all the rooms, video message system, and express video checkout. 333 S. Figueroa (phone: 213-617-1133 or 800-325-3535; fax: 213-613-0291; telex: 677003).

Westwood Marquis A favorite among businessfolk who appreciate quality. The attractive high-rise holds 258 suites, and the bustling college town of Westwood is all around. The *Garden Terrace Room* is popular for Sunday brunch, and the elegant *Dynasty Room* (see *Eating Out*) serves California-French food. The UCLA running track is less than a half-mile away. There's also a lovely pool surrounded by cabañas. Secretarial assistance is available, as are A/V equipment, photocopiers, computers, and express checkout. There's also a concierge desk. 930 Hilgard Ave., Westwood (phone: 310-208-8765 or 800-421-2317; fax: 310-824-0355; telex: 181835MARQUIS).

EXPENSIVE

Beverly Hilton It's not quite as convenient to downtown Beverly Hills as the *Regent Beverly Wilshire* (see above), but if you plan to spend a lot of time in the hotel, you'll be happy in this self-contained establishment. *Trader Vic's* is a consistently good restaurant, and *L'Escoffier*, under the exclusive direction of executive chef Michel Blanchet, now offers superb food along with entertainment and dancing (see *Eating Out*). Meeting rooms hold up to 1,200, and there are secretarial services, a concierge desk, A/V equipment, photocopiers, computers, and express checkout. 9876 Wilshire Blvd., Beverly Hills (phone: 310-274-7777; 800-922-5432; fax: 310-285-1313; telex: 194683HILTONBVHL).

Biltmore The grande dame of downtown hotels offers dramatic interiors that combine the classical architecture typical of European palaces with contemporary luxury. There are 700 well-appointed rooms, an indoor pool, and Jacuzzi. Other pluses include the fine French restaurant *Bernard's* and the *Grand Avenue* bar, with great jazz nightly. Business amenities include meeting rooms that hold up to 1,000, a concierge, secretarial services, photocopiers, A/V equipment, and express checkout. 506 S. Grand Ave. (phone: 213-624-1011 or 800-245-8673; fax: 213-612-1545; telex: 677686).

Hyatt Regency This 487-room super-modern place is another convention favorite. Meeting rooms hold up to 6,600, and secretarial services, a concierge, A/V equipment, photocopiers, and express checkout are available. There are also 2 restaurants, the *Brasserie* and the *Pavan* (serving northern Italian fare). 711 S. Hope St. (phone: 213-683-1234; fax: 213-629-3230).

Inter-Continental Los Angeles Downtown's newest hotel, this massive 469-room establishment is geared to business travelers. There is a fully equipped business center: fax, computer, and modem capabilities are in each room; and two Club Inter-Continental floors provide business conference and secretarial facilities. Other amenities include 2 restaurants, a pool, and a health club. 251 S. Olive (phone: 310-670-7284 or 800-327-0200).

Loews Santa Monica Loews' first venture on the West Coast, this 349-room property provides 20th-century comfort in a 19th-century setting, an era when the area flourished as a resort community. A 5-story atrium affords spectacular Pacific views; there also are an extensive fitness center with a top-notch personal trainer, an indoor/outdoor swimming pool, a Jacuzzi, and the beach a few steps away. The decor features antique ironwork, cool Pacific colors, and marine themes in paintings and sculptures by local artists. There are 2 restaurants, the contemporary Italian *Riva* and the more casual *Coast Café,* and a lobby bar that also serves afternoon tea. There are 5 meeting rooms, secretarial services, a concierge, A/V equipment, photocopiers, and express video checkout. 1700 Ocean Ave., Santa Monica (phone: 310-458-6700; fax: 310-458-6721).

Le Mondrian This contemporary 188-room establishment on the Sunset Strip pays homage to Piet Mondrian and attracts rock stars, models, and other Hollywood types. The suites provide stunning city views, and the decor is upbeat and sophisticated. There's a pool, fitness center, beauty salon, and restaurant featuring northern Italian cooking. The jazz lounge provides entertainment nightly. Business amenities include a state-of-the-art computer center, which also has drafting tables and video editing equipment for project work, meeting rooms for up to 120, secretarial services, photocopiers, and A/V equipment. There is also a concierge desk. 8440 Sunset Blvd., W. Hollywood (phone: 213-650-8999 or 800-255-5168; fax: 213-650-5215; telex: 4955516).

Le Montrose This property is considered one of the best bargains (a relative term in LA) in the city. The 107 rooms are all suites; some have balconies and kitchenettes. A favorite extended-stay place for people in the music and movie industries. There is a rooftop pool, Jacuzzi, and tennis courts. Meeting rooms accommodate up to 50, and there are secretarial services and photocopiers. 900 Hammond St., W. Hollywood (phone: 310-855-1115 or 800-424-4443 fax: 310-657-9192; telex: 4955516LEGG).

Nikko Beverly Hills East meets West in this high-tech, Japanese-style hostelry. Busy executives will appreciate the full-service business center as well as the guestrooms, each of which is equipped with a fax, computer hookup, voice mail, oversize desk, and a multi-line computer phone that also controls the lights, stereo, and TV set. Other features include a private bar, terry robes, and a Japanese soaking tub in each striking, black marble bathroom. The hotel also has a small swimming pool; a well-equipped fitness center; the *Matrixx* restaurant, which serves marvelous pasta and Japanese noodles with fish, chicken, and beef; and the recently opened *Arnie Morton's of Chicago,* located next door (see *Eating Out* for both). 465 S. La Cienega Blvd. (phone: 310-247-0400 or 800-NIKKO-US; fax: 310-247-0315).

Radisson Bel Air Summit Ideally located, this spot offers a light, breezy atmosphere. All 162 rooms have balconies, and there is a swimming pool, tennis court, cocktail lounge, and dining room. Free parking. Meeting rooms accommodate 400. Secretarial services are available, as are A/V equipment, photocopiers, and express checkout. 11461 Sunset Blvd. (phone: 310-476-6571 or 800-333-3333; fax: 310-471-6310).

Ritz-Carlton, Huntington Pasadena's Spanish-style landmark, razed after it was declared earthquake-unsafe, has risen like the proverbial phoenix, Ritz-Carlton–style — a country-estate setting on 23 acres. The 1920s building has been reconstructed, complete with its imposing Alamo Arch at the entrance, Japanese horseshoe gardens, 6 cottages, and leaded crystal chandeliers. Other features include the hotel chain's signature dark woods, art and antiques in 385 guestrooms, an Olympic-size pool, Jacuzzi and fitness center, 3 tennis courts, 3 restaurants, and 3 lounges. Business facilities include meeting rooms that seat 1,000, a concierge, secretarial services, A/V equipment, photocopiers, computers, and express checkout. 1401 S. Oak Knoll Ave., Pasadena (phone: 818-568-3900 or 800-241-3333; fax: 818-568-3159).

Sheraton at LAX This conference center at the airport features 810 rooms, comprehensive convention facilities, and *Landry's,* a fine restaurant with an excellent sushi bar. Additional amenities include meeting rooms that can hold up to 800, a concierge, secretarial services, A/V equipment, photocopiers, computers, and express checkout. 6101 W. Century Blvd. (phone: 310-642-1111; fax: 310-410-1276; telex: 4720230).

Sofitel Ma Maison The broad carved staircase, country French furniture, and gaily patterned wall-and-window treatments create a fittingly homey atmosphere in this 311-room, château-style property called "My House." The *Ma Maison* restaurant, airy and plant-filled, features expertly prepared French-California fare. For less formal dining, there's the bistro, *La Cajole,* an approximate re-creation of an old Parisian artists' hangout. On the Beverly Hills–Los Angeles border, it offers complimentary limousine service once a day to *Mann's Chinese Theatre* (6925 Hollywood Blvd., phone: 213-464-8111) and to Rodeo Drive. Additional pluses are meeting rooms that can accommodate 440, secretarial services, a 24-hour concierge desk, A/V equipment, photocopiers, and express checkout. 8555 Beverly Blvd. (phone: 310-278-5444 or 800-521-7772; fax: 310-657-2816).

Sunset Marquis If you're looking for a romantic hideaway, this Mediterranean-style paradise is just the ticket. Lush tropical gardens with koi ponds and exotic birds shelter guests from the outside world, which is just what the many celebrities who stay here are looking for. Its 118 luxury suites and villas are furnished with canopy beds, fireplaces, saunas, and Jacuzzis; each has its own butler to cater to guests' needs. Amenities include 2 restaurants, 2 pools, a full health club with personal trainers available, a concierge, and full business services. 1200 N. Alta Loma Rd., West Hollywood (phone: 310-657-1333 or 800-858-9758).

Westin Bonaventure This 1,474-room giant is a major downtown convention hotel. Its cylindrical, mirrored towers are an LA skyline landmark, and it is especially convenient for downtown activities. This city within a city has 20 restaurants and lounges. Note that the rooms do not live up to the promise of the lobby and public spaces. Extras are a concierge desk, meeting rooms that seat 3,000, secretarial services, A/V equipment, photocopiers, computers, and express checkout. 404 S. Figueroa St. (phone: 213-624-1000; fax: 213-612-4800; telex: 677628).

Westin, LA Airport If it's Tuesday, this must be LA — a mile from the airport, this 750-room hotel (formerly the *Stouffer Concourse*) announces the day of the week — on its elevators' carpets. With travelers often adjusting to time changes from places as far away as the Orient, this amenity could save a day. There is an outdoor swimming pool and a health club, the *Trattoria Grande,* and the *Charisma Café.* No surcharges on collect, 800-number, or credit card calls. Twenty-one suites have private outdoor Jacuzzis. The meeting rooms seat up to 1,300. Additional amenities include a concierge desk, A/V equipment, photocopiers, and express checkout. 5400 W. Century Blvd., Los Angeles (phone: 310-216-5858 or 800-228-3000; fax: 310-645-8053; telex: 5106017169).

MODERATE

Barnabey's Possibly the best value in Southern California, with the charm of an English country inn, less than 3 miles from the airport and within walking distance of Manhattan Beach. All rooms are furnished with antiques and breakfast is included in the rate. Dine in *Barnabey's* restaurant and drink in *Rosie's Pub*. Complimentary 24-hour shuttle service to the airport, beach, and shopping. Room service is available until 10 PM. Meeting rooms seat 125, and A/V equipment and photocopiers are available for guests' use. Sepulveda Blvd. at Rosecrans Ave., Manhattan Beach (phone: 310-545-8466 or 800-552-5285; fax: 310-545-8621).

Beverly Prescott Hotelier Bill Kimpton took over the former *Beverly Hillcrest* and transformed the place into another one of his snazzy boutique hotels. Perched on a hilltop — with private balconies overlooking Beverly Hills, Century City, Hollywood, and the Pacific Ocean — this 140-room hostelry has a palm-tree-lined, canopied entrance, a jewelry-box reception desk inlaid with onyx and mother of pearl, and gardens in its indoor/outdoor lobby. Each room has its own balcony; executive suites come with fax machines, computers, and printers. There are full secretarial services, a concierge, health club, outdoor pool with cabañas and food service, daily newspaper delivered to your door, room service, and a restaurant. 1224 S. Beverwil Dr., W. Los Angeles (phone: 310-277-2800 or 800-421-3212).

Century Wilshire In Westwood, the movie theater capital of LA and home of UCLA, this 99-room spot offers kitchen units, complimentary coffee, and continental breakfast. No room service is available. There's a concierge desk, and secretarial services can be arranged. Photocopiers also are on the premises. 10776 Wilshire (phone: 310-474-4506; 800-421-7223, outside California; fax: 310-474-2535).

Hollywood Roosevelt Once the social center of old Hollywood, this 322-room establishment has LA-Spanish charm and an essence of the not so distant past. Traces of Tinseltown still remain — photographs of movie celebrities grace the walls, the Hollywood sign is up the hill, and the star-studded Walk of Fame is right outside. A swimming pool, Jacuzzi, and weight room are on the premises. No room service is available. Meeting rooms can accommodate up to 300, and there are a concierge desk, A/V equipment, photocopiers, and express checkout. 7000 Hollywood Blvd., Hollywood (phone: 213-466-7000; fax: 213-462-8056; telex: 194404 HOLLYROOSVLAS).

Mikado Best Western The twisting canyon roads separating Hollywood from the San Fernando Valley are among the most scenic parts of LA. Set between Coldwater and Laurel canyons, where cottages and modern glass and wood homes hang dramatically from cliffs, propped up only by stilts, the 58-room hostelry has a pool, a Jacuzzi, a restaurant, and a cocktail lounge.

No room service is available, but guests receive complimentary American breakfast. Photocopiers are available. 12600 Riverside Dr. (phone: 818-763-9141; 800-433-2239 within California; 800-826-2759 elsewhere in the US).

New Otani Within walking distance of the *Music Center*, it has 448 rooms featuring Japanese luxury and service in a lovely garden-like setting — a soothing respite from the madness of downtown LA. The suites have an authentic tatami room and futon bedding as well as deep bathtubs. *A Thousand Cranes* is its serene Japanese restaurant (see *Eating Out*). For more casual dining, the cheery *Azalea Restaurant & Bar* serves breakfast, lunch, and dinner. Amenities include a shopping arcade and a Japanese health club with shiatsu massage and acupuncture therapy, as well as meeting rooms that hold up to 750, a concierge, secretarial services, A/V equipment, photocopiers, and express checkout. 120 S. Los Angeles St. (phone: 213-629-1200; 800-252-0197 within California; 800-421-8795 elsewhere in the US; fax: 213-622-0980; telex: 4720429).

Le Rêve With 80 suites, this is a small, modest hotel with a European flair similar to *L'Ermitage* (they used to be under the same ownership). The decor and atmosphere are country French. There is a rooftop swimming pool, a Jacuzzi, self-service laundry, and full room service from early morning until 11 PM but no restaurant. Secretarial services are on call, and there's also A/V equipment. 8822 Cynthia St., W. Hollywood. (phone: 310-854-1114 or 800-424-4443; fax: 310-657-2623; telex: 4955516LEGG).

INEXPENSIVE

Beverly Garland Close to Universal Studios, here's a real charmer with 258 pleasant rooms at very appealing rates (their weekend package features breakfast and free accommodations on Sunday night). Amenities include an outdoor pool, sauna, putting green, tennis, free parking, room service from 6 AM to 11 PM, and a restaurant. 4222 Vineland Ave., Studio City (phone: 818-980-8000 or 800-BEVERLY).

Chesterfield A real find, this charming, 133-room hotel provides guests with all the amenities of higher-priced hostelries: a concierge, fine continental fare at the *Butler Grill* restaurant, afternoon tea. In the rooms, you'll find complimentary mineral water, bathrobes, hair dryers, and even potpourri sachets. 10320 W. Olympic Blvd., W. Los Angeles (phone: 310-556-2777; fax: 310-203-0563).

Figueroa Downtown's best buy, this venerable, still gracious Spanish hotel has tile floors, patio dining, a pool, and 280 large guestrooms. The *Firenze*, a lobby café, serves three meals a day; the *Music Room*, featuring American cooking, is open for dinner only. There is no room service. Photocopiers are available. 939 S. Figueroa St. (phone: 213-627-8971; 800-331-5151 or 800-421-9092 outside California; fax: 213-689-0305).

Safari Inn If you're planning to visit the studios in Burbank, this will be more convenient than Beverly Hills or downtown LA hotels. The spacious valley environment also provides more of a sense of being in the open. There are 85 rooms and 20 suites. Meeting rooms can accommodate up to 50, and there are photocopiers. 1911 W. Olive Ave., Burbank (phone: 818-845-8586 or 800-STAHERE; fax: 818-845-0054).

EATING OUT

These days, Los Angeles may be the country's most exciting restaurant town. Only the purest of purists still go completely by L'Escoffier's book. Ethnic places abound in all price ranges, and imaginative chefs meld superb raw materials, ethnic ingredients, and nutritional caveats into pots of culinary gold. Though popularity with the show-biz crowd is often inversely proportional to the quality of a kitchen and the maître d's treatment of non-celeb guests, good manners are creeping back. Regrettably, dining in din is still in, even when the food is exquisite, but some new restaurants have rediscovered the joy of calm. As of last year, Los Angeles has banned smoking in all restaurants in the city proper (alfresco dining places, bars, and nighclubs are exempt, however). Our choices are below. Expect to pay $100 or more for two at those places we've listed as very expensive; $75 to $90 at places in the expensive category; $40 to $70 for moderate; and under $30 for inexpensive. Prices do not include drinks, wine, or tips.

Note: All telephone numbers below include their area codes.

For an unforgettable dining experience, we begin with our culinary favorites, followed by our recommendations of cost and quality choices listed by price category.

INCREDIBLE EDIBLES

Arnie Morton's of Chicago, the Steakhouse Direct from the Windy City comes this LA steakhouse franchise where beef is the name of the game. Porterhouse, New York strip, and rib eye steaks — served in man-size portions — are the raison d'être for eating here. Many confirmed carnivores claim the steaks are the best in town. The veal and lamb chops and the Maine lobsters are also scrumptious, and the side dishes — especially the hash browns and giant mushroom caps — are almost meals in themselves. Open daily. Reservations necessary. Major credit cards accepted. 435 S. La Cienega Blvd. (phone: 310-246-1501) and several other locations around LA.

Bistro This old standard Beverly Hills rendezvous of the rich and famous is as popular today as the day it opened. Back in 1963, Kurt Niklas — who earned his stripes at the famous *Romanoff's* — convinced producer Billy Wilder and 60 of Hollywood's biggest names (Jack Lemmon, Laurence Harvey, Tony Curtis, Robert Stack, Otto Preminger, Swifty Lazar, Alfred

Bloomingdale, Frank Sinatra, and Louis Jourdan, to name a few) to invest in the restaurant. The food is simple bistro style, updated to suit today's tastes. Go Friday nights to see the *real* Hollywood wives (and non-wives) exchanging gossip in this most glamorous setting. Serves dinner only; closed Sundays. Reservations essential. Major credit cards accepted. 240 N. Canon Dr., Beverly Hills (phone: 310-273-5633).

Ca'Brea A touch of *Locanta Veneta* spills over to this 2-level restaurant owned by Antonio Tommassi and Jean Louis de Mori. Everything about this place is earthy — from its ocher-walled dining area to a menu of simple dishes at down-to-earth prices. Specialties include tortelloni filled with spinach and ricotta and grilled lamb chops with a robust mustard sauce and truffles. Be sure to leave room for the *tiramisù* — it's worth every calorie. Yes, trivia fans, this is the same spot once occupied by the legendary eatery *Robaire's;* mementos of that past have been carefully preserved in the third-floor private dining room. Open for lunch and dinner weekdays; Saturdays for dinner. Reservations advised. Major credit cards accepted. 346 S. La Brea (phone: 213-938-2863).

California Pizza Kitchen *Spago* for the masses, it's Beverly Hills' favorite pizza place. Upscale fast food served in a sleek black-, white-, and yellow-tiled environment — this is not your average neighborhood pizzeria. Nouvelle cuisine pizza specialties, served straight from a wood-fired oven, include such delights as Original BBQ Chicken Pizza, Thai Chicken Pizza, Tandori Chicken Pizza, Peking Duck Pizza, BLT Pizza, and Tuna-Melt Pizza. There also is fresh pasta with interesting sauces, and yummy desserts on the menu. Open mid-morning to late evening daily. Unlike *Spago,* there's no need for a reservation here — but there'll probably be a line here, too. Major credit cards accepted. 207 S. Beverly Dr., Beverly Hills (phone: 213-272-7878) and several other locations around LA.

Campanile Named for the tower that crowns this 1928 Charlie Chaplin–built landmark, this stunning place is run by the husband and wife team of Mark Peel and Nancy Silverton, veterans of *Michael's* and *Spago.* Enter through a delightful, skylit café and walk through a long, cloister-like room with tables on one side and the kitchen on the other to get to the balcony-rimmed dining room in the rear. The food is California-Italian, with other Mediterranean influences. The tastes of Tuscany — like antipasto and poached mozzarella — abound, and the all-American grilled prime ribs and the sinfully delicious desserts are out of this world. Serves breakfast and dinner; closed Sundays. Reservations essential (the farther in advance the better). Major credit cards accepted. 524 S. La Brea Ave. (phone: 213-938-1447).

Le Chardonnay In an unlikely setting on bustling Melrose Avenue, this Belle Epoque dining place is reminiscent of a 1920s Left Bank bistro. Owners Robert Bigonnet and Claude Alrivi have combined beautiful decor — rich mahogany, mirrored walls, hand-painted French tile — and first-rate food — roast venison, terrine of squab and sweetbreads, and goat cheese–filled ravioli with Italian parsley sauce — to create an extraordinary dining experience in the heart of Los Angeles. Reservations advised. Major credit cards accepted. 8284 Melrose Ave. (phone: 213-655-8880).

Chaya Venice The family responsible for the *Chaya* (Japanese for tea house) chain has been running tea houses in Japan for 3 centuries now. Also owners of the *Chaya Brasserie* and *Chaya Diner*, their latest venture blends Japanese and American cuisines with such dishes as Hawaiian-tuna spring rolls accompanied by a spicy salsa, charred rare tuna *niçoise*, and broiled sea eel with julienned vegetables. The look is hot, and very high-tech — an eclectic mix of chrome, copper, stone, and wood, reflecting the diversity of its menu. Dinner nightly, lunch Sundays through Fridays. Reservations are at a premium. Major credit cards accepted. 110 Navy St., Venice (phone: 310-396-1179).

Chinois on Main At *Spago*, Wolfgang Puck makes pizza topped with goat cheese and grills tuna to perfection. At *Chinois*, Puck's cooking leans more toward French-Chinese cuisine — goose liver with marinated pineapple and ginger-cinnamon sauce, barbecued squab with scallion noodles, and charcoal-grilled Szechuan beef in a cilantro-shallot sauce. The upscale, contemporary dining room boasts track lighting and pastel-colored walls covered with modern art. It's lovely, but as noisy as most in LA. If you show up without a reservation (which is impossible to get, anyway), you wait at a counter in front of the kitchen and watch the chefs at work. Dinner nightly, lunch Wednesdays through Fridays. Reservations essential. Major credit cards accepted. 2709 Main St., Santa Monica (phone: 310-392-9025).

Cicada Former *L'Orangerie* chef Jean Francois Meteigner has created a menu to delight all palates in this charming, auberge-like dining room. The John Dory en papillote melts in your mouth, and the Norwegian smoked salmon is simply superb. Pining for pasta? Try the linguine with scallops. Plan on a long, leisurely evening of fine food, and some serious "star gazing." Open daily. Reservations necessary. Major credit cards accepted. 8478 Melrose Ave., W. Hollywood (phone: 213-655-5559).

David Slay's La Veranda Owner David Slay is a talented chef and a gracious host who has won a place in the hearts of all who have discovered this Beverly Hills spot. Decorated in soft cream hues, the dining room is comfortable and inviting. The menu offers contemporary California-Italian fare, such as a robust roasted garlic soup, roast veal loin, and salmon tartare with waffle-cut potatoes. Save room for one (or two or three) of the homemade pastries, especially the tiny puffs filled with vanilla cream and caramel sauce. For social nibblers, the new Sunday night "grazing" menu features delightful samples of grilled Japanese eggplant, salmon tartare, and quesadillas with grilled chicken and cheddar cheese. Closed Sundays. Reservations advised. Major credit cards accepted. 225 S. Beverly Dr., Beverly Hills (310-274-7246).

Le Dôme This Art Deco setting in the heart of the Sunset Strip is great for star watching, especially at lunch on Saturdays and after midnight at the magnificent bar. The rooms up front are stylish and casual, but the super-agents, with their star clientele, negotiate contracts with big-name directors in the back. These rooms are more formal — velvet upholstery and candlelight — with magnificent views of the city. The food is French-continental; there's also an extensive wine list. Closed Sundays. Reservations necessary. Major credit cards accepted. 8720 Sunset Blvd. (phone: 310-659-6919).

Maple Drive From the folks who brought you Venice's own *72 Market St.*, Dudley Moore, Tony Bill, and Julia Stone have combined their talents once again to create this trendy restaurant — often loud, but always fun. You'll taste the best meat loaf you've ever had *and* the best chili. The roast turkey, bouillabaisse, and Caesar salad (made without eggs) have their fans, too. Live entertainment nightly, and who knows, the piano-playing Moore might even stop by to tickle the ivories. Open weekdays for lunch; Mondays through Saturdays for dinner. Reservations necessary. Major credit cards accepted. 345 N. Maple Dr. (phone: 310-274-9800).

L'Orangerie One of LA's truly elegant French dining places, this posh, flower-filled, special-occasion spot is one of the most beautiful in town. Pastel furnishings, flickering candlelight, stunning mirrors, and high-arched windows add to the romance. The delicacies served here include coddled eggs with caviar, rack of lamb, roasted squab, lobster fricassee, and scrumptious desserts. Open daily for dinner. Reservations necessary. Major credit cards accepted. 903 N. La Cienega Blvd. (phone: 213-652-9770).

Patina Superchef Joachim Splichal has really pulled out all the stops with a whimsical menu that includes a corn blini "sandwich" filled with marinated salmon; a soufflé (how French) of grits (how American) with Herkimer cheddar and an apple-smoked bacon sauce; or New York duck liver with blueberry pancakes and blueberry sauce. Open weekdays for lunch; daily for dinner. Reservations necessary. Major credit cards accepted. 5955 Melrose Ave., W. Hollywood (phone: 213-467-1108).

Pinot Housed in a charming yellow brick building, *Patina*'s bistro sister offers many of the same culinary delights as its sibling, but in a more casual atmosphere. The menu features a salad of wild greens with a poached egg, bacon, and toasted country bread; blinis topped with creamy goat cheese and ratatouille; and roasted duck confit. Dessert is a must — try the lemon tart with baked strawberries or the flourless chocolate cake with coffee sauce. This eatery is a favorite among the trendsetters and mega-stars —

Warren Beatty is one of the regulars. Open for lunch and dinner; closed Sundays. Reservations necessary. Major credit cards accepted. 12969 Ventura Blvd., Studio City (phone: 818-990-0500).

Spago When you're hot, you're hot. Superchef Wolfgang Puck turned pizza making into an art form. His are baked in wood-burning brick ovens and topped with shrimp, duck, sausage, and goat cheese. Celebrity diners also munch on Sonoma lamb, Washington oysters, North Pacific salmon, and grilled free-range chickens. Be sure to leave room for one of the incredible desserts. Open daily. Since this still is one of the most popular spots in town, make reservations weeks in advance. Major credit cards accepted. Also see *Quintessential Los Angeles* in DIVERSIONS. 1114 Horn Ave., W. Hollywood (phone: 310-652-4025).

VERY EXPENSIVE

Citrus Dining here means strictly California fare. Owner Michel Richard's French-Provençal-California cuisine with delicate seasonings and creative touches turns ordinary entrées into masterpieces — grilled swordfish with lentils, pepper tuna steaks, roast veal, and rack of lamb. Don't miss the tasty fish specialties or his famous signature desserts. Closed Sundays. Reservations necessary. Major credit cards accepted. 6703 Melrose Ave. (phone: 213-857-0034).

Geoffrey's The wings of Eros beat here, for whether you fall in love with the views of the Pacific, the tasty food, or your dinner companion, it's nigh impossible not to find contentment here. Rich, roasted garlic soup topped with parmesan cheese, addictive rosemary muffins, and hearty braised veal ribs are the stars of the menu. The gallant service continues through the end of the meal, when ladies are offered a rose. Open daily. Reservations advised. Major credit cards accepted. 27400 Pacific Coast Hwy. (phone: 310-457-1519).

Rex II Ristorante Filled with Lalique, oak paneling, and brass, this downtown eatery in an Art Deco building duplicates the dining room of the *Rex*, an Italian passenger liner popular during the 1920s. Each evening there's a six-course special dinner or à la carte dining. There's a full bar featuring soft dance music on the mezzanine level. Closed Sundays; open for lunch Thursdays and Fridays. Reservations necessary. Major credit cards accepted. 617 S. Olive (phone: 213-627-2300).

EXPENSIVE

Adriano's High atop the Hollywood hills is this picturesque restaurant decorated with a vaulted ceiling and a brass-trimmed sculpture surrounded by flowers. A favorite with celebrities, it offers tasty northern Italian fare, with perfect pasta and superb Caesar salad. Open daily for lunch and dinner.

Reservations advised. Major credit cards accepted. 2930 Beverly Glen Blvd. (phone: 310-475-9807).

Bikini The young, the hip, and the beautiful squeeze into this stunning, Japanese-style eating emporium. The eclectic, health-conscious menu offers everything from East Indies enchiladas to dim sum dumplings. The high-tech Japanese decor spreads over 2 stories with a rooftop garden patio. Open Mondays through Fridays for lunch; daily, except Sunday, for dinner. Reservations advised. Major credit cards accepted. 1413 5th St. (phone: 310-395-8611).

Bistro 45 Just a short drive from the city, this splendid Pasadena dining place with pale pink walls, skylights, and a separate trellised outdoor dining area excels in a California-French menu of fish stews and Hawaiian tuna sashimi with lemon-Dijon vinaigrette. Desserts are just as tempting, especially the chocolate hazelnut torte. Open for lunch Tuesdays through Fridays; dinner Tuesdays through Sundays. Reservations advised. Major credit cards accepted. 45 S. Mentor Ave., Pasadena (phone: 818-795-2478).

Champagne Bis The owner/chef is American, but the food is French — traditional, contemporary, and spa. The crispy Norwegian salmon and the veal shanks are most popular, and the restaurant is simple, elegant, and blissfully quiet. Lunch on weekdays; closed for dinner on Mondays. Reservations advised. Major credit cards accepted. 10506 Little Santa Monica Blvd. (phone: 310-470-8446).

Chasen's A somewhat stuffy LA institution for over 50 years, this celebrity favorite has shed its former image for a more casual atmosphere. There's a new, more budget-friendly, prix fixe menu. Frank Sinatra, Rosemary Clooney, and Jimmy Stewart are regular patrons. Specialties include scampi maison, signature chili, and chicken pot pie. Open for lunch Tuesdays through Fridays; dinner, Tuesdays through Sundays. Reservations advised. American Express accepted. 9039 Beverly Blvd. (phone: 310-271-2168).

La Chaumière Despite its location — the fifth floor of the tower at the *Century Plaza* hotel in a bustling area off Santa Monica Boulevard — this dining room evokes the charm of a French country manor, where diners can look out over the city while enjoying such California-French inspirations as cold lobster stew with Japanese cucumbers or roast rack of Sonoma lamb with dried figs and peanut sauce. In addition to some of the best California vintages, the wine list offers fine French and German selections as well. Open nightly for dinner, lunch on weekdays only. Reservations advised. Major credit cards accepted. 2055 Ave. of the Stars (phone: 213-551-3360).

Chianti Tasty Italian and continental fare are served in a romantic, old-fashioned room with cozy banquettes and extremely professional service. Some favorites are veal piccata and angel hair pasta with shrimp and crabmeat. Open daily for dinner. Reservations necessary. Major credit cards accepted. 7833 Melrose Ave., W. Hollywood (phone: 213-653-8333).

Drago One of Santa Monica's trendy spots, chef-owner Celestino Drago orchestrates his culinary talents with such stylish Sicilian dishes as cannellini beans and tuna and *tramezzino di polenta* with wild mushrooms. A good finish to any meal is the cheesecake with an espresso. Open daily for dinner, Mondays through Fridays for lunch. Reservations necessary. Major credit cards accepted. 2628 Wilshire Blvd., Santa Monica (phone: 310-828-1585).

Dynasty Room California-French food is served in a dining room that showcases original artwork and artifacts from China's T'ang Dynasty. The creative cuisine coupled with an eye-opening Sunday brunch are among the reasons it's remained one of the most popular dining spots in town. Baby abalone and pink-lip scallops on green beans with sauce *citronette* is just one of several winning combinations. Open daily for dinner. Reservations advised. Major credit cards accepted. *Westwood Marquis Hotel,* 930 Hilgard Ave., Westwood (phone: 310-208-8765).

L'Escoffier This once formal and somewhat snobby local landmark now boasts a brighter, more casual look and is under the direction of the celebrated culinary genius Michel Blanchet. The inviting room, high atop the *Hilton,* offers a spectacular view of Beverly Hills and an equally wonderful menu of such Blanchet specialties as tartlet of shrimp with asparagus, Maine lobster in lemon and vegetable broth on couscous, and *côte de boeuf* with grilled vegetables and choron sauce. For dessert, the chocolate and Grand Marnier soufflés are to die for. Open for dinner Tuesdays through Saturdays. Reservations necessary. Major credit cards accepted. *Beverly Hilton Hotel,* 9876 Wilshire Blvd., Beverly Hills (phone: 310-274-7777).

Café Four Oaks One of LA's loveliest cafés, this indoor/outdoor spot is unashamedly romantic. Indoors, there's a roaring fireplace. Outdoors, a fabulous garden with lush flora and bubbling fountains that make you feel you're no longer in the city. The food here is a visual treat and a pleasure to eat, especially the gorgeous salads and the lightly sauced, grilled fish dishes. There are fabulous goodies for dessert and the service is friendly and unobtrusive. One of the best locations in LA for a leisurely Sunday brunch. Closed Mondays. Reservations suggested. Major credit cards accepted. 2181 N. Beverly Glen Blvd., Bel-Air (phone: 310-470-2265).

Granita Wolfgang Puck's Malibu entry. Designed by his wife, Barbara Lazaroff, the restaurant has an aquarium theme: mosaics, shells, and a koi fishpond. Puck's designer pizzas still rank among the best, and the seafood is superb. But the star-struck staff tends to ignore anybody less famous than the local celebrities who flock from their nearby beachfront homes. Open daily for dinner; Wednesdays through Sundays for lunch. Reservations necessary. Major credit cards accepted. 23725 W. Malibu Rd., Malibu (phone: 310-456-9488).

Ivy A favorite venue for lunchtime power deals, it is an anomaly — an old brick farmhouse on bustling Robertson Boulevard, bordering Beverly Hills. Its rustic decor is the perfect setting for the eclectic (with a Southern accent) American menu; it's also a great place for outdoor dining. Corn chowder with fresh tarragon, warm mesquite-grilled salad with chicken or shrimp, and twice-cooked Cajun prime ribs — first oven-seared and then grilled — are standouts on the changing menu. Desserts are the likes of which mama could only dream of making. Open for lunch and dinner daily. Reservations necessary (during evening hours, expect at least an hour's wait even with reservations). Major credit cards accepted. 113 N. Robertson Blvd. (phone: 310-274-8303).

Jimmy's Popular with the Beverly Hills set, this elegant dining place is unbeatable for a romantic dinner or late-night supper. Try the peppered salmon on a bed of spinach or grilled veal chop with chanterelles. Leave room for the delicious chocolate truffle cake with espresso sauce; insulin shock aside, it's a knockout. Open weekdays for lunch; Mondays through Saturdays for dinner. Reservations advised. Major credit cards accepted. 201 Moreno Dr., Beverly Hills (phone: 310-879-2394).

Locanda del Lago A spunky Italian trattoria-style eatery set along Santa Monica's Third Street Promenade. The oversize windows afford a great view of the eclectic crowd strolling by. Favorite menu selections include wild mushroom polenta, grilled eggplant, *osso buco con risotto alla Milanese,* and just about any pasta. Open daily for lunch and dinner, no lunch on weekends. Reservations advised. 231 Arizona Ave., Santa Monica (phone: 310-451-3525).

Locanda Veneta A tiny trattoria filled with some of the most sophisticated Italian food this side of Rome. Try the arugula, mushroom, and parmesan salad; the veal chop is nearly perfect, juicy and charred just so. For dessert, the *tiramisù* is a must. Open daily for lunch and dinner; no lunch Saturdays; closed Sundays. Major credit cards accepted. Reservations necessary. 8638 W. 3rd St. (phone: 310-274-1893).

Michael's Now that prices have dropped closer to the level of LA's other high-priced restaurants, this pioneer eatery — where California nouvelle was first new — just may be affordable. The gorgeous garden and contemporary art add visual pleasure to the gustatory feats. Dinner nightly, lunch weekdays, brunch on weekends. Reservations advised. Major credit cards accepted. 1147 3rd St., Santa Monica (phone: 310-451-0843).

Orso Although the outside decor is extremely unassuming, this popular northern Italian trattoria more than compensates for its decor inside, with a charming patio framed by ficus trees and candlelit tables. Earthy country salads, pizza with all-but-transparent crusts, grilled meat, and delicious calf's liver are served on attractive Italian pottery plates. There is an extensive wine list as well. Well-known actors frequent this spot, and the bar becomes lively after theater hours. Open daily. Reservations advised. MasterCard and Visa accepted. 8706 West 3rd St. (phone: 310-274-7144).

Pacific Dining Car Steaks — cut on the premises from aged, corn-fed beef — are the house specialty, although the menu also offers four types of fresh fish every day. The layout is a real dining car (plus an additional building) that's been at the same downtown location since 1921. This is a good place for early dinner or late supper when you have tickets for a show at the *Music Center*. Open 24 hours daily. Reservations necessary. MasterCard and Visa accepted. 1310 W. 6th St. (phone: 213-483-6000).

Remi Evocative of a tony seaside Italian restaurant (even though it's 3 blocks from the sea), and named for Venetian gondoliers' oars, this eatery serves ambrosial Venetian fare in a casually elegant atmosphere. The rich wood, gleaming brass, and nautical theme provide an airy backdrop for this eatery, which presents dishes such as whole fish infused with herbs and a wonderful selection of grappas. The outdoor tables are ideal for people watching on Santa Monica's Third Street Promenade. Open daily. Reservations necessary. Major credit cards accepted. 1451 Third St. Promenade (phone: 310-393-6545).

Le Restaurant A quaint and unassuming decor provides the backdrop for yet another of LA's fine French establishments. All entrées and appetizers are carefully prepared. Service is just as meticulous. Closed Sundays. Reservations necessary. Major credit cards accepted. 8475 Melrose Pl. (phone: 213-651-5553).

Tatou This lavish, 1930s-style supper club, where the dressed to the nines clientele dine under a 25-foot-high, tented ceiling showcasing a crystal chandelier, is patterned after the legendary *Coconut Grove* nightclub. Plush banquettes line the ornate walls, and center stage tables are shaded by faux palm trees. Live entertainment accompanies chef Desi Szonntagh's "traditional, hearty American-French-Provençal cuisine." A sampling might include Maine lobster, Caesar salad, crispy roast duck with ginger and black currants, and herb-packed red snapper with oven-dried tomatoes. Desserts are a chocolate lover's paradise. After dinner, go upstairs and dance off those calories (the club is open until 2 AM on weekdays, 4 AM on Fridays and Saturdays). Jackets required for men. Open for lunch and dinner; closed Sundays. Reservations necessary. Major credit cards accepted. 233 N. Beverly Dr., Beverly Hills (phone: 310-274-9955).

La Toque A fine French restaurant, arguably the best in the city. Small, intimate, and very romantic. Since only the freshest ingredients are used, the menu changes daily to reflect seasonal availability and quality. There are usually at least four fish dishes; another four or more meat dishes, including, each autumn, game; plus an extensive wine list — about half are California labels — with some real treasures (for instance, the 1974 Beaulieu Vineyards Cabernet Reserve). Closed Sundays; open for lunch weekdays. Only 20 tables, so reservations necessary. Major credit cards accepted. 8171 Sunset Blvd. (phone: 213-656-7515).

Valentino Devotees generally describe the food as Italian, and the homemade pasta certainly bears them out. But there's also a world of other choices on the eclectic menu — starters such as *timballo* (rolled baby eggplant) or *crespelle* (corn crêpes stuffed with seafood) and entrées like grilled fresh shrimp wrapped with swordfish and dressed with lime juice. The casually elegant spot boasts an impressive wine cellar: more than 50,000 bottles, including Italian, French, German, and California labels. Closed Sundays; open for lunch Fridays. Reservations necessary. Major credit cards accepted. 3115 Pico Blvd., Santa Monica (phone: 310-829-4313).

Val's Good food such as grilled calf's liver, fried shrimp, and all kinds of pasta are dished out to the crew of regulars who jam this favorite spot. Open Mondays through Fridays for lunch and dinner; Saturdays for dinner. Reservations advised. Major credit cards accepted. 10130 Riverside Dr., Toluca Lake (phone: 818-508-6644).

Water Grill The only oyster bar in the downtown area is located in this handsome spot where eight varieties of the mollusk are served along with a wide selection of fresh regional seafood: Atlantic soft-shell crabs with cranberries, northern pike with succotash, and California cioppino are just a hint of what you can experience. Open Mondays through Saturdays for dinner; Mondays through Fridays for lunch. Reservations advised. Major credit cards accepted. 523 W. 6th St. (phone: 213-891-0900).

MODERATE

Benvenuto A tiny trattoria offering friendly service and exquisitely prepared Italian food. This cozy café is a popular hangout for celebs, artists, entertainers, and other assorted Hollywood types. Although chef Mustapha

Sadd's menu is the main attraction — designer pizza, fresh fish, pasta, baked rabbit, *tiramisù* — lingering over an espresso in the candlelit dining room or on the patio overlooking Santa Monica Boulevard while watching the celebrity parade pass by makes this place hard to leave. Open weekdays for lunch and dinner; dinner only on weekends. No reservations. Major credit cards accepted. 8512 Santa Monica Blvd., W. Hollywood (phone: 310-659-8635).

Bistro Garden The very same Beverly Hills celebrities who have parked their Rolls-Royces up the street at the *Bistro* for years have made its sister restaurant the "in" spot. Lunch is especially chic with fare like baked sea scallops with a muscat-ginger sauce. The garden-like patio is *the* place to be seen, and it's quite a pretty place. Closed Sundays. Reservations necessary. Major credit cards accepted. 176 N. Canon Dr., Beverly Hills (phone: 310-550-3900).

Café La Bohème This whimsical West Hollywood eatery attracts a lively, eclectic crowd who comes mostly for the ambience: The high-ceilinged nouveau baroque dining room is draped in faded velvet and adorned with gilded mirrors. The menu has something for everybody — pizza, pasta, salads topped with garlic-seared beef, and filet mignon with shiitake mushrooms. Open daily. Reservations advised. Major credit cards accepted. 8400 Santa Monica Blvd., W. Hollywood (phone: 213-848-2360).

Carroll O'Connor's Place Hollywood celebrities have really taken to the actor's local branch of New York's *Ginger Man* (formerly with the same name). At dinner, the specialties are a good choice, and the country pâté makes a fine starter. Open for breakfast Mondays through Fridays; open for lunch and dinner except Sundays. Reservations advised. Major credit cards accepted. 369 N. Bedford Dr., Beverly Hills (phone: 310-273-7585).

Celestino The young Italian chef draws on his Sicilian roots and Tuscan training for a limited menu with innovative twists, such as the highly praised seafood baked in a paper bag. The restaurant is airy and unpretentious. The art exhibit changes and so does the menu. Open daily for dinner, weekdays for lunch. There's a wonderful Sunday brunch, and late-night suppers Fridays and Saturdays until 1 AM, accompanied by jazz until 2 AM. Reservations advised. Major credit cards accepted. 236 S. Beverly Dr. (phone: 310-859-8601).

Chez Mélange This South Bay eatery is true to its name, offering an international variety of victuals. There is a vodka, oyster, and caviar bar; a wine bar with tastings on Tuesdays; and a dining room, all in a former coffee shop of a motor inn. Open daily for breakfast, lunch, and dinner. Reservations advised. Major credit cards accepted. 1716 Pacific Coast Hwy., Redondo Beach (phone: 310-540-1222).

Il Cielo A brick cottage, with several romantic dining rooms (a fireplace glows in the winter), and a heated patio. Its northern Italian food is excellent. During quiet hours the staff treats guests as if they were at a family reunion. On a balmy evening, eating in the garden feels like dining in Tuscany. Closed Sundays. Reservations advised. Major credit cards accepted. 9018 Burton Way, Beverly Hills (phone: 310-276-9990).

Engine Co. No. 28 This converted firehouse re-creates an American grill of 50 years ago, with what chef Naomi Serizawa calls old-fashioned comfort food combined with a health-conscious attitude that uses less cream, butter, and salt: popular dishes include seafood salad, turkey burgers on whole-wheat buns, a light Firehouse chili, and special pastas. Recipes created by firehouse cooks from around the country make up the weekly specials. Dinner daily, breakfast and lunch weekdays only. Reservations advised. Major credit cards accepted. 644 S. Figueroa St. (phone: 213-624-6996).

Epicentre Although some Angelenos fail to see the humor in the faux post-earthquake damage decor presented here, the place attracts a steady clientele. Gimmicky food names — "seismic entrées" — include quesadillas, crab cakes in corn chili sauce, curries, and homemade ice cream. Open for lunch and dinner, closed Sundays. Reservations advised. Major credit cards accepted. *Kawada Hotel,* 200 S. Hill St. (phone: 213-625-0000).

Fresco It looks Italian, and the menu sounds Italian, yet both stretch tradition with twists such as lobster and spinach filling for cannelloni, and duck in port sauce wrapped in corn crêpes. Closed Sundays; open for lunch weekdays. Reservations advised. Major credit cards accepted. 514 S. Brand Blvd., Glendale (phone: 818-247-5541).

Gilliland's The owner is Irish but the product is Californian — with an Irish accent, such as soda bread on Sundays. Open daily for dinner, weekdays for lunch, Sunday brunch. Reservations necessary on weekends. Major credit cards accepted. 2425 Main St. (phone: 310-392-3901).

Joss The austere decor makes this a high-style showcase for unfamiliar regional Chinese delicacies, such as glazed ginger venison with *quei hua* wine. The waiter shows off the whole perfectly crisped, golden brown Hong Kong Pin-Pei chicken before carving and preparing it in the style of Peking duck on a side table. Open daily for dinner; closed for lunch on weekends. Reservations advised. Major credit cards accepted. 9255 Sunset Blvd. (phone: 310-276-1886).

Lawry's, the Prime Rib What's billed is what you get — delicious prime ribs with horseradish sauce, perfect Yorkshire pudding, mashed potatoes, and salad — at this reliable eatery. The room is paneled but bright, the better to see the immense portions. Dinner daily. Reservations advised. Major credit cards accepted. 100 N. La Cienega Blvd., Beverly Hills (phone: 310-652-2827).

Mandarin Northern Chinese cooking in elegant surroundings instead of the usual plastic, pseudo-Oriental decor. Not on the menu, but well worth remembering as an appetizer, is the minced squab wrapped in lettuce leaves; also be sure to try the spicy prawns. Open daily for dinner; closed Sundays for lunch. Reservations advised. Major credit cards accepted. 430 N. Camden Dr., Beverly Hills (phone: 213-272-0267).

Matrixx This exceptional dining spot is attractively designed in modern, casual Art Deco with faux Tiffany lamps and floor-to-ceiling windows. Specialties include superbly prepared dishes with pasta or Japanese noodles combined with fish, beef, or chicken; there also are more traditional entrées such as steaks and sandwiches. Open daily for breakfast, lunch, and dinner. Reservations advised. All major credit cards accepted. In the *Nikko Beverly Hills Hotel,* 465 S. La Cienega Blvd. (phone: 310-247-0400).

Matsuhisa The fare here — Japanese with Peruvian accents (honest) — is described by its chef as "new wave seafood." The most popular dishes are squid cut like pasta, with an asparagus topping, and seafood with soy, *wasabi,* and garlic. Open daily for dinner, weekdays for lunch. Reservations necessary 2 to 3 days in advance. Major credit cards accepted. 129 N. La Cienega Blvd. (phone: 310-659-9639).

Mon Kee's Amazing seafood combinations are the draw at this bustling Chinese dining spot which caters to downtown LA's business crowd, as well as tourists. "Live" lobster, 15 squid dishes (try the crispy squid with special salt), steamed or fried salt- and fresh-water fish are the mainstays of the seafood menu, and for those not compelled by the above or the conch, clams, or oysters, there are dozens of traditional pork, poultry, beef, and vegetable dishes by which to be dazzled. Open daily. Reservations advised. Major credit cards accepted. 679 N. Spring St. (phone: 213-628-6717).

Musso & Frank Grill It really is a grill, in Hollywood since 1919, and apparently not redecorated once (not that its regulars — film people, journalists, the moiling LA middle class — want it to change one iota). Orthodox American food and the kind of place whose cachet is having none at all; it's okay if you like nostalgia and surly waiters. Try the sand dabs and creamed spinach. Open for lunch and dinner; closed Sundays. Reservations advised. Major credit cards accepted. 6667 Hollywood Blvd. (phone: 213-467-7788).

Pane Caldo Bistro An unpretentious Italian *ristorante* with a great view of the city's famed hills. What it lacks in fancy appointments, it more than makes up for with careful food preparation, generous portions, and reasonable prices. A complimentary appetizer and basket of *focaccia* arrive with the menu to ease the difficult task of choosing from among Tuscan specialties such as warm bell-pepper salad, risotto specials, tagliatelle with porcini mushrooms, spinach tortelloni with butter and sage, osso buco, and a selection of 14 kinds of individual pizza. Try the ultra-rich *tiramisù* for dessert. Open daily for lunch and dinner. Reservations advised. Major credit cards accepted. 8840 Beverly Blvd. (phone: 310-274-0916).

Parkway Grill California cooking is served in a cozy, informal Pasadena eatery without the glitz and prices of *Spago*. The innovative cuisine features mesquite-grilled fish and game, fresh pasta, and pizza lovingly baked in an oak-burning oven. Its late hours make it convenient for supper after the theater or a concert. Open daily for dinner, weekdays for lunch, and Sundays for brunch. Reservations advised. Major credit cards accepted. 510 S. Arroyo Pkwy. (phone: 818-795-1001).

Rockenwagner It's loud, even raucous, but the food's great at this Frank Gehry–designed, high-tech eatery. Set behind a glass façade with chimerical decorations, booths lighted by modern streetlamps, and a huge German countryside mural, its creative menu features tasty appetizers of garlic flan, goat cheese, and beet terrine with grilled radicchio, and entrées of cilantro fettuccine with chicken, mild chilies, onion, and roasted jalapeño tomato sauce. Desserts highlights include caramelized pear Napoleon, crisp warm apple pizza, and scrumptious signature cookies. Open weekdays for breakfast, lunch, and dinner; brunch and dinner on weekends. Reservations advised. Major credit cards accepted. 2435 Main St., Santa Monica (phone: 310-339-6504).

Siamese Princess This Oriental eatery, which predates the Thai proliferation, looks like an antiques shop. European furniture and collectibles vie for space with Siamese gift items and photos of British, Thai, and show-biz royalty. The food, billed as "Royal Thai" and beautifully presented, ranks high above run-of-the-mill. Slivers of orange peel turn rice noodles into a delicacy. Dinner daily; lunch Tuesdays through Fridays. Reservations necessary. Major credit cards accepted. 8048 W. 3rd St. (phone: 213-653-2643).

A Thousand Cranes Besides having such a beautiful name, this Japanese spot is well versed in the traditional art of serving beautiful food. It has several tatami rooms and a Western dining room. Go for Sunday brunch, a spectacular Japanese buffet accompanied by live music. Open daily. Reservations advised. Major credit cards accepted. In the *New Otani Hotel,* 120 S. Los Angeles St. (phone: 213-629-1200).

INEXPENSIVE

Chianti Cucina Sister to the far pricier *Chianti* (right next door), this casual trattoria specializes in great-tasting pasta and pizza. Open daily. Reservations necessary. Major credit cards accepted. 7383 Melrose Ave. (phone: 213-653-8333).

Chicago Pizza Works The pizza are deep-dish-style and served with your choice of a wide range of toppings. Other offerings include lasagna, spaghetti, salads, and desserts. There also are more than 100 brands of beer. Open daily. Reservations unnecessary. Visa and MasterCard accepted. 11641 W. Pico Blvd. (phone: 310-477-7740).

Chin Chin Delicious dim sum and traditional Chinese food, cooked without MSG, account for its ongoing popularity as do its quick service and low prices. Takeout also is available. Open daily. Reservations unnecessary. Most major credit cards accepted. Five locations: 8618 Sunset Blvd., Sunset Plaza (phone: 213-652-1818); 11740 San Vicente Blvd., Brentwood (phone: 213-826-2525); 12215 Ventura Blvd., Studio City (phone: 213-985-9090); 16101 Ventura Blvd., Encino (phone: 818-783-1717); and 13455 Maxella Ave., Marina del Rey (phone: 213-823-9999).

El Cholo LA is glutted with places promising authentic south-of-the-border cooking, but this is the best, without question. Around for more than 60 years, its burritos and combination plates are real knockouts. Open daily. There's usually a wait even with reservations; they're advised anyway. Major credit cards accepted. 1121 S. Western Ave. (phone: 213-734-2773).

Chopstix A small chain turning out novel variations on Chinese themes, including Chinese pizza. Open daily for lunch and dinner (closes late). No reservations. Major credit cards accepted. Main location: 7229 Melrose Ave. (phone: 213-937-1111).

Gladstone's Malibu One of the best beachfront restaurants for casual dining, this funky fish house offers alfresco, picnic-style dining on wooden tables stationed on a floor rife with peanut shells and sawdust (or you can eat indoors, but you'll miss the fresh sea air). The menu offers a variety of seasonal seafood in assorted recipes, soups, and salads. Bring a hearty appetite because portions are generous. Open daily for breakfast, lunch, and dinner. Major credit cards accepted. Reservations unnecessary. 17300 Pacific Coast Hwy., Pacific Palisades (phone: 310-454-3474).

Hamayoshi One of the reasons Japanese diplomats request appointments to Los Angeles is this sushi bar for connoisseurs favoring flatfish of all kinds — a list unequaled almost anywhere. The place is small and simple, and customers sometimes have to wait outside for a spot. Free parking. Open daily for dinner; lunch weekdays. Reservations advised. Major credit cards accepted. 3350 W. 1st St. (phone: 213-384-2914).

Hugo's This charming, country-style café with attentive waiters and great coffee is the home of the "power breakfast" for studio heads, stars, and starlets (Julia Roberts, Bette Midler, and Geena Davis are regulars) — where million-dollar deals are made over pumpkin pancakes, pasta *alla Mama* (the house specialty: linguine, eggs, garlic, and Hugo's secret seasoning), and smoked salmon omelettes with tomatoes and sour cream. Get here early; window tables go fast. Lunch and dinner have a calmer atmosphere, but the food is equally first-rate: pasta carbonara, fresh fish, veal parmesan, and so forth. Open daily. No reservations. Major credit cards accepted. 8401 Santa Monica Blvd., W. Hollywood (phone: 213-654-3993).

Katsu Sushi artistry in both preparation and presentation, in a stark setting. How much you pay depends entirely on the number of tidbits you order, and you can personalize your order from a list at the table. Traditional cooked Japanese dishes also are served. Dinner nightly; lunch weekdays. Reservations necessary. Major credit cards accepted. 1972 Hillhurst Ave. (phone: 213-665-1891).

Nosh of Beverly Hills Stop in for a quick, delicious bite of "authentic delicatessen" at this New York–style eatery, where the man-size portions will make any Jewish mother proud. Everything from bagels and lox to chicken soup to incredible cheesecake is offered. Open daily. No reservations. Major credit cards accepted. 9689 Little Santa Monica Blvd., Beverly Hills (phone: 310-271-3730).

Old Town Bakery A real charmer. Chef-owner Amy Pressman's bakery-cum-restaurant caters to hefty appetites, offering giant country crêpes (filled with chicken, herb pesto, ratatouille, or ricotta), great rotisserie chicken tacos, crisp bow tie pasta, and homestyle pan pizzas. Leave room for delectable desserts — bittersweet chocolate terrine, orange poppyseed cake, and Amy's hand-spun ice cream. Open daily. No reservations. No credit cards accepted. 166 W. Colorado Blvd., Pasadena (phone: 818-792-7943).

Original Pantry The decor is early greasy spoon — the food, waiters, and prices ditto — yet long lines at lunch have forced expansion after 67 years. A potful of raw vegetable sticks precedes big portions of basic food. If the mood for a big American breakfast strikes at 3 AM, one might even find a parking place outside. Open nonstop. Reservations unnecessary. No credit cards accepted. 877 S. Figueroa (phone: 213-972-9279).

Original Pizza Small and family run, this place is renowned for its New York–style crisp-crust pizza, with gobs of mozzarella cheese and all the toppings you can name. Open daily. Reservations unnecessary. No credit cards accepted. 2121 Balboa Blvd., Newport Beach (phone: 714-673-1451).

Twin Dragon As inexpensive as Chinese food used to be, with a solid repertoire of topnotch northern Chinese dishes. A lot of families bring their children here, but it's not too noisy. Open daily. Reservations advised. Major credit cards accepted. 8597 W. Pico Blvd. (phone: 310-657-7355).

Whitney's A special little place where chef/owner Whitney Werner and wife, Cheryl Kunitake Werner, work their culinary wonders: seared sea bass with tomatillo and black bean salsa or peppered tuna with crispy wontons and *ponsu* sauce. If pasta's your passion, try the linguine with Norwegian smoked salmon or *Arrabiata penne* (fresh parsley and tomato sauce over quill-shape pasta) with Japanese eggplant smothered with warm goat cheese. Open for lunch and dinner Mondays through Fridays; dinner only on Saturdays. Reservations unnecessary. Major credit cards accepted. 1518 Montana Ave., Santa Monica (phone: 310-458-4114).

> **THE FINAL TOUCH** For dessert, try the luscious ice cream made by *Robin Rose* (215 Rose Ave. in Venice; phone: 310-399-1774). Also sold in Old Pasadena (at 35 S. Raymond St.; phone: 818-577-7676); downtown in the Wells Fargo Center (333 S. Grand Ave.; phone: 310-687-8815); and in Brentwood (11819 Wilshire Blvd.; phone: 310-445-2771).

TAKING TEA

The ritual of afternoon tea has become quite popular in Los Angeles in recent years. Even the "ladies who lunch" pause for a mid-afternoon break from their shopping sprees. Visitors to the city should definitely consider doing the same — it's a very Los Angeles thing to do. And it's done at some of the very best places.

Checkers Kempinski A fine addition to the downtown hotel scene, *Checkers* is one of the city's more elegant tea stops. Afternoon tea served in the lounge features wonderful baked goods made fresh on the premises every day. 535 S. Grand Ave. (phone: 213-624-0000).

Lobby Lounge The elegantly furnished *Regent Beverly Wilshire* has become quite the place for tea; at peak hours, expect a bit of a wait. And no wonder: The *Lounge* is lovely, and the feeling very cosmopolitan. The afternoon tea served here — an infused pot, tiny sandwiches, excellent scones with rich Devonshire cream and jam, and a selection of pastries — is exemplary. A pianist plays tunes ranging from Cole Porter to Chopin, and you feel as though you've been transported from tacky old LA to a plush European salon. *Regent Beverly Wilshire Hotel,* 9500 Wilshire Blvd., Beverly Hills (phone: 310-275-5200).

Paddington's Tea Room A charming little tearoom/curio shop that's an homage to Paddington Bear. Owned by an expatriate Australian, the afternoon tea consists of a pot of one of Fortnum & Mason's various blends, a platter of the usual finger sandwiches (cucumber and cream cheese, ham, curried egg), crackers, crudités with a very good spinach dip, and finally, a plate of butter cookies. The shop is filled with tea-brewing paraphernalia, kitchen gadgets, and packaged Australian foodstuffs. 729 N. La Cienga Blvd., W. Hollywood (phone: 213-652-0624).

Rose Tree Cottage Owners Edmund and Mary Fry have created a wonderful English cottage ambience in their Pasadena tearoom. In addition to serving their own specially blended tea — which took some 6 years to perfect — the Frys pride themselves on their scones, homemade jams, Scottish shortbread, and finger sandwiches. After tea, enjoy browsing in the on-premises curio shop. 824 E. California Blvd., Pasadena (phone: 818-793-3337).

Diversions

Exceptional Experiences for the Mind and Body

Quintessential Los Angeles

Rarely, if ever, does a native Angeleno step out onto the deserted sidewalk in front of his or her well-manicured home and start walking somewhere. The joke about Los Angeles consisting of 72 suburbs in search of a city sometimes seems more truth than parody. Just look around: It seems almost impossible to find the essence of the place amidst so much diversity and distracting clutter.

In addition, stereotypes abound. Yes, it seems that most of the people who live here are under 25 and blond. Yes, jogging (never walking) is the local religion. And yes, everyone seems to be either seeking or giving autographs. But look beyond those trim bronzed bodies running along the Esplanade (you're probably green with envy anyhow) and immerse yourself, even just for a while, in the magic that is Los Angeles. The truth is that quintessential Los Angeles is found in all kinds of places — from a chichi restaurant to a funky beach town to a day at an amusement park to watching a whale blow its top. Wild, weird, whacky, wonderful — it's all that and much, much more.

A DAY AT DISNEYLAND The original dream of Walt Disney, celebrating its 39th anniversary this year, is as irresistible as you've probably heard, as magical as Tinker Bell's fairy dust, and perfect to the last detail. Thrill rides aren't the big deal. Instead, there are "adventures" — you get bombarded by cannonballs fired by Pirates of the Caribbean, visit a haunted mansion, explore the frontier, or fly through outer space. The special effects are truly astounding. During summer evenings, the Main Street Electrical Parade — floats and creatures outlined in thousands of tiny white lights — is supercalifragilisticexpialidocious, and the fireworks are stupendous. Ditto for Fantasmic!, a high-tech battle between the forces of good (led by Mickey Mouse) and several classic Disney villains; and Fantasyland, whose old-fashioned kiddie attractions have been treated to some $55 million of Disney's most magical special effects. Speaking of special effects, George Lucas designed a few for one of the park's most popular attractions, Star Tours, a flight simulator in which riders experience a *Star Wars*-type journey to the moon of Endor, home of the Ewoks. Mickey's

Toontown, the park's newest neighborhood, is "home" to many of the Disney characters. And then there is Splash Mountain, the ultimate flume ride. Not to be overlooked is the techno-spectacular Imagination, where classic animated Disney films and live performers are staged in an after-dark show on Tom Sawyer's Island.

If you can't get enough Disney, you can stay at the adjacent *Disneyland* hotel. Future plans include WESTCOT Center — inspired by Florida's EPCOT — that showcases foreign lands and theme pavilions. (*Birnbaum's Disneyland* provides complete details about this still-expanding wonderland.) For information, contact the Guest Relations Office, *Disneyland*, 1313 Harbor Blvd., Anaheim, CA 92803 (phone: 714-999-4565). For a list of nearby lodgings, an area map, and other vacation aids, write to the Anaheim Area Visitor and Convention Bureau, PO Box 4270, Anaheim, CA 92803 (phone: 714-999-8999).

AN AFTERNOON AT THE MALL Los Angeles is the "Land of Malls," and no wonder: In a city that spreads over 464 square miles, the mall is what holds it all together. It's a shopper's lifeline, and what's more, it's become a social hub at which otherwise isolated Angelenos can mingle. Near the center of the mall zone (which includes the *Sherman Oaks Galleria, South Coast Plaza,* and *Woodland Hills Promenade*), on the border between West Hollywood and Beverly Hills, stands the mother of all malls: the *Beverly Center*. A massive bunker, it's home to an impressive assortment of upscale shops, restaurants, and a multiplex movie theater.

Here you can shop till you drop at more than 200 stores, then revive yourself with a meal at the *Hard Rock Café* (a brat-pack hangout with great burgers) or the *California Pizza Kitchen* (18 different toppings). Just for the fun of it, do some fancy food shopping at the *Irvine Ranch Market* and then treat yourself to a movie — all without losing your parking space.

SHOPPING THE FARMERS' MARKET With its giddy assortment of shops and restaurants, this is like a hokey country fair with European sidewalk-café overtones and some Ghirardelli Square know-how thrown in for good measure. Some people say it's too touristy. We say, don't leave LA without seeing it. Started as a cooperative during the Depression years, the market has evolved into quite an attraction.

Don't just walk through the market — become a part of it. You're outdoors — enjoy the people watching, buy some overpriced souvenirs, soak up the sunshine, snack on an ice-cream cone. Instead of charging through the aisles, mill around; nibble on goodies from the various food stalls — Chinese, Japanese, French, Italian, Spanish; relax at one of the colorful umbrella-shaded tables; and shop! Here there is something for everyone — clothes, jewelry, toy stores, art galleries, and, yes, even fresh produce stands. It's comforting to know that in the the midst of this star-struck world, there's still a wonderful, down-to-earth place to spend the afternoon!

DINNER AT SPAGO When Wolfgang Puck first opened his celebrity restaurant back in the early 1980s, he said he just wanted to create a pleasant pizza and pasta shop where friends could come by for a late-night snack. Puck got more than he bargained for. The hottest restaurant in LA (even if you call 6 months in advance, you'll be told reservations are only available at 6 AM and 11 PM), this is a regular haunt of Sylvester Stallone, Arnold Schwarzenegger, Tom Cruise, Meryl Streep — and just about anyone else who's anyone in this image-conscious town.

If you do manage to secure a table, you'll have a chance to sample the *Spago* magic. The paparazzi outside will clue you in to who's inside munching away on Puck's legendary goat cheese–topped pizza, cooked in a wood-burning oven. *Spago* has also earned the reputation for serving the best grilled fish and fowl in town. The noise level is astounding, the bustle (thanks in part to the open kitchen) is maddening, and the waving and air-kissing is right out of a scene penned by Jackie Collins (who also happens to be a regular). A far cry from a simple pasta shop, it's the place everyone wants to see — or be seen at. 1114 Horn Ave. at Sunset Blvd. (phone: 310-652-4025).

SATURDAY ON MELROSE AVENUE Like wow, man. Awesome. Fer sure, you're in LA. Melrose Avenue is Soho West, only more so. It's Main Street with a dose of California weird. It's the hippest stores, the hottest restaurants, the coolest street scene. If it's true that the West Coast is the birthplace of the way-out and radical in food, fashion, and art, then Melrose Avenue is its spawning grounds. Even if you don't go into a single shop (but please do), just walking down Melrose is a perfect way to experience this very LA shoppers' row. Enjoy it. Groove on the consumer madness. Take in the sights. Sip a cappuccino at a sidewalk café and watch the madding crowds. Step into *Soap Plant* or *Wacko* and pick up some things you really need — like an inflatable Japanese monster or a book on the history of miniature golf. Pick up a basket handwoven of telephone wire at *New Stone Age*. Stop in at one of the local eateries — we recommend *Citrus* or *Patina* — or grab a chili dog at *Pink's*. With tourists, trendies, and punks alike now drawn to this shoppers' paradise, the hottest club-and-café center in the city, it's LA at its zaniest. Sample the flavor. Cowabunga!

SUNDAY ON THE VENICE PROMENADE This 300-ring circus that spins into high gear on the weekends typifies what most people believe all of Southern California is like. The setting is complete with performing daredevils juggling chain saws, rappers, bikini-clad roller skaters, and jocks flexing their pectorals on Muscle Beach (an exercise zone in the center of it all). Add to this street vendors selling sunglasses of every imaginable hue, T-shirts from the sublime to the ridiculously obscene, and beachwear so miniscule it's a wonder anyone bothers to put it on — and you've got a scene that amazes even the most jaded locals.

Venice originally was the dream of tobacco heir Abbot Kinney, who (in 1905) created an American version of his favorite Italian city. In its heyday, Kinney's Venice was replete with gondoliers, swank seaside hotels, bathhouses, bazaars, honky-tonk entertainment, and an amusement park. Today, only a few of the old canals remain (most of the original 16 miles of waterways were filled in by the city in 1929), but the carnival atmosphere remains. Fast-food stands line the 3-mile strip: For the best hot dogs in Southern California, head over to *Jody Maroni's Sausage Kingdom* (2011 Ocean Front Walk), and try the Yucatán chicken dogs and sausages made with bacon and maple syrup. Since the roller-skating craze started in Venice, you might want to work off your lunch by renting a pair of Rollerblades and becoming part of the liveliest sideshow in Los Angeles. Though it bears no resemblance to the Piazza San Marco, this Venice is as memorable in its own way.

WHALE WATCHING Every year (between December and mid-April) hundreds of humpback whales migrate south to their spawning ground in Baja, California, from Alaska. And every year, thousands of tourists stand along the piers or go out on boats to try and spot them. Actually, when they're in the area, the whales are pretty hard to miss: Measuring from 40 to 50 feet long and weighing about 40 tons, they are agile and even graceful swimmers. In one incredible display known as "breaching," the whale will propel its entire body up out of the water and then land on its back or side, sending up a wall of spray. Whether it breaches to communicate its location, to dislodge the many barnacles and lice that cling to its ample body, or simply to express a natural exuberance, no one knows for certain. But the display is undeniably impressive.

Best whale watching times are early in the morning or late in the afternoon. Be patient. Scan the horizon till you see what looks like an explosion of smoke about 18 feet high. That's the blow of the humpback. Don't forget your binoculars — or your camera. This is one sight you'll want to preserve in your memory and your scrapbook. Whale watching cruises are offered by *Buccaneer-Mardi Gras Cruises* (Ports O' Call Village, Berth 76, San Pedro; phone: 310-548-1085), *Redondo Sport Fishing* (Sport Fishing Pier, 233 N. Harbor Dr., Redondo Beach; phone: 310-772-2064), *Cabrillo Whale Watch* (3720 Stephen White Dr., San Pedro; phone: 310-548-7563), and *Whale Watch Cruises* (Sport Fishing Pier, 233 N. Harbor Dr., Redondo Beach; phone: 310-372-3566).

To learn more about the humpback and the Pacific gray whale, visit the *American Cetacean Society Library,* open Mondays through Fridays by appointment only; no admission charge. 807 Paseo del Mar, San Pedro (phone: 310-548-6279).

HIKING MALIBU CREEK STATE PARK Driving into this 4,000-acre sylvan hideaway, just minutes off the freeway, you'll be struck by the resemblance the California hills have to the mountains of Korea. For nearly a decade, this was the location for the filming of the popular TV series "MASH." In fact, over the years, this well-maintained park has been the setting for many a movie memory: *How Green Was My Valley* (1940), *Love Is a Many-*

Splendored Thing (1955), *Love Me Tender* (1959), *Planet of the Apes* (1968), *Butch Cassidy and the Sundance Kid* (1969), and *The Towering Inferno* (1974), to name a few.

There are more than 15 miles of trails to be explored here. For nature lovers, there's a wide variety of flora and fauna; it's also possible to spot great blue herons, violet-green swallows, hawks, woodpeckers, and redwing blackbirds. Rabbits, coyotes, foxes, and bobcats also inhabit the richly adorned Southern California hills. Stay alert: You might even get a glimpse of a movie star out bird watching.

If you're interested in seeing the former "MASH" set, there's a memorable 5-mile round-trip hike that goes past Rock Pool (used in many a Western and jungle adventure), past Century Lake (a great picnic spot), right up to the very edge of Malibu Lake. At the end of the trail there's a wide clearing — an open-air museum of "MASH" memorabilia: the helicopter landing pad, a rusted jeep, and what remains of the 4077.

On Sundays, the nearby *Saddle Peak Lodge* (phone: 818-340-6029) serves an excellent brunch. As you look out over the rolling hills, it's hard to imagine that the burgeoning population of Los Angeles is just minutes away. To get to Malibu Creek State Park, take the Ventura Freeway west out of Los Angeles through the San Fernando Valley, to the Las Virgenes exit, and make a left. (For a more scenic trip, take Malibu Canyon Road up from the Pacific Coast Highway.)

A DAY AT THE BEACH: MALIBU One of Southern California's most famous stretches of sand, a favorite haven of celebrities and surfers, and the place where movie stars have been frolicking in the surf here since the 1920s. Today, the likes of Johnny Carson, Jack Lemmon, Goldie Hawn, Kenny Rogers, Linda Ronstadt, Barbra Streisand, and Steven Spielberg call this 27-mile-long strand of pearly beaches home.

Although local residents act as if theirs is a private beach community, the state of California thinks otherwise. And there are now several clearly marked public accessways along the Pacific Coast Highway, Malibu Road, and Broad Beach Road. Even in Malibu Colony — where the "in" crowd lives — ownership extends only to the mean high-tide line (stick to the hard-packed sand down by the water and you'll be okay). If you need some incentive, know that Alexis Maas — Johnny Carson's current wife — met him as she walked by his Malibu house wearing a bikini.

Start your surfside sojourn with a bite to eat on the Malibu Pier. At *Alice's Restaurant* (23000 Pacific Coast Hwy.; phone: 310-456-6646) there are magnificent views extending up the beach and out across the ocean. The Malibu Surf Riders State Beach is just north of the Pier and very popular with the hang-ten crowd. The *Pro Surfing Tour* is held here in August (phone: 310-372-0414). Up the coast just shy of Point Dume, Paradise Cove is a wonderful spot, with a sheltered white beach, sandstone cliffs, and fishing and boating facilities (see *Best Beaches*).

If you're ready for some celebrity gazing, stop in at *Granita* (23725 W.

Malibu Rd.; phone: 310-456-0488), where Wolfgang Puck's designer pizza makes this the hottest spot in Malibu. Or, if you prefer, try *La Salsa* (22800 Pacific Coast Hwy.; phone: 310-456-6299) for good Mexican food. Local luminaries often can be found at *Saint Honoré* (22943 Pacific Coast Hwy.; phone: 310-456-2651); the lures here are the fabulous French pastries. *Geoffrey's* (27400 Pacific Coast Hwy.; phone: 310-457-1519), a cliffside restaurant overlooking the ocean, is a longtime favorite.

Zuma Beach County Park, on the other side of Point Dume, is one of Malibu's largest beaches, and the recreational possibilities — playgrounds, volleyball courts, and surfing — attract large crowds. As you wander along these beaches lined with the "cottages" of the rich and famous, you might decide to stay a while. Try the *Casa Malibu* motel (22752 Pacific Coast Hwy.; phone: 310-456-2219), right in the middle of Malibu, or the *Malibu Beach Inn* (22878 Pacific Coast Hwy.; phone: 310-456-6444) on the beach 1 block from the Malibu Pier. Sit out on your private balcony and pretend you're one of the locals — even if only for a little while.

Performing Arts

It's worth a trip to LA just to spend an evening listening to fabulous music under the stars. And seeing "stars" is another good reason to attend the theater out here. In between projects, big-name film stars and your favorite television actors like to take a turn on the boards. You might even get to brag about seeing future superstars when they were unknown, struggling thespians.

AHMANSON Part of the world-famous *Music Center* in downtown LA, the *Ahmanson* has been host to such musical hits as *Phantom of the Opera* and a cadre of Neil Simon winners — *Biloxi Blues, Brighton Beach Memoirs,* and *California Suite.* Among the many great talents who have performed on its stage are Ingrid Bergman, Richard Chamberlain, Faye Dunaway, Katharine Hepburn, and Elizabeth Taylor. The *Ahmanson's* bold design and dramatic, plush interior make it the gem of the *Music Center,* and an enchanting place to spend the evening. Information: *Ahmanson Theater,* 135 N. Grand Ave. (phone: 213-972-7211).

GREEK THEATRE A beautiful outdoor theater that features such eclectic musical talents as Hall & Oates, Peter, Paul & Mary, Air Supply, Michael Feinstein, and Reba McIntyre. It's just a few steps south of Griffith Park, a wooded, hilly retreat in Los Angeles, so make an evening of it — enjoy a picnic dinner and listen to some great music under the stars. Information: *Greek Theatre,* 2700 N. Vermont Ave. (phone: 213-480-3232).

HOLLYWOOD BOWL One of the loveliest places to spend an evening in all Los Angeles, this natural amphitheater seats 17,620 and is the summer home of the *Los Angeles Philharmonic*. Have a pre-concert picnic on the park-like grounds or an alfresco supper on the patio of the *Bowl*'s restaurant (phone: 213-851-3588). The musical program (held from July to mid-September) ranges from jazz to pop to classical. Actor and pianist Dudley Moore has been a popular performer. It gets chilly in the evenings, so remember to bring a sweater and a blanket (and a cushion for the hard wooden seats). Parking can be difficult, so inquire about the park-and-ride service from several LA locations. Information: *Hollywood Bowl,* 2301 N. Highland Ave. (phone: 213-850-2000).

MARK TAPER FORUM One of the nation's most respected resident theaters. The *Mark Taper* production of *Children of a Lesser God* went on to win Broadway's Tony Awards for best play, best actor, and best actress in 1979, and for overall theatrical excellence in 1977, the same year Michael Cristofer's *Shadow Box,* which was produced here, won a Pulitzer. On the main stage, you'll see many premieres and an occasional revival; the subject matter tends toward the timely, the currently problematic. Also under the *Taper* wing are the *Improvisational Theatre Project,* the intimate *Taper, Too* house, and the Sunday afternoon *Literary Cabaret.* Information: *Mark Taper Forum,* 135 N. Grand Ave. (phone: 213-972-7211).

PALOMINO Originally opened in 1951 exclusively as a country-and-western music venue, it has featured most of country's top performers: Waylon Jennings, Johnny Cash, Linda Ronstadt, and Dwight Yokum. To this day, Jerry Lee Lewis stops by to tickle the ivories. Over the last few years, the club has expanded its musical horizons and now features a variety of musical groups playing country, jazz, rock 'n' roll, and bluegrass. Information: *Palomino,* 6907 Lankershim Blvd., North Hollywood (phone: 818-764-4010).

PASADENA PLAYHOUSE Founded in 1925, this lovely 700-seat theater is on the National Registry of Historic Places; the Spanish-baroque architecture is just one of its appeals. The theater offers a wide variety of stage plays and musicals (it was the first American theater to stage the entire 37-play Shakespearean cycle). An added incentive is that celebrities such as Dustin Hoffman and Gene Hackman often grace the stage. Since Pasadena is evolving into one of LA's most popular nightspots, make an evening out of your visit to the playhouse and dine in one of the many fine restaurants in the area. Information: *Pasadena Playhouse,* 39 S. El Molino Ave., Pasadena (phone: 818-356-7529).

ROXY A very hip club/music hall with atmosphere. It's dark, sometimes crowded, and a lot of fun. A great place to go for the evening — you'll feel like you're part of the "in-crowd" (even though it's too dark to see who's "in") in this LA hot spot. Entertainment is offered by up-and-coming local and national groups; about 60% of the music is rock 'n' roll and progressive; the other 40% ranges from jazz to country. The *Roxy* has a history of showcasing talents before they hit the big time, like Bruce Springsteen, Whitney Houston, and Bob Marley. David Bowie is among those who cut his teeth here, and he still stops by to play when he's in town. Information: *Roxy,* 9009 Sunset Blvd., West Hollywood (phone: 310-276-2222).

SHUBERT A wonderful, modern space that is especially good for musicals because of its fine acoustics and unobstructed views. The large (1,830-seat) theater is in the very contemporary ABC Entertainment Center, which also houses a movie theater, shops, and restaurants. This is the perfect place for a special evening out — enjoy a good musical and relax afterwards in the outdoor mall. Information: *Shubert Theatre,* 2020 Ave. of the Stars, Century City (phone: 800-233-3123).

UNIVERSAL AMPHITHEATRE Built in 1973, this enclosed ampitheater on Universal Studios' grounds features a wide array of talent (this is the place where you'll see Linda Ronstadt, Barry Manilow, Diana Ross, and Julio Iglesias), although it shies away from heavy metal. A nice place to take the whole family. Stroll along the quaint walks and visit one of the pleasant restaurants on the grounds. Information: *Universal Amphitheatre,* 100 Universal Plaza, Universal City (phone: 818-777-3931).

WESTWOOD PLAYHOUSE A charming 498-seat theater housed in a historic Spanish colonial revival building, it offers a wide variety of Broadway and off-Broadway productions, often with celebrity headliners. Information: *Westwood Playhouse,* 10886 Le Conte Ave., Westwood (phone: 310-208-5454).

WILTERN The name is a combination of Western Avenue and Wilshire Boulevard — it's located on the corner of those two streets. Built in 1931, this is one of LA's favorite music venues, as well as one of the best examples of Art Deco architecture in the city. The tall, green building showcases a wide range of musical talents from rock 'n' roll to bluegrass and jazz. The elaborately decorated Art Deco interior is a show in itself. Information: *Wiltern Theatre,* 3790 Wilshire Blvd. (phone: 213-380-5005).

Audience Participation: Getting into the Act

If you didn't make it as a star of stage and screen, there's still hope for you — as a member of the audience. It's a tough job, but somebody's got to do it. Tickets are free and it's a fun way to experience the glamour of Hollywood.

Pick up tickets at the TV stations' ticket counters or write for them. (Tickets are not sent out of state. You will receive a "guest" letter or card redeemable for tickets.) But having a ticket (or a guest letter) doesn't necessarily guarantee a seat. Generally, you'll still have to wait in a long, first-come, first-served line to get in. If you're traveling with young children, remember there are minimum-age requirements that vary from show to show, so be sure to check. When in doubt, call the hotline numbers provided below.

ABC-TV Ticket information hotline: 213-520-1ABC. Write to: ABC Tickets, 4151 Prospect Ave., Los Angeles, CA 90027. Requests should be sent at least a month in advance. Enclose a self-addressed, stamped envelope. Indicate the name of the show, number of tickets, and date. Age minimums and ticket limits vary from show to show. You will receive tickets or a guest card redeemable for tickets.

ABC does not have a ticket counter. When you call the hotline number, your name will be put on the list for the show and date you want. Show up at least an hour ahead of taping time.

CBS-TV Ticket information hotline: 213-852-2458. Write to: CBS Tickets, 7800 Beverly Blvd., Los Angeles, CA 90036. Requests should be sent at least a month in advance. Enclose a self-addressed, stamped envelope. Indicate the name of the show, number of tickets, and date. Age minimums and ticket limits vary from show to show. You will receive tickets or a guest card redeemable for tickets.

For day-of-the-show tickets: CBS Information Window, CBS Television City, 7800 Beverly Blvd., Los Angeles (near the *Farmers' Market*). Hours are 9 AM to 5 PM Mondays through Fridays; weekend hours vary depending on taping schedule. Arrive early.

FOX-TV Ticket information hotline: 818-506-0067, or call 213-462-7111. Write to: Fox Tickets, 5746 Sunset Blvd., Hollywood, CA 91608. Requests for tickets to "Married with Children" and "In Living Color" should be enclosed in a self-addressed, stamped envelope. Indicate the name of the show, number of tickets, and date. Or, simply show up at the studios (same address) on Wednesday, a week before scheduled taping.

NBC-TV Ticket information hotline: 818-840-3537. Write to: NBC Tickets, 3000 W. Alameda Ave., Burbank, CA 91523. Requests should be sent at least a month in advance. Enclose a self-addressed, stamped envelope. Indicate the name of the show, number of tickets, and date (if you can plan that far ahead). Remember there are age minimums and a limit on tickets for some shows (four per request for "The Tonight Show"). You will receive tickets or a guest letter redeemable for tickets.

For day-of-the-show tickets: NBC-TV Ticket Counter, 3000 W. Alameda Ave., Burbank. Hours are 8 AM to 5 PM Mondays through Fridays; weekend times vary according to taping schedules. Tickets are distributed on a first-come, first-served basis — arrive early! Tours of Studio 1 (home of "The Tonight Show") are also available.

ON STAGE

So, you wanna be a game-show contestant — here's your chance. Although there's no need to make a special trip out to Hollywood to try out for these shows, if you're a game-show devotee and you're planning to be in town, it's worth a try. Be aware that while the shows are happy to have you audition, they don't want people to have unrealistic hopes of being chosen. If you try out, do it just for the fun of it, with no expectations. If you're not chosen, think of what an interesting experience you've had. And if you are selected, think of all the great prizes you could win!

Although game shows appear on network television, most are produced by independent production companies. Contact each show for details on auditioning.

FAMILY FEUD Contestant hotline: 213-965-9999. Call 3 months in advance with the dates of your visit. You will receive an information sheet detailing the audition procedure. All five family members who hope to participate (related by blood or marriage) must be present. Each family plays a mock version of the game and is auditioned twice, so make sure you will be out in LA long enough to do this. The show does not tape every day or even every week.

JEOPARDY Contestant hotline: 213-466-3931. Call a month in advance to check the production schedule and to make an appointment. At the audition, you will be given a written test; if you pass, you will be asked to perform a mock version of the game. Your name will then be placed in a contestant pool for up to 6 months — but there is no guarantee you will be chosen.

WHEEL OF FORTUNE Contestant hotline: 818-972-8088. Call 3 weeks in advance for an appointment. At the audition, you'll take a 5-minute written test and play an hour-long, mock version of the game followed by a very brief interview. If you pass, you'll be called back within a week to play a longer version of the mock game (2½ hours). If chosen as a contestant, an out-of-towner will be notified within 2 weeks.

Oddities, Insanities, and Just Plain Fun

This is soooo California! If you're into oddball architectural wonders, or just fun places to visit, Southern California is the place to be. For those who want to experience the offbeat side of LA, these are places about which to write home.

PHOTO EXPRESS An architectural curiosity that is pure Americana, this is a photo shop in the shape of an old-time box camera. One picture is worth a thousand cocktail-party conversations — have a friend snap a shot of you getting film developed here. Take the San Diego Freeway No. 405

south and get off at the Golden West St./Bolsa exit. Head south toward the beach. Information: *Photo Express,* 15336 Golden West St., Westminster (phone: 714-897-4777).

DONUT HOLE Another of America's classic roadside attractions, a donut-shape donut shop. They say it's good luck for newlyweds to drive through the hole. The donuts are pretty good, too. Take the Pomona Freeway No. 60 to the Hacienda Boulevard exit and turn left (north) and drive about 2 miles until you come to Amar Road, make a right (east), and the giant confection will be right in front of you. Open 24 hours. Information: *Donut Hole,* 15300 E. Amar Rd., La Puente (phone: 818-968-2912).

EXOTIC FELINE BREEDING COMPOUND Lovers of big cats will enjoy this place, where the focus is on research and breeding of endangered big cats including the Siberian tiger, puma, snow leopard, black Asian, and other wild animals. This decade-old habitat also offers visitors informative slide shows and lectures. To get here, take Highway 14 and exit at Rosemond Boulevard; follow signs to the compound. Information: *Exotic Feline Breeding Compound,* Mohave-Tropico Rd., Rosamond (phone: 805-256-3332).

LITTLE SHOP OF FLOWERS Even if you're not in the market to send a dozen red roses, it's well worth a trip to *Finley & Gibbons Fashion Flowers* just to get a glimpse of Liz Taylor's favorite sterling silver roses (yes, they're the real thing!). This is also the place that furnished floral arrangements for Roseanne and Tom Arnold's splash wedding and where other Hollywood types such as Kevin Costner, Barbra Streisand, and Cher pick their blooms. Also interesting and worth a look are the adorable animal creations artistically fashioned from chicken wire and covered entirely in ivy and flower petals. Pick up a few for your stars back home. Information: *Finley & Gibbons Fashion Flowers, Inc.,* 9960 Santa Monica Blvd. (phone: 310-275-0159 or 800-356-1325).

IT'S A SMALL WORLD Less is certainly more at the *Petite Elite Miniature Museum & Gallery.* Its collection of handcrafted miniatures includes tiny figurines of contemporary personalities such as Count Basie, Nancy Reagan, and Michael Jackson; detailed historic rooms, each no larger than a matchbox; and minute mansions, palaces, and castles. Open Mondays through Saturdays by appointment only. Admission charge. Information: *Petite Elite Miniature Museum & Gallery,* 1901 Avenue of the Stars, Suite 500 (phone: 310-277-8108).

SPORT WALK OF FAME Unlike the Hollywood version devoted to screen celebrities past and present, this walk of fame — complete with handprints and signatures — is dedicated strictly to professional athletes, Olympic medalists, and collegians who have made outstanding contributions to their respective sport. Most notable honorees include Mark Spitz, Fred Dryer,

Wilt Chamberlain, Ron Cey, and Jackie Joyner-Kersee. Information: *Sport Walk of Fame,* located along Sixth St., San Pedro.

SILENT MOVIE Not just another movie house, this historic 1942 theater showcases classic films from days gone by (when admission was a mere 10¢). Former owners John and Dorothy Hampton accumulated a vast number of screen favorites; now the property of Larry Austin, a film historian and lover of silent films, the library ranks as the largest private collection of silent movies in the world. This is the only theater of its kind where fans can enjoy vintage footage to the sound of live organ music. Open Wednesdays, Fridays, and Saturdays, 8 to 10:30 PM. Admission charge. Information: *Silent Movie,* 611 N. Fairfax Ave., Los Angeles (phone: 213-653-2389).

Grave Matters

Movie stars are an elusive bunch — slipping in and out of chauffeured limousines, traveling incognito. If you're getting frustrated trying to spot them, consider going someplace where they're a captive audience — the cemetery. Although the idea may seem a little macabre, the cemeteries in Los Angeles are a fascinating microcosm of Hollywood lore. Anybody who was anybody is buried here — from Marilyn Monroe to Rudolph Valentino.

Pick up a copy of *Permanent Californians: An Illustrated Guide to the Cemeteries of California* (Chelsea Green; $16.95), a scintillating tome on Hollywood's legends and where they were laid to rest, and set out on this unique star-gazing adventure.

WESTWOOD MEMORIAL PARK Dwarfed by tall buildings, Westwood is a small, tranquil spot within the boundaries of LA. Office workers and students from nearby UCLA use the exquisitely planted grounds as a lunchtime retreat. The most famous crypt is Marilyn Monroe's, and she is in good company — Natalie Wood, Donna Reed, Oscar Levant, drummer Buddy Rich, producer Darryl F. Zanuck, and renowned industrialist Armand Hammer are all laid to rest here.

Joe DiMaggio no longer sends roses to Marilyn's grave every week, but faithful fans keep up the tradition. Sugar cubes are left on Natalie Wood's grave. Before he died, Armand Hammer had a stereo system installed in the Hammer family mausoleum that plays classical music when the door is opened. Maybe you *can* take it with you, after all! *Directions:* Take the San Diego Freeway No. 405 to the Wilshire Boulevard exit. Go east on Wilshire about a half mile to Glendon Avenue. Turn right onto Glendon; the cemetery is up ahead on the left. 1218 Glendon Ave. (phone: 310-474-1579).

HOLLYWOOD MEMORIAL PARK It is fitting that Cecil B. De Mille is buried here: The place looks like one of the elaborate sets in *The Ten Commandments.* Greek, Roman, and Egyptian temples, incredible statues and obelisks, grand old tombstones, a small lake, and breathtaking mausoleums are ringed by tall, majestic palms. The final resting places of De Mille, director John Huston, Tyrone Power, Marion Davies (William Randolph Hearst's paramour), and a Jayne Mansfield memorial are around the lake.

Rudolph Valentino, the cemetery's most famous permanent guest, rests in the Cathedral Mausoleum (No. 1205). Peter Lorre and Peter Finch are neighbors. A stone staircase leads to the magnificent Sunken Garden and Douglas Fairbanks's reflecting pool and monument (reportedly paid for by Mary Pickford, his ex-wife). Also interred here is mobster Bugsy Siegel, whose dream of a resort in the desert grew into a reality called Las Vegas. The famed "Hollywood" sign is visible from the cemetery, which is right next door to Paramount Studios — bittersweet reminders that life goes on. *Directions:* Take the Hollywood Freeway No. 101 north to the Santa Monica Boulevard exit. Follow Santa Monica west a few blocks; the cemetery is on the left between Gower Street and Van Ness Avenue. 6000 Santa Monica Blvd. (phone: 213-469-1181).

FOREST LAWN MEMORIAL PARK The list of those buried here reads like a "Who's Who" of Hollywood — Humphrey Bogart, Spencer Tracy, Clark Gable, Carole Lombard, Errol Flynn, Jean Harlow, Mary Pickford, W.C. Fields, Nat King Cole, and Walt Disney, to name just a few.

Disney should be resting in peace because this place is as Disneyesque as a cemetery could get — sections are named Slumberland, Lullabyland, Everlasting Love, and Inspiration Slope. The 300-acre plot was designed as an "enchanting park with sparkling lawns, shaded arborways, garden retreats, and noble statuary." This is almost an understatement. On the grounds are copies of Michelangelo statues including his *David,* a stained-glass interpretation of Leonardo da Vinci's *The Last Supper,* churches modeled after 10th-century English and 14th-century Scottish ones (popular for weddings, as well as funerals), a swan lake, and last, but not least — Casey Stengel. This is an incredible place around which to wander — be aware that several of the areas are private, so go to see the setting, not necessarily the grave sites. *Directions:* Take Golden State Freeway No. 5 north and exit east at Glendale Boulevard. Turn right onto Forest, then left onto Glendale Avenue. 1712 S. Glendale Ave., Glendale (phone: 818-241-4151).

FOREST LAWN HOLLYWOOD HILLS The sister cemetery to the one in Glendale is sort of a theme park. The subject: America and the ideal of liberty. A 60-foot statue of George Washington and a replica of the Liberty Bell set the tone. There are reproductions of historic American places of worship and a huge mosaic depicting major events in American history. Interestingly enough, in keeping with the Americana theme, D.W. Griffith filmed scenes for *The Birth of a Nation* on this site in 1915. Buster Keaton, Stan Laurel, Liberace, Ozzie Nelson, and Andy Gibb enjoy a patriotic rest here. *Directions:* Take the Hollywood Freeway No. 101 to the Ventura Freeway No. 134 and go east to Forest Lawn Drive. The cemetery is on your right. 6300 Forest Lawn Dr., Burbank (phone: 818-254-7251).

HOLY CROSS CEMETERY In Europe, grottoes are believed to be favorable settings for miracles. This cemetery, the permanent home of some of Hollywood's most famous Roman Catholic stars, has an absolutely stunning one. The Grotto of the Holy Cross shelters a graceful statue of the Virgin Mary in prayer. Resting in the grotto's tranquil shadows are Rita Hayworth, Charles Boyer, Bing Crosby, Jack Haley, and Jimmy Durante. Rosalind Russell has her own impressive memorial farther on. On a truly tragic note, Sharon Tate Polanski and her unborn child, victims of the Manson Family massacre in 1969, are laid to rest here. *Directions:* Take the San Diego Freeway No. 405 to the Slauson Avenue exit going east. The cemetery will be on your left. 5835 W. Slauson Ave., Culver City (phone: 213-670-7697).

HILLSIDE MEMORIAL PARK This is a resting place for those of the Jewish faith, and Al Jolson and some of his cronies do it proud. Jolson's presence here is as dramatic as it was in life. His tomb, a Greek temple–like structure with a cascading waterfall, is visible from the freeway. There's also a statue of the jazz singer down on one knee with arms outstreched in his classic "Mammy" pose. Keeping him company are the likes of George Jessel, Eddie Cantor, and Jack Benny. *Directions:* Take the San Diego Freeway No. 405 and exit at Sepulveda-Centinela. Go south on Sepulveda Boulevard, then turn left and proceed to the cemetery. 6001 Centinela Ave. (phone: 213-641-0707).

> **GHOULISH GOOD FUN** If seeing where Janis Joplin overdosed, Marilyn Monroe bought her last prescription, and George Reeves (Superman) put a "speeding bullet" through his head is your kind of thing, have we got a tour for you. On a *Grave Line Tour,* you'll be whisked around in a renovated hearse, past 85 sites of celebrity scandal and tragedy. The cost for the 2½-hour tour is $30 per person. Reservations necessary. PO Box 931694, Hollywood, CA, 90093 (phone: 213-469-3127).

Spas

After several days of hardcore sightseeing, come back to life with a rejuvenating visit to a spa — the ultimate indulgence. Unlike traditional European spas, which use mineral waters as therapy, the typical American spa considers a fully equipped gym its epicenter. In addition to such old standbys as massages, herbal wraps, and facials, many spas and wellness centers now offer such treatments as fruit showers (hot water scented with citrus) and "sound massages" (where classical or New Age music is played in the background). Sophisticated equipment and specialized treatments, such as aromatherapy (where the skin is treated with herbal oils and then wrapped in dry sheets), are combined to relax the mind as well as strengthen the body. Most spas have a beauty salon, where guests can change nail color, have their hair cut, dyed, or curled, or enjoy a professional makeup session. Most programs emphasize exercise sessions, hikes, and nutritious diets.

BURKE WILLIAMS DAY SPA & MASSAGE CENTRE, Santa Monica, California This elegant 7,000-square-foot facility draws a celebrity crowd, including Michele Phillips, Gene Wilder, and Oliver and Susan Stone, for a 1-day experience of primal pampering. Although you may choose from a variety of à la carte treatments, indulge yourself with a package such as the "Pure Bliss Spa Day" — 5½ hours of ecstasy starting with a private herbal or marine whirlpool bath followed by a massage, an exfoliation scalp treatment, an aromatherapy facial, a full-body mud masque, and a manicure and pedicure. Other options include "Stress Therapy," "Aromatherapy Escape," and "Gentlemen's Choice." Amenities include lockers, showers, a full supply of toiletries, all the purified water and juice you can drink, and conference rooms for business meetings. Limousine transportation from anywhere in the Greater Los Angeles area is available. Open weekdays from 10 AM to 11 PM; Saturdays and Sundays, from 9 AM to 10 PM. Information: *Burke Williams Day Spa & Massage Centre,* 1460 4th St., Santa Monica, CA 90401 (phone: 310-587-3366).

LA COSTA, Carlsbad, California Just 90 minutes from Los Angeles, this immensely popular spa offers a variety of beauty and health treatments including Swiss showers, herbal wraps, and a hydrotherapy tub; the massage rooms are often crowded, which may hamper one's ability to relax. Other activities include aerobics, tennis, jogging trails, outdoor heated swimming pools, and two fine 18-hole golf courses. The 23 tennis courts (13 lighted) include grass, clay, and hard surfaces. The *Spa Dining Room* offers nutritionally balanced, surprisingly good-tasting, low-calorie meals. Celebrities typically laud *La Costa,* but be forewarned that not everyone is the recipient of the obsequious Tinseltown treatment. Information: *La Costa Resort and Spa,* Costa del Mar Rd., Carlsbad, CA 92009 (phone: 619-438-9111; for reservations, 800-854-5000).

GLEN IVY HOT SPRINGS, Corona, California The perfect 1-day getaway, this is a Mediterranean-style, natural hot springs spa. Relax in the natural mineral water pools and red-clay mud bath. Pamper yourself with a massage or beauty treatment. Enjoy the aqua-aerobics class, delightful gardens, wholesome food, and friendly staff.

Tucked away in a hidden canyon, these hot springs have been popular with the Hollywood set since the 1930s, when W.C. Fields, Paul Muni, and Ronald Reagan rolled around in the mud. In recent years, Reggie Jackson and Dan Aykroyd have followed in the footsteps of the ancient Indians, who believed the soothing waters had spiritual power to heal illness of the body, mind, and spirit.

No miracle cures promised, but you'll certainly be in a better mood by the end of the day. Open daily 10 AM to 6 PM. Admission charge includes use of the pools, spas, sauna, and mud bath (massage and salon services are extra). Reservations required in advance for massage or salon appointments. There are no overnight accommodations, but management can recommend nearby inns if you want to indulge for more than a day. *Directions:* Glen Ivy Hot Springs is about 90 minutes south of Los Angeles. Take the No. I-5 Santa Ana Freeway to eastbound Highway No. 91. In Corona, take I-15 south toward Elsinore. Continue 8 miles to Temescal Canyon Road. Exit right onto Temescal Canyon Road, go 1 mile, then turn right onto Glen Ivy Road and follow it to the end. Information: *Glen Ivy Hot Springs,* 25000 Glen Ivy Rd., Corona, CA (phone: 714-277-3529).

MARRIOTT'S DESERT SPRINGS, Palm Desert, California Although conventions tend to gravitate to this 892-room mega-resort, the spa here manages to keep the ambience intimate and tranquil. The 27,000-square-foot spa area has separate facilities for men and women, and a 22-station gym is the focal point of the fitness program. Facials, loofah scrubs, paraffin hand and foot treatments, and algae treatments leave skin smooth and glowing; if the pampering doesn't lift your spirits, try relaxing in the steam or sauna rooms. There are also 21 tennis courts, two 18-hole golf courses, and a nearby racquet club. Meals are served at the hotel. Information: *Marriott's Desert Springs,* 74855 Country Club Dr., Palm Desert, CA 92260 (phone: 619-341-2211; for reservations, 800-228-9290).

THE OAKS AT OJAI, Ojai, California Ninety minutes north of Los Angeles, owner Sheila Cluff has created a spa that practices fitness with fervor. Evening programs and special-interest theme weeks — such as high-energy workshops and celebrity chefs who prepare spa fare — are so numerous that Cluff publishes a quarterly magazine to update guests on the latest spa news. Classes include high- and low-impact aerobics, toning, and stretching; there also are programs to help guests stop smoking or learn how to cook low-calorie dishes. The 44 guestrooms are simply decorated and very comfortable. Fishing, tennis, and golf are nearby — and you can always embark on an 8-mile hike if you feel a need to commune with nature. Information: *The Oaks at Ojai,* 122 E. Ojai Ave., Ojai, CA 93203 (phone: 805-646-5573).

TWO BUNCH PALMS, Desert Hot Springs, California A world away from the glitzy image promoted by neighboring Palm Springs, this 44-room mineral water spa prides itself on pampering its guests in privacy. Film stars who wish to remain almost anonymous come to be rubbed at this highly touted center for massage therapy. From shiatsu to watzu (Japanese acupressure and massage), which is enhanced by enriching oils, the reverberation of gongs, and the flicker of candlelight, this spa concentrates seriously on the release of body energy. You can do as much or as little as you please; schedules, evening programs, and crash courses on counting calories do not exist at this sanctuary. There is no room service, no gift shop, no valet parking, and no children are allowed. If you've been dreaming about dropping out for a few days, by all means sample the curative powers on tap here. Information: *Two Bunch Palms Resort,* 67-425 Two Bunch Palms Trail, Desert Hot Springs, CA 92240 (phone: 619-329-8791; 800-472-4334 in Southern California).

WHEELER HOT SPRINGS, Ojai, California This spot, 1½ hours north of LA, has drawn people to its therapeutic waters since the early 1800s. Today, the waters can be taken in private redwood rooms, outfitted with hot and cold tubs and a skylight view of towering oak trees. Follow this up with a massage and a meal in their health-food restaurant and be born again. Located in a canyon, this desert oasis is surrounded by a grove of tall palms fed by the natural springs. In addition to the hot tubs, there is an outdoor pool filled with mountain spring water. The spa is open from 10 AM to 9 PM weekdays, except Tuesdays; Saturdays from 9 AM to 10 PM; Sundays from 9 AM to 9 PM.

The *Wheeler* restaurant is open for dinner Thursdays through Sundays from 5 to 9:30 PM and for Sunday brunch from 10 AM to 2 PM. At other times, bring fixings for a picnic — the grounds are lovely. *Directions:* From Los Angeles, take Highway No. 101 west to Highway No. 33 going north (the last exit in Ventura says "33 North Ojai"). Follow Highway 33 for 13 miles, turn left to stay on 33 (look for a traffic light and a shopping center at this intersection). Continue on 33 for another 6.5 miles. Look for the *Wheeler* sign on the left. No rooms, but if you'd like to spend more time in Ojai, they will recommend nearby overnight accommodations. Information: *Wheeler Hot Springs,* 16825 Maricopa Hwy., Ojai, CA 93024 (phone: 805-646-8131).

Best Beaches

Along the 60 miles of California coastline that curve by Los Angeles are more than 20 beaches — some best suited for swimming, others for catching a wave, still others just for sunning. Most Angelenos pick their turf according to proximity, so "best" beach has as much to do with convenience as wonderful waves and superb sand. Below are some of our favorite strands, in order of proximity to LA.

WILL ROGERS STATE BEACH At the bottom of Santa Monica Canyon, this is a wide, sandy beach with even surf and the dramatic cliffs of the Pacific Palisades rising in the background. Different groups — families, surfers, teens, gays — stake out their own territory. Good swimming and surfing. Parking, restrooms, lifeguard. Located along the Pacific Coast Hwy. at Sunset Blvd. in Pacific Palisades.

Temescal Beach is part of Will Rogers, at the bottom of Temescal Canyon. This wide, sandy strand is one of those hidden treasures. Just a short drive from LA, it's practically unknown, which keeps most sun worshipers at bay. There are convenience stands and a play area for kids. It adjoins Temescal Canyon Park, so beachgoers can picnic on the grass if they choose. Parking fee. Pacific Palisades.

MALIBU Although residents like to give the impression that it's all private and off-limits to the public, the state of California says ownership extends only to the mean high-tide line (wherever that is) and there are now several clearly marked accessways along the Pacific Coast Highway, Malibu Road, and Broad Beach Road. The beaches are quiet and pristine, most of the homes along the shore are pretty spectacular, and celebrities often wander by. Here are some of the truly wonderful spots along this stretch:

Paradise Cove A lovely, sheltered beach with a scenic fishing pier. The *Sand Castle* restaurant (phone: 213-275-2503) attracts big crowds for the fabulous ocean views. Parking fee, restrooms, lifeguard (summer only), food. Off the Pacific Coast Hwy. on Paradise Cove Rd., just east of Point Dume.

Robert H. Meyer Memorial State Beaches This complex comprises three hidden beaches — El Matador, La Piedra, and El Pescador — which are among the nicest along this strand. Long walkways lead down to the little-known, deserted beauties. Since there are no lifeguards, be careful swimming. There are fabulous rock formations and magnificent Malibu mansions to admire along El Matador. Parking fee, but no amenities such as food, restrooms, or a lifeguard. On the Pacific Coast Hwy. about 11 miles west of Malibu. Signs will lead the way 1 mile west of Trancas Canyon. Malibu.

Leo Carillo State Beach Named after the actor who played Pancho in *The Cisco Kid,* this incredibly scenic mile-long stretch is much more rustic than the beaches closer into the city (it's about 40 minutes from Santa Monica). There are tidepools, interesting rock formations, nature trails, and campsites. Parking fee, restrooms, showers, lifeguards. Public barbecue grills but no food. On the Pacific Coast Hwy. about 14 miles west of Malibu.

CABRILLO Known as *the* windsurfing place, this popular San Pedro strand is about 21 miles due south of Los Angeles. It's hard to miss: Nearby are docks harboring huge cruise ships bound for Alaska and the Mexican Riviera. Even if you're not into windsurfing, there's lots more to do here: Try jetskiing, swimming, or simply sunning. Parking is available. For more information contact the *San Pedro Peninsula Chamber of Commerce* (phone: 310-832-7272).

LAGUNA This artsy beachside community, framed by graceful hills and valleys sloping toward the jagged coastline, is well worth the 2-hour drive south on Highway No. 1 from Los Angeles. The popular resort was once the residence of John Steinbeck (he wrote *Tortilla Flat* here) and was home to Bette Davis during the 1940s. The action is primarily limited to the 3-mile stretch of beach, where volleyball players of every description play hard and fast. Join them for a turn or, if you prefer, browse along the avenues lined with small craft shops.

Great Sailing and Cruising

Most of the Los Angeles coastline is so sail-happy that you'd think everybody there owns a boat; if you don't, you usually can charter. Expect to be asked about your sailing experience; most boats are handled by brokers for private owners. Your experience will determine which boat you get; which one you want will depend on how long you plan to cruise, since boats under 26 feet can be a little too cozy for a week on the water.

LONG BEACH With its canal-like waters, ideal for gondola rides, it may not be Italy, but California's version of Venice is the next best thing. *Gondola Getaway* (phone: 310-433-9595) offers a 1-hour tour through the canals with a basket of bread, salami, and cheese (bring your own wine). Also, *Hornblower Dining Yachts* (phone: 310-519-9400) features a fun-filled sail around Long Beach with food, drink, and dancing.

MARINA DEL REY Ever since this marina, the largest manmade recreational-boat harbor in the world, was built in the 1960s, pleasure boaters have been passing through in droves; there are 6,000 slips and plenty of docks and sailing schools. Transient boat rentals are available for overnight or up to 1 week. You can even rent the *Wild Goose* (phone: 310-574-6611), the late John Wayne's 36-foot yacht for a sail on the bay. The vessel boasts a fireplace, a helicopter landing pad, a wet bar, and an entertainment center. *Sunset Sail Charter Company* (phone: 310-578-9248) offers romantic sails aboard their 120-foot luxury yachts or 34-foot sloops, including candlelit dinner, wine, or champagne. Information: *Department of Beaches and Harbors,* 13837 Fiji Way, Marina del Rey, CA 90292 (phone: 310-305-9545).

NEWPORT BEACH Local celebs and some 10,000 others keep boats in this big, beautiful, busy Southern California harbor, an hour to the south of LA, the largest pleasure-boat harbor in the world. There are dozens of marinas. Information: *Newport Harbor Area Chamber of Commerce,* 1470 Jamboree Rd., Newport Beach, CA 92660 (phone: 714-644-8211).

Best Golf Outside the City

While many of the golf courses in the Los Angeles area are part of private clubs, some of the most spectacular ones allow public access. These three have been highly rated by *Golf Magazine.*

MONARCH BEACH Located about halfway between San Diego and Los Angeles in the city of Dana Point. With much of the course on the water, only the most diligent duffer will be able to ignore the fabulous scenery and concentrate on golf. Designed by Robert Trent Jones, Jr., the golf course is a true "links," bordering the Pacific Ocean. The course features rolling terrain, bent-grass greens, and spectacular views. The elevated greens and ocean breezes add to the challenge. Rates vary depending on the day you play. Weekdays (Mondays through Thursdays), greens fees are $50 per person for 18 holes of golf, including a cart. On weekends, during the day, you will pay $75 per person. During twilight hours, play will cost you only $50. 33080 Niguel Rd., Dana Point (phone: 714-240-8247).

MORENO VALLEY RANCH This 27-hole property, designed by Pete Dye, is set on hilly terrain. The views are kind of stark, but it's the best deal around price-wise: 18 holes cost only $35 on weekdays and $50 on Fridays, Saturdays, and Sundays. All greens fees include a golf cart. About an hour's drive from Los Angeles. 28095 John F. Kennedy Ave., Moreno Valley (phone: 714-924-4444).

OJAI VALLEY COUNTRY CLUB A 90-minute drive from LA, it features one of the most lavish golf courses in the US — the waiting list attests to it. Be sure to make reservations well in advance. When you do actually get onto the fairways, be sure to raise your head every now and again to appreciate the panoramic views of the mountain-capped valley. A favorite of pros Jimmy Demaret and Doug Sanders, and a host of Hollywood stars, the course — originally designed by George Thomas, Jr. — got a face-lift from golf architect Jay Morrish. Greens fees are $75 per person for 18 holes, plus a $14 per person cart fee. Country Club Rd., Ojai (phone: 805-646-5511).

A Shutterbug's Los Angeles

With all its pastels, seascapes, and picturesque neighborhoods, Los Angeles is a very photogenic city. There is architectural variety: Art Deco is juxtaposed with modern, ornate with ordinary, and a skyline bristling with the temples of modern commerce with the seashore reaching to meet it. There also is natural variety: Flowers embroider a park footpath, a palm tree waves in the breeze, and a sunrise sparks the horizon over the ocean. There's human variety, as well: Immigrants exchange the latest news from the Old Country in Korean, Spanish, and Vietnamese, ruddy fishermen return with their catch, and beachcombers flaunt their tans on the boardwalk. The thriving city, the shimmering sea, the parks, the people, and most of all, the views, make Los Angeles a fertile stomping ground for shutterbugs. Even a beginner can achieve remarkable results with a surprisingly basic set of lenses and filters. Equipment is, in fact, only as valuable as the imagination that puts it into use.

LANDSCAPES, SEASCAPES, AND CITYSCAPES Los Angeles's populated beaches and chrome and glass skyscrapers are most often visiting photographers' favorite subjects. But the city's green spaces and waterways provide numerous photo possibilities as well. Be sure to look for natural beauty: the tropical gardens, the well-manicured plots of flowers in the public parks, the San Gabriel mountains in the background, and the rolling waves of the Pacific.

Although a standard 50mm to 55mm lens may work well in some landscape situations, most will benefit from a 20mm to 28mm wide-angle. The Los Angeles skyline from the top of the *Bonaventure* hotel, for example, is the type of panorama that fits beautifully into a wide-angle format, allowing not only the overview, but the opportunity to include people or other points of interest in the foreground. A fruit stand, for instance, may be used to set off a view of the *Farmers' Market;* or people can provide a sense of perspective in a shot of a café on Melrose Avenue.

To isolate specific elements of any scene, use your telephoto lens. Perhaps there's a particular carving in a historic theater that would make a lovely shot, or it might be the interplay of light and shadow on the façade of an old Spanish church. The successful use of a telephoto means developing your eye for detail.

PEOPLE As with taking pictures of people anywhere, there are going to be times in Los Angeles when a camera is an intrusion. Consider your own reaction under similar circumstances, and you have an idea as to what would make others comfortable enough to be willing subjects. People are often sensitive to having a camera suddenly pointed at them, and a polite request, while getting you a share of refusals, will also provide a chance to shoot some wonderful portraits that capture the spirit of the area as surely as the scenery does. For candids, an excellent lens is a zoom telephoto in the 70mm to 210mm range; it allows you to remain unobtrusive while the telephoto lens draws the subject closer. And for portraits, a telephoto can be used effectively as close as 2 or 3 feet.

For authenticity and variety, select a place likely to produce interesting subjects. *Knott's Berry Farm* is an obvious spot for visitors, but if it's local color you're after, try to capture the fitness scene at the boardwalk in

Venice or the Esplanade in Redondo Beach. Aim for shots that tell what's different about Los Angeles. In portraiture, there are several factors to keep in mind. Morning or afternoon light will add richness to skin tones, emphasizing tans. To avoid the harsh facial shadows cast by direct sunlight, shoot in the shade or in an area where the light is diffused.

SUNSETS When shooting sunsets, keep in mind that the brightness will distort meter readings. When composing a shot directly into the sun, frame the picture in the viewfinder so that only half of the sun is included. Read the meter, set, and shoot. Whenever there is this kind of unusual lighting, shoot a few frames in half-step increments, both over and under the meter reading. Bracketing, as this is called, can provide a range of images, the best of which may well be other than the one shot at the meter's recommended setting.

Use any lens for sunsets. A wide-angle is good when the sky is filled with color-streaked clouds, when the sun is partially hidden, or when you're close to an object that silhouettes dramatically against the sky.

Telephotos also produce wonderful silhouettes, either with the sun as a backdrop or against the palette of a brilliant sunset sky. Bracket again here. For the best silhouettes, wait 10 to 15 minutes after sunset. Unless using a very fast film, a tripod is recommended.

Red and orange filters are often used to accentuate a sunset's picture potential. Orange will help turn even a gray sky into something approaching a photogenic finale to the day, and can provide particularly beautiful shots linking the sky with the sun reflected on the ocean. If the sunset is already bold in hue, however, the orange will overwhelm the natural colors. A red filter will produce dramatic, highly unrealistic results.

NIGHT If you think that picture possibilities end at sunset, you're presuming that night photography is the exclusive domain of the professional. If you've got a tripod, all you'll need is a cable release to attach to your camera to assure a steady exposure (which is often timed in minutes rather than fractions of a second).

For situations such as evening concerts or nighttime cruises, a strobe does the trick, but beware: Flash units are often used improperly. You can't take a view of the skyline with a flash. It may reach out as far as 30 feet, but that's it. On the other hand, a flash used too close to a subject may result in overexposure, resulting in a "blown out" effect. With most cameras, strobes will work with a maximum shutter speed of 1/125 or 1/250 of a second. If you set the exposure properly and shoot within range, you should come up with pretty sharp results.

CLOSE-UPS Whether of people or of objects such as antique door knockers, close-ups can add another dimension to your photography. There are a number of shooting options, one of which is to use a 70mm or a 210mm lens at its closest focusable distance. Unless you're working in bright sunlight, a tripod will be worthwhile. If you are very near your subject and there is a good deal of reflective light, it may pay to underexpose a bit in relation to the meter reading.

If you do not have a telephoto lens, you can still shoot close-ups using a set of magnification filters. Filter packs of one-, two-, and three-time magnification are available, converting your lens into a close-up lens. Even better is a special macro lens designed for close-up photography.

A SHORT PHOTOGRAPHIC TOUR

Here are a few of Los Angeles's most photogenic places.

EL PUEBLO DE LOS ANGELES Juxtaposing the old with the new always makes for an interesting shot. In the heart of downtown Los Angeles, towering skyscrapers form the backdrop to the sights and sounds of an old-time, Mexican marketplace. El Pueblo is as close as you can get to what Los Angeles was like in the very early days. The structures in El Pueblo de Los Angeles Historic Park date from the 1800s and look quite striking against the modern-day skyline. Be sure to get the buildings on the Old Plaza into the shot — the Old Plaza Church, built in 1818; the Italianate Pico House, built in 1870; and the Firehouse, built in 1884. As you snap away, imagine how startled the original 44 settlers, who came from Sonora, Mexico, in 1781, would be to see the old town now! On Olvera Street, you also can get some great "people" shots of folks browsing through the colorful, hand-crafted Mexican wares and stopping for a taco or burrito at the outdoor cafés. When you look at the slides back home, make sure you have mariachi music playing in the background.

VENICE BEACH Should your friends and relations doubt you went to California, just show them your way-out, wacky shots of a day in the life of Venice Beach. The heart of the scene runs from about Windward Avenue, at the Venice Pavilion, south to the Venice Pier at Washington Street. The weekend is the best time to capture the outrageous sights at this open-air carnival. You can get clowns, jugglers, panhandlers, and the bikini-clad all in one shot. For some real-life art forms, walk north to 18th Avenue and capture the modern-day strongmen flexing their pecs at Muscle Beach. Another of the town's artistic manifestations are the outdoor murals. Check out Rip Cronk's *Venice Reconstituted* (Venus on roller skates) at 25 Windward Avenue, his van Gogh-esque *Homage to a Starry Knight* on Ocean Front Walk, Christina Schlesinger's *Marc Chagall Comes to Venice Beach* at 201 Ocean Front Walk at Ozone, and Emily Winters's *Endangered Species* at Ocean Front Walk and Park. To get more details on the murals, contact the *Social and Public Arts Resource Center* (*SPARC*), 685 Venice Blvd.; phone: 310-822-9560).

ARCHITECTURAL WONDERS Los Angeles has an incredible collection of architectural gems sprinkled throughout its many neighborhoods, which means: Take the camera with you at all times. Lovingly restored examples of

Spanish colonial, Spanish baroque, Art Deco, and Italianate structures from the 1920s and 1930s can be found all over town. In Hollywood, aim your camera at the theater façades of *Pantages,* the *Hollywood Egyptian, El Capitan,* and *Mann's Chinese.* In Beverly Hills, the "Maya Deco" Civic Center is a nice architectural counterpoint to some of the city's more renowned hotels, like the Italian Renaissance–Beaux Arts *Regent Beverly Wilshire* and the Mission Revival *Beverly Hills.* In Westwood, you'll be dazzled by the Spanish colonial sights — *Mann's Village Theatre, Mann's Bruin Theatre,* and the temple-like *Contempo Casuals.*

WHALES FOR POSTERITY Whether you try to catch a glimpse of them by standing on your tiptoes along the shoreline or go out on a whale watching cruise, it's a great thrill to bring home some snapshots of Moby Dick's friends and relatives. During the winter months, these fascinating creatures head south along the coastline from Alaska to Baja, California. Watch for rolling humps, a slapping tail, or a spuming spout of water. Early morning or late afternoon is the best time to spot them. If you're really lucky, you might capture a breach on film. That's when the whale (all 40 tons of it) leaps out of the water and dives back in with a thunderous splash.

STAR-STRUCK In a city where stars come out at all times of day and night, a sharp eye and an instant-focus lens can yield all manner of candid shots of those people you're accustomed to viewing only in the movies. And keep your flash handy. Remember that some LA stars like to act like their heavenly counterparts and shine only at night. Happy hunting.

Directions

Introduction

Walking is a relatively alien concept in Los Angeles. People here worship at the shrine of the internal combustion engine, and genuflect at the sight of a Mercedes-Benz hood ornament. Walking occurs only because, as yet, Angelenos can't be "beamed" straight from their bedrooms to the garage. And after their car has been valet-parked, they do still have to get from the curb to the restaurant.

It's really too bad that they've bought the myth of themselves as part of a freeway society, because there are some pretty places within the city limits to be discovered on foot. You still have to drive and park to get to them, but they're there for the exploring.

Because so many people's experience of Los Angeles is through a car window, Gertrude Stein's lament that "There's no there there" seems appropriate. But the truth is that there is a "there," and it's quite fascinating once you find it. Second, there is so much focus on the LA of today — the hot, new, chic, hip, burgeoning metropolis — that the compelling historical sites — and authentic early architectural gems — often get lost in the shuffle.

To break this ugly cycle of neglect and misunderstanding, it helps to know that this city is really a collection of neighborhoods — little "villages," if you will — downtown, Hollywood, West Hollywood, Beverly Hills, Westwood. The most rewarding way to explore it, therefore, is one neighborhood at a time. It's also wise to note that a lot of what you'll see can be credited to a man named De Mille.

Back in 1913, the great Cecil B. De Mille shot one of the first movies ever to be made in Hollywood, and things were never the same again. As he and nascent stars such as Mary Pickford and Douglas Fairbanks gained popularity and financial position, they began to build homes, offices, and studios. Their style was unprecedented opulence — a hybrid of fantasy and royalty, to the manor born à la Hollywood. Around the same time, other men with equally grandiose real-estate visions began breaking new ground: Beverly Hills started as a sort of high-minded subdivision, the master plan for Westwood called for a Spanish colonial shopping center, and so on.

As the salaries of other stars — Valentino, Jean Harlow, Gloria Swanson — rose into the stratosphere, they, too, acquired lavish homes. Soon, whole neighborhoods of magnificent villas and private palaces sprung into being. It was as if fairy-tale characters (with lots of money) had come to life and designed a city. For apart from the early Spanish and Mexican influences, Los Angeles was shaped by the affluence and vision of this emerging motion-picture elite.

In the late 1920s and early 1930s, as the building frenzy continued, Los

Angeles became a town of architectural wonders. Truly spectacular, lovingly restored Spanish baroque and Art Deco buildings from that period can be found all over town. Recently, Angelenos have taken an interest in the city's historic architecture, and several preservationist organizations have emerged. Two — the *Los Angeles Conservancy* (phone: 213-623-CITY) and *Hollywood Heritage* (phone: 213-874-4005) — offer fascinating walking tours focusing on the architecture and history of various sections of town.

So we invite you to join us. Our driving and walking tours will give you a view of Tinseltown that is off the beaten track.

Tour 1: Downtown

Any walking journey through Los Angeles should begin downtown, for this is where Los Angeles was born on September 4, 1781, as El Pueblo de la Reina de Los Angeles (The Town of the Queen of the Angels). The area, El Pueblo de Los Angeles, has now been turned into a state historic park.

To reach downtown, take the Hollywood Freeway No. 101. Exit at the Union Station–Alameda Street off-ramp, then follow the signs to Union Station. El Pueblo de Los Angeles is directly across the street. The park is bordered by Alameda Street (east), Arcadia Street (south), Spring Street (west), and Macy Street (north). Park at Union Station or in the parking lots at El Pueblo.

El Pueblo de Los Angeles, a 44-acre, Mexican-style site, has 27 historic buildings, dating from 1818 to 1926. The park's main attraction is the festive Olvera Street (closed to traffic, as is most of the park). With its cobblestone walkways and outdoor vendors selling all manner of food and trinkets, Olvera has the feel of a Mexican marketplace.

It shouldn't take more than 2 hours to explore the park and visit the shops on Olvera Street. Enjoy your wanderings, but as in any big city, be mindful of your belongings and surroundings. For anyone unfamiliar with the streets of Los Angeles, the *Los Angeles County Street Guide and Directory* (Thomas Bros.) is an invaluable tool.

There is a large directory in the middle of the park near the gazebo to help you get your bearings. Start your visit at the Visitor Information Center on Olvera Street (open 10 AM to 3 PM Mondays through Fridays, and 10 AM to 4:30 PM Saturdays).

If you want to learn about the colorful history of the area, free guided tours are given on the hour from 10 AM to 1 PM Tuesdays through Saturdays. Meet next door to Firehouse No. 1. For a self-guided tour, pick up the El Pueblo de Los Angeles brochure with a detailed map and brief history of the area.

At the center of El Pueblo de Los Angeles sits the Old Plaza, a lovely Spanish square with a gazebo in the center. The rising towers of downtown Los Angeles can be seen in the distance — one glance takes you from the past to the present.

Olvera Street is the bright, bustling hub of activity in the park, a good place to pick up Mexican souvenirs, browse, or grab a snack. Lining the street are some of LA's oldest buildings, landmarks in the history of Los Angeles, a city that first belonged to Spain (1781), then to Mexico (1822), and finally to the United States (1847).

The Zanja Madre, a section of the Pueblo's original irrigation system, dates from 1783. The Avila Adobe (10 Olvera St.), the oldest house in Los Angeles, was built in 1818. It was home to Don Francisco Avila, the first

Downtown

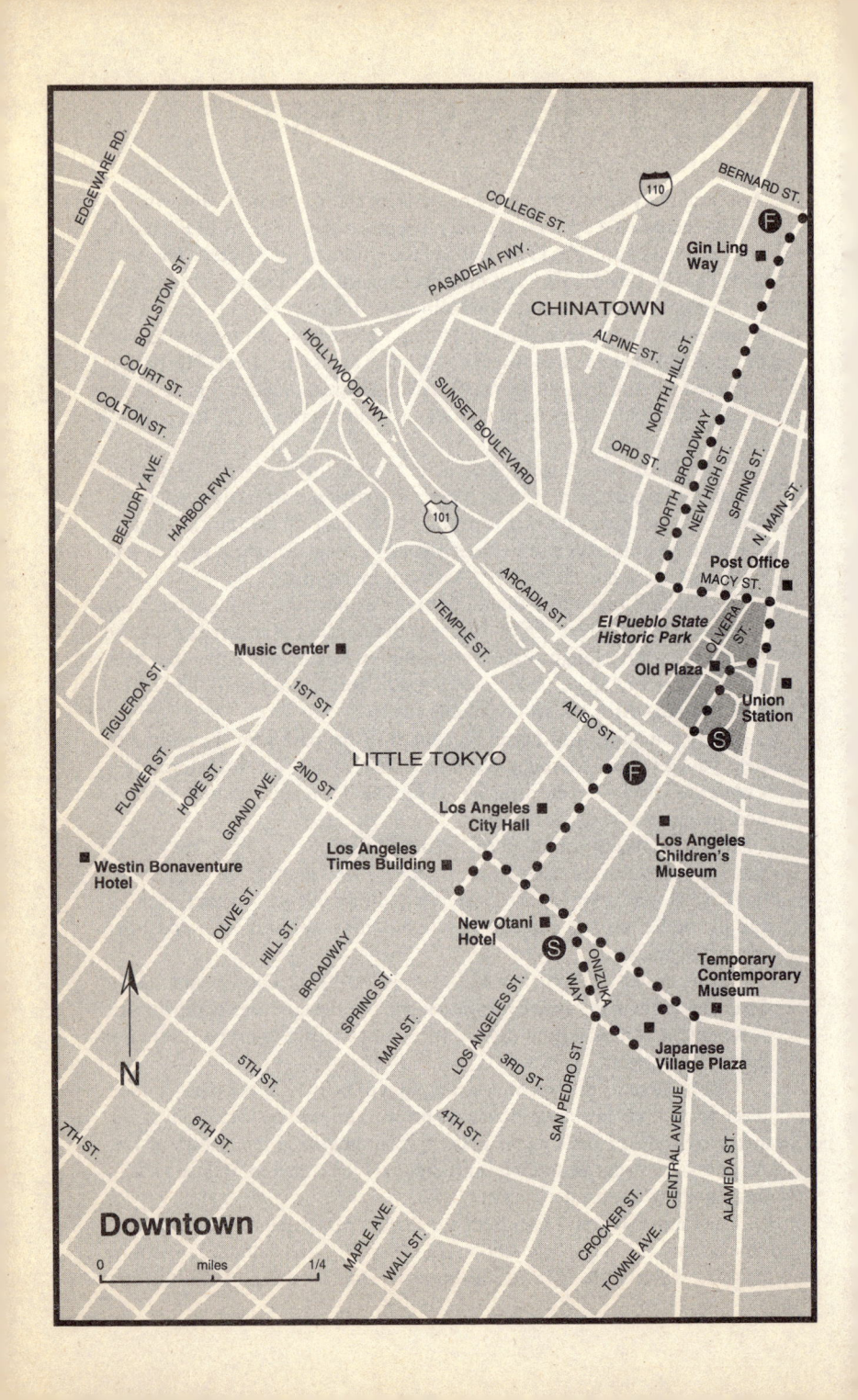

- BERNARD ST.
- Gin Ling Way
- CHINATOWN
- COLLEGE ST.
- PASADENA FWY.
- ALPINE ST.
- NORTH HILL ST.
- ORD ST.
- NORTH BROADWAY
- NEW HIGH ST.
- SPRING ST.
- N. MAIN ST.
- Post Office
- MACY ST.
- El Pueblo State Historic Park
- OLVERA ST.
- Old Plaza
- Union Station
- EDGEWARE RD.
- BOYLSTON ST.
- COURT ST.
- COLTON ST.
- BEAUDRY AVE.
- HARBOR FWY.
- HOLLYWOOD FWY.
- SUNSET BOULEVARD
- ARCADIA ST.
- TEMPLE ST.
- Music Center
- 1ST ST.
- ALISO ST.
- LITTLE TOKYO
- Los Angeles City Hall
- Los Angeles Times Building
- Los Angeles Children's Museum
- FIGUEROA ST.
- FLOWER ST.
- HOPE ST.
- GRAND AVE.
- 2ND ST.
- Westin Bonaventure Hotel
- OLIVE ST.
- HILL ST.
- BROADWAY
- SPRING ST.
- MAIN ST.
- LOS ANGELES ST.
- New Otani Hotel
- ONIZUKA WAY
- 3RD ST.
- SAN PEDRO ST.
- Temporary Contemporary Museum
- Japanese Village Plaza
- CENTRAL AVENUE
- ALAMEDA ST.
- 4TH ST.
- 5TH ST.
- 6TH ST.
- 7TH ST.
- MAPLE AVE.
- WALL ST.
- CROCKER ST.
- TOWNE AVE.

N

0 miles 1/4

Mayor of the Pueblo. The Pelanconi House (17 W. Olvera St.), constructed in 1855, was one of Los Angeles's first brick buildings. (There's a mariachi show inside every evening at *La Golondrina* restaurant; phone: 213-628-4349). The Sepulveda House was constructed by Eliosa Martinez de Sepulveda in 1887 as a hotel/boarding house. Today it houses the Visitor Information Center.

The Old Plaza Church, built in 1818, is the city's oldest Catholic church, boasting California's largest Hispanic congregation. Also worth a look is Firehouse No. 1, built in 1884. Although it's been a saloon, a store, and a boarding house, it is now a great museum of late 19th-century fire-fighting equipment. Behind the firehouse, the Victorian Garnier Building, built in 1890, was once part of the original Chinatown (parts of which were bulldozed in the late 1930s to make way for Union Station).

As you leave the park, be sure to stop across the street to admire the Spanish-Mission-style Union Station. Built in 1939 as the western terminus for the *Southern Pacific, Union Pacific,* and *Santa Fe* rail lines, it's one of the country's last great (and still operative) railroad cathedrals. The waiting room has a 52-foot ceiling, marble floor, and grand seating areas. (The *LA Conservancy* runs guided tours focusing on the architecture; phone: 213-623-CITY.)

Just north of Union Station on Alameda Street, note the 1930s Works Progress Administration murals depicting the history of communications (in the Main Post Office-Terminal Annex; 900 Alameda St.). Stop for a snack at *Philippe's Original Sandwich Shop* (1001 N. Alameda St.; phone: 213-628-3781). Allegedly, the French dip sandwich was invented here in 1918. It's still a fine old spot, where a cup of coffee costs only a dime. It's a favorite of the mayor's, as well as the down-and-outers snoozing at corner tables. But you might want to save your appetite for the culinary treats in Chinatown.

At the corner of Alameda and Macy Streets, go west on Macy Street for a few blocks until you come to North Broadway. Make a right (north) onto North Broadway. This is the beginning of Chinatown. It's an easy walk, but some stretches are quite dull and Los Angeles can get very hot and smoggy. If you choose to drive, there is ample parking along North Broadway and a nice garage on Bernard Street and North Broadway at *Bamboo Plaza* mall. Exploring this area could take from 2 to 4 hours. There's lots to see.

Unlike the Chinatowns of New York and San Francisco, this is not a bustling community of narrow alleyways. This Chinatown has broad streets lined with modern structures, and boasts a fair-size Vietnamese population as well. A vibrant, colorful, and crowded section of Los Angeles, it has dozens and dozens of terrific restaurants and hundreds of small shops; try to come here toward the evening, when the place really hums.

Chinatown runs along North Broadway (east) and North Hill Street (west). It is bordered by Sunset Boulevard (south) and Bernard Street (north). You can do some interesting shopping for Oriental goodies and eat very well at the *Empress Pavilion* (988 N. Hill St.; phone: 213-617-9898), *Ocean Seafood* (747 N. Broadway; phone: 213-687-3088), the *Mandarin Deli* (819 N. Broadway; phone: 213-625-0811), *Yang Chow* (819 N. Broadway; phone: 213-625-0811), or at *Mon Kee* (679 N. Spring St.; phone: 213-628-6717), where lobsters and crabs are plucked live from bubbling tanks.

The farther you walk up North Broadway, the closer you'll come to the heart of Chinatown. The area to which everybody flocks is between College and Bernard Streets. Just north of College Street are the famous Oriental arches with "Chinatown" emblazoned above them and pagoda-style buildings. This is Gin Ling Way — the formal entrance to Chinatown.

North of Gin Ling Way, on the corner of North Hill and Bernard Streets, is *Bamboo Plaza,* a quiet, low-key mall with restaurants and shops. Just south of College Street is *Saigon Plaza,* an outdoor shopping area teeming with stores and eateries attesting to the large influx of Vietnamese. Another find in the heart of Chinatown is *Little Joe's* (900 N. Broadway; phone: 213-489-4900), one of Los Angeles's most popular Italian restaurants.

Once you've done the historic El Pueblo de Los Angeles area and Chinatown, you might want to call it a day. But if you have any energy left, the next stop is Little Tokyo and the contemporary art museums. Otherwise, save this excursion through another interesting section of downtown for another time.

To get to Little Tokyo, take the Hollywood Freeway No. 101 south to the Union Station–Alameda off-ramp. At the end of the exit, make a right. The first signal will be Alameda Street. Make a left (south) on Alameda Street. Drive south for about a half mile. When you come to 2nd Street, make a right (west). Park at any of the lots on 2nd Street, between San Pedro and Los Angeles Streets. (The parking garage underneath Onizuka Way on 2nd Street is a very convenient place.)

This neighborhood of small plazas and gardens, dating back more than a century, contains the largest Japanese community outside of Japan. No pagodas here, though; this is a stark, modern setting. The best place to begin an excursion into Little Tokyo is at *Weller Court,* a multilevel plaza with a nice fountain in the middle. It houses a variety of shops, including a branch of *Matsuzakaya,* the Japanese department store.

Weller Court connects to the ultramodern *New Otani* hotel (120 S. Los Angeles St.; phone: 213-629-1200), which caters to Japanese tourists. The hotel's restaurant, *A Thousand Cranes,* has some of the best food in Little Tokyo. Just off the restaurant level, you'll find a serene, Japanese-style garden to soothe the spirit in the midst of the hustle and bustle of downtown Los Angeles. The hotel also features *Kinokuniya,* a marvelous bookstore filled with excellent, English-language guides to Japan and its culture.

Walking south along Onizuka Way, there are several stores in which to browse. (This is like a low-key Rodeo Drive with Japanese salespeople.) When you come to 2nd Street, make a left (east) and walk a few blocks down to the *Japanese Village Plaza,* the heart of Little Tokyo. This mall is filled with a curious combination of inexpensive Japanese and American take-out eateries and stores. Across the street is the *Japanese American National Museum* (369 E. 1st St.; phone: 213-625-0414); it boasts the largest collection of Japanese-American artifacts ever assembled in the US.

Although Little Tokyo caters primarily to Japanese visitors and businesspeople, if you want to spend an hour or two soaking up an Asian atmosphere, this is a good spot. (The *LA Conservancy* brings this area to life on a walking tour that relays the history of the Japanese immigrant experience in Los Angeles; phone: 213-623-CITY.)

From Little Tokyo, walk or drive to one of the variety of museums and city landmarks: the *Temporary Contemporary Art Museum,* the *Los Angeles Children's Museum, Los Angeles City Hall,* and the *Los Angeles Times* building, among others.

It is a quick trip from the center of Little Tokyo to the *Temporary Contemporary.* Continue walking north along the *Japanese Village Plaza* up to 1st Street. Turn right (east) and walk to Central Avenue. Make a left (north) at Central and the museum will be right in front of you. (If you drive, be sure to take 1st Street to Central; it's not possible to enter Central from the north. There's plenty of parking at the museum.)

The *Temporary Contemporary* (152 N. Central Ave.; phone: 213-626-6222), an annex of the *Museum of Contemporary Art (MOCA;* 250 S. Grand Ave.; phone: 213-621-2766), is itself a striking work of modern art. The building often is used to house oversize exhibits. There is a free shuttle service between the two museums; just show your admission ticket (see *Special Places,* THE CITY).

For the motivated walker, a trip to the Los Angeles City Hall (200 N. Spring St.) and the *Los Angeles Times* building (1st and Spring Sts.) is next. If you're starting from the *Temporary Contemporary,* walk back to 1st Street and head west. This is a fairly short walk, but it could be driven. City Hall is about a quarter of a mile down 1st Street on the right, between Main Street and Spring Street. The *Times* building is across the street on the corner.

City Hall is a majestic structure. Television viewers might recognize it as the *Daily Planet* newspaper building — where Superman had his day job. An observation deck on the 27th floor is open to the public and informative tours are given by appointment (phone: 213-485-4423/24). If you want to see how a newspaper is put together, tour the "new" and "old" *Los Angeles Times* buildings. The original Art Deco plant (at 202 W. 1st St.) is a step back in history while the ultra-modern facility (at 2000 E. 8th St.) is replete with robotics and a streamlined interior (phone: 213-237-5757).

The next stop, 1 block north of City Hall, is for the young at heart.

From the corner of 1st Street and Main, head north on Main Street. Go 1 block past Temple Street to the *Los Angeles Children's Museum* (310 N. Main, phone: 213-687-8825). This place will fascinate even the most hard to please youngsters. The museum is part of *Fletcher Bowron Square,* with shops and restaurants frequented by downtown denizens.

If you drive to the museum on a separate trip, take the Hollywood Freeway No. 101. Coming southbound, exit on Los Angeles Street and turn right. Northbound, take the Alameda Street–Union Station off-ramp and continue west past Alameda to Los Angeles Street and turn left.

At night, the skyline of downtown Los Angeles is magnificent. The lights on the imposing First Interstate Bank building on Hope Street illuminate the sky, and the pyramid-shape towers of several Los Angeles landmarks can be seen in the distance. From the top of the *Westin Bonaventure* hotel (404 S. Figueroa St.; phone: 213-624-1000), you can see it all.

To reach the circular, silver towers of the *Bonaventure,* go north on the Harbor Freeway No. 110. Take the 3rd Street off-ramp and stay to the right. Turn right on Flower Street. The hotel's parking lot is on your right between 4th and 5th Streets. This is a tricky part of Los Angeles, with lots of one-way streets, so drive cautiously.

The *Bonaventure* is definitely worth an evening out. There are 8 levels of shopping and dining in this sleek, futuristic hotel. Enjoy stunning views of the city from the revolving bar and restaurant. Have drinks at the *Bonavista Lounge* on the 34th floor. If you're hungry, visit the elegant *Top of the Five* restaurant on the 35th floor. You also can get some spectacular views just riding up and down in the glass-enclosed elevators.

If you are in the mood for a play, the *Music Center* (135 N. Grand Ave.; phone: 213-972-7211) affords theatergoers a wide choice of theaters in the heart of Los Angeles. The center also houses the *Dorothy Chandler Pavilion* (site of the annual Academy Awards ceremony), where the *Los Angeles Philharmonic, Los Angeles Opera,* and *Joffrey Ballet* perform regularly; the *Ahmanson Theatre,* a venue for musical comedies; and the *Mark Taper Forum,* a space for experimental theater. An evening spent here is a lovely way to end a trip to downtown LA (see *Performing Arts,* DIVERSIONS).

Should you get tired of walking, hop aboard a *DASH* minibus (phone: 213-626-4455). Three *DASH* routes travel through downtown's most scenic areas — from the Civic Center district to California Plaza, Broadway, or Pershing Square — 24 hours a day, Mondays through Saturdays. The fare is a mere 25¢.

Tour 2: Melrose Avenue

Melrose Avenue is where it's at. Everyone comes here to shop for the latest cutting-edge fashions, to see and be seen, to dine in the trendy ethnic restaurants, and to promenade down the avenue. Until the early 1980s, Melrose was just another street lined with small shops and a few restaurants of no particular distinction — then something happened. Beginning around 1982, shops and restaurants catering to the yuppie crowd opened and, within a few years, Melrose became the single most interesting street in Los Angeles. (Certainly, it's become one of the toughest to park near.) On a warm weekend afternoon, half the population of Los Angeles seems to be swarming through the stores and filling the restaurants. Melrose has come to define hip and trendy, in a city where hip and trendy is a way of life.

The transformation began in 1979 when the owners of *LA Eyeworks* (outré eyeglass frames) decided to open a restaurant. The tiny *City Café* put fabulous food on its tables, contemporary art on the walls, and new-wave music in the air. At the same time, *Ma Maison* (now in the *Sofitel Ma Maison* hotel) was giving *Chasen's* a run for its money as the latest celebrity hot spot. The decor was an exercise in reverse snobbism (astroturf and lawn furniture), but every star and power broker in town fought for a good table, and Wolfgang Puck became Southern California's first superstar chef. The new, chic Melrose was born.

Any journey down Melrose begins and ends with the restaurants along the street, with shopping in between. Along with all the new places, Melrose Avenue lays claim to the city's oldest continually operating restaurant, *Chianti* (opened in 1939; 7383 Melrose Ave.; phone: 213-653-8333), and the famous and exclusive *Steak Pit* (7529 Melrose Ave.; 213-653-2011), where you have to know someone to get in. Start out at the east end of town at *Cha Cha Cha,* the sizzling Caribbean celebrity hangout, and wind up at *Café Figaro,* at the west end, for a cappuccino.

Melrose begins at Hoover Street near downtown LA, goes through the Wilshire district, and ends in West Hollywood at Doheny Drive. Since it stretches on for miles and miles, it's best to tackle Melrose Avenue in sections. First, an overview:

Hoover Street to Highland Avenue is the least developed section of Melrose, with a few interesting sights and hip restaurants scattered along the way. (Although parking is practically impossible on Melrose, in this section you can try to park as close to your destination as possible.)

Highland Avenue to Fairfax Avenue is the trendy section, with a color-

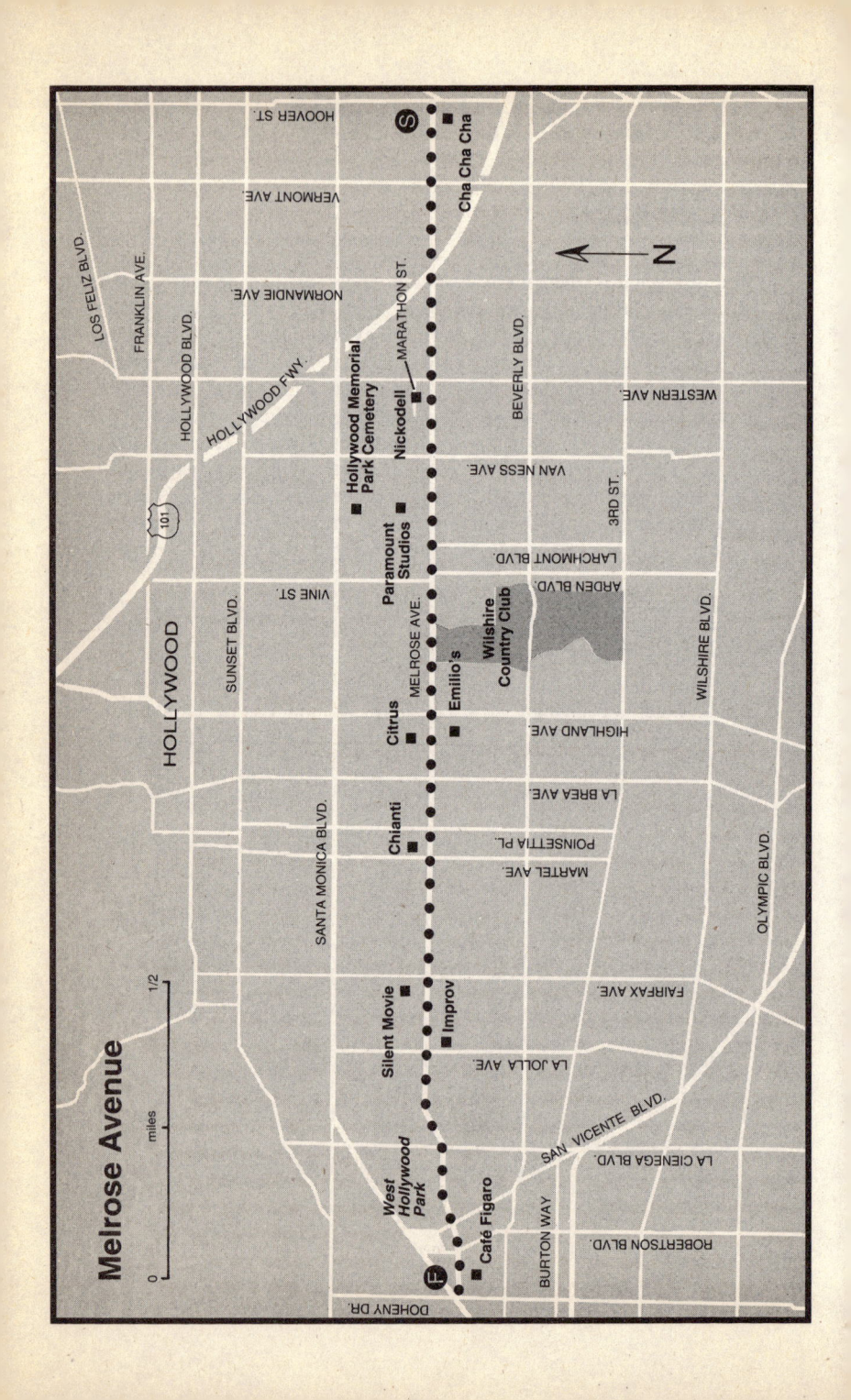

Melrose Avenue

ful concentration of small boutiques, specialty shops, and restaurants. Since this area of Melrose is the most popular, parking is next to impossible. Consider combining a visit here with a trip to Fairfax Avenue and the *Farmers' Market*. You could then park at the market and walk up Fairfax to Melrose.

Fairfax Avenue to San Vicente Boulevard marks the end of the energetic, hip scene, and moves into higher gear. There are fewer stores, but they tend to be more expensive — elegant clothing stores, restaurants, antiques shops, and pricey home furnishing stores stretch from here to San Vicente Boulevard.

The area from San Vicente Boulevard to Doheny Drive, known as Decorators' Row, is strictly for professional decorators. There are some interesting bookstores and celebrity restaurants, however, for visitors to check out. Melrose ends at Doheny Drive.

If you're going to start at the east end of Melrose, have lunch at Mario Tamayo's *Cha Cha Cha* (656 N. Virgil Ave.; phone: 213-664-7723). A funky, little blue-stucco bungalow, it's the hottest scene in town for Cuban-Caribbean cuisine. Tamayo also runs a nifty shop called *Modern Objects* (4355 Melrose Ave.) that specializes in 1940s-style clothing for rock stars. (You might catch Joe Jackson selecting a wardrobe for an upcoming tour.) Just across the street, *Rincon Chileno* (4352 Melrose Ave.; phone: 213-666-6075) serves delicious seafood, empanadas, and *papas mayonesas* at affordable prices. This friendly little café is a favorite among Melrose's Latino population.

At this point, drive west to Paramount studios. Although closed to the public, you can get a good feel for the studios by walking around the outside. There's an entrance on Melrose Avenue, but if you turn onto Marathon Street you'll come up to that beautiful, wrought-iron gate made famous in the film *Sunset Boulevard*. Adjacent to Paramount, *Nickodell* (5511 Melrose Ave.; phone: 213-469-2181) is a popular old restaurant, considered the studios' unofficial commissary. The Hollywood Memorial Park Cemetery — resting place of Rudolph Valentino, Tyrone Power, and other heartthrobs — abuts Paramount, and also is worth a detour (see *Grave Matters*, DIVERSIONS).

Between the studio and Larchmont Boulevard, there are a number of interesting antiques stores and *Elizabeth Marcel's Hat Gallery* (5632 Melrose Ave.; phone: 213-463-3163), where new hats are made from old designs.

If hunger strikes, try *Patina* (5955 Melrose Ave.; phone: 213-467-1108), which some consider to be the best restaurant in Los Angeles. Although the menu is somewhat eccentric, the food is wonderful, the prices are high (but not outrageous), and the decor is very understated — a great dining experience.

Get back in the car and head for the corner of Highland and Melrose, where the truly trendy section begins. Once you find a parking spot, you'll want to walk this stretch, so wear comfortable shoes. The restaurant on the corner is *Emilio's* (6602 Melrose Ave.; phone: 213-935-4922), a wonderful Old World Italian eatery. Next door is the far more modern *Il Piccolino* (641 N. Highland Ave.; phone: 213-936-2996), run by Emilio's son. This reasonably priced spot serves good *nuova cucina*.

Perhaps the most famous restaurant on Melrose is *Citrus* (6703 Melrose Ave.; phone: 213-857-0034). Its gorgeous glassed-in kitchen is one of the best culinary shows in town, turning out superb French-California cooking for a fashionable crowd of foodies and celebrities. If you have time for only one meal, this may well be the best spot.

Heading farther west, stroll past *New Living* (6812 Melrose Ave.; phone: 213-933-5553), a furniture shop where chairs masquerade as art. Be sure to drop in at the *Rock Store* (6817 Melrose Ave.; phone: 213-930-2980). The memorabilia ranges from a silver sequined dress worn by Diana Ross in *Lady Sings the Blues* to one of Paul McCartney's guitars — a museum of rock history for sale!

As you cross La Brea Avenue, keep an eye out for *Pink's Famous Chili Dogs* (711 N. La Brea Ave.; phone: 213-931-4223), a Los Angeles institution fabled for its chili dogs — and the heartburn that goes with them. (If you have the energy, check out La Brea to the south. Due to the rising rents on Melrose, some of the more offbeat stores have moved here.)

At this point, you're on the fashionable, boutique-lined side of Melrose, where most shops open about 11 AM. Madonna wannabes flock to *Retail Slut* (7264 Melrose Ave.; phone 213-934-1339); it's one of her favorite stores. *Unit 7301* (7301 Melrose Ave.; phone: 213-933-8391) sells reproduction Bauhaus furniture. *A Star Is Worn* (7303 Melrose Ave.; phone: 213-939-4922) sells clothing once worn by stars, complete with authenticated histories of who wore what where. *Vinyl Fetish* (7305 Melrose Ave.; 213-935-1300) has a great selection of underground and alternative records — not for the easy-listener. *Zero for Men* (7310 Melrose Ave.; phone: 213-931-8296), a color-blind man's dream, sells hip black and white clothing with matching accessories. *Betsey Johnson* (7311 Melrose Ave.; phone: 213-931-4490) has striking hot-pink walls and paisley decor, with campy women's wear to match. *Off the Wall Antiques* (7325 Melrose Ave.; phone: 213-930-1185) has bright, colorful collectibles, from gas pumps to jukeboxes to life-size horse, cow, and chicken statues, as well as carnival rides from the 1930s.

If you need a little sustenance, pop into *Chopstix* (7229 Melrose Ave.; phone: 213-937-1111) for what they call "Really Risqué Rice" before moving on. A neon Indian head sign will direct you to *American Classics* (7368 Melrose Ave.; phone: 213-655-9375) for an excellent selection of Westernwear — cowboy boots, suede jackets, Levi's, and fancy belt buckles. *Vacationville* (7372 Melrose Ave.; phone: 213-653-6683) has every T-shirt you ever wanted but were afraid to buy — at reasonable prices.

Less than 2 blocks away, at the corner of Martel Avenue and Melrose, are a pair of stores, the *Soap Plant* (7400 Melrose Ave.; phone: 213-651-5587) and *Zulu* (7402 Melrose Ave.; phone: 213-651-4857), which many consider to be the apex of Melrose shopping. Housed in a brightly hand-painted building, these zany shops carry just about anything, as long as it's peculiar. The *Soap Plant* has offbeat sundries and *Zulu* carries vividly colored spandex dresses, plus gaudy accessories.

The entranceway to *Wacko* (7416 Melrose Ave.; phone: 213-651-3811) takes you down a hallway of carnival mirrors. This place lives up to its name — inflatable sharks, books on loud ties, weird windup dolls, and Mexican *Day of the Dead* artifacts. If you've seen it in a dream, it's here in bold colors.

Farther along is *Antonio's* (7472 Melrose Ave.; phone: 213-655-0480), one of the oldest Mexican restaurants in the city, specializing in a variety of spicy, unusual dishes. And when Rob Lowe took Princess Stephanie out for an evening on the town, they headed for *Johnny Rocket's* (7507 Melrose Ave.; phone: 213-651-3361), a spiffy 1950s diner serving great burgers, shakes, and fries.

Some of the interesting shops along the way are *Ecru* (7428 Melrose Ave.; phone: 213-821-9962), with cutting-edge fashions from new international designers; *Leathers & Treasures* (7511 Melrose Ave.; phone: 213-655-7541), a popular clothing shop for rock stars (Bruce Springsteen has been sighted here); and *Grau Design* (7520 Melrose Ave.; phone: 213-651-0487), for Guatemalan- and Japanese-inspired creations.

Continuing west, there's *Fantasies Come True* (8012 Melrose Ave.; phone: 213-655-2636), specializing in Walt Disney memorabilia, and *Fred Segal* (8100 Melrose Ave.; phone: 213-651-3342), an entire department store of interconnecting boutiques filled with trendy togs for kids and adults.

For entertainment try the *Matrix* (7657 Melrose Ave.; phone: 213-852-1445), one of the best Equity-waiver playhouses in Los Angeles, and the *Improv* (8162 Melrose Ave.; phone: 213-651-2583), where Robin Williams likes to pop in to try out new material. Just 1 block south of Melrose, on Fairfax Avenue, there's a special treat for silent-movie aficionados. According to its owner, *Silent Movie* (611 N. Fairfax; phone: 213-653-2389) is now the only silent-movie theater in the world dating back to 1942.

At the far end of Melrose is Decorators' Row, just down the street from the Pacific Design Center, a big, blue behemoth. Although most of the stores here are for professional decorators only, the lavish window displays are reason enough for a visit. There are also several interesting shops open to the public. Be sure to browse in the specialized bookstores: the *Heritage* (8540 Melrose Ave.; phone: 310-652-9486), for original manuscripts and first editions; *Elliott Katt* (8570 Melrose Ave.; phone: 310-659-1753), for books on the movies; and the *Bodhi Tree* (8585 Melrose Ave.; phone: 310-659-1733), one of Shirley MacLaine's favorite haunts, for arcana and esoterica.

One of LA's celebrity restaurants — *Morton's* (8800 Melrose Ave.; phone: 310-276-1253) — is at this end of town. The food served here is really beside the point; this power eatery is about movie muscle, mega-deals, who's hot, and who's not.

Or relax at *Café Figaro* (9010 Melrose Ave.; phone: 310-274-7664), where the food is still great and the prices are low. Next, stroll 2 blocks east on Melrose to *Maxfield* (8825 Melrose Ave.; phone: 310-274-8800), where you'll find an impressive collection of chic European and American designer fashions, and perhaps spot some superstars — Jack Nicholson and Cher are regulars.

Nearby is *Melrose Place* (650 N. La Cienega Blvd.; phone: 310-657-2227). Named for the hit Fox TV show, this trendy eatery is a favorite watering hole for the cast of the nighttime soap. It's hard to believe that Melrose — this Soho of the West Coast — was once just a street lined with nothing but drab storefronts.

Tour 3: Fairfax/Farmers' Market

The predominately Jewish section of Fairfax Avenue runs from about Beverly Boulevard to Melrose. To get to Fairfax, go west on Melrose and turn left (south) onto Fairfax Avenue. Or take the No. 10 Freeway west and get off at the Fairfax Exit. Go north and you'll reach the *Farmers' Market*. Park here and walk up Fairfax Avenue.

Fairfax Avenue has long been the heart of Jewish life in Los Angeles — a taste of the old *shtetl* in the midst of the City of Angels. It's as close as LA gets to the sights and sounds of New York's Lower East Side. Along with the city's best delis, the area has half a dozen blocks of kosher butchers, Israeli restaurants (try *Shula & Esther's,* 519 Fairfax Ave.; phone: 213-852-9154), and shops selling Judaica — Hebrew books and Jewish religious artifacts.

The smells of herring and corned beef waft from the center of life along Fairfax, the legendary *Canter's Delicatessen* (419 Fairfax Ave.; phone: 213-651-2030). Known for its hearty breakfasts and triple-decker combination sandwiches and sometimes crabby waitresses, you can get heartburn here any time of day or night (*Canter's* is one of the few restaurants in Los Angeles open 24 hours a day).

A walk down Fairfax offers a fascinating glimpse into a vanishing world. Most of the businesses are mom-and-pop shops with Hebrew signs. After sampling the deli fare, go into *Hatikvah, International Records and Tapes* (436 N. Fairfax; phone: 213-655-7083) for a wide selection of recordings by Jewish artists. If you've been searching for a particular book in Hebrew, try *Atara's Books, Gifts and Israeli Souvenirs* (452 N. Fairfax; phone: 213-655-3050) — the name says it all.

The Jewish ghetto here is rapidly being replaced by a world of young professionals, happy to live close to CBS Television City (7800 Beverly Blvd.) in a quiet neighborhood adjacent to the hustle of Hollywood. The Fairfax district's younger residents hang out at the nearby *Nowhere Café* (8009 Beverly Blvd.; phone: 213-655-8895), a vegetarian dining spot, or at the *Authentic Café* (7605 Beverly Blvd.; phone: 213-939-4626), serving Southwestern-style cooking. Drive by at any hour of the day or night and you'll see a hipper-than-thou crowd waiting out front for tables.

Just south of the old Fairfax district is the *Farmers' Market,* a Los Angeles institution dating back to the Depression. The market also can be

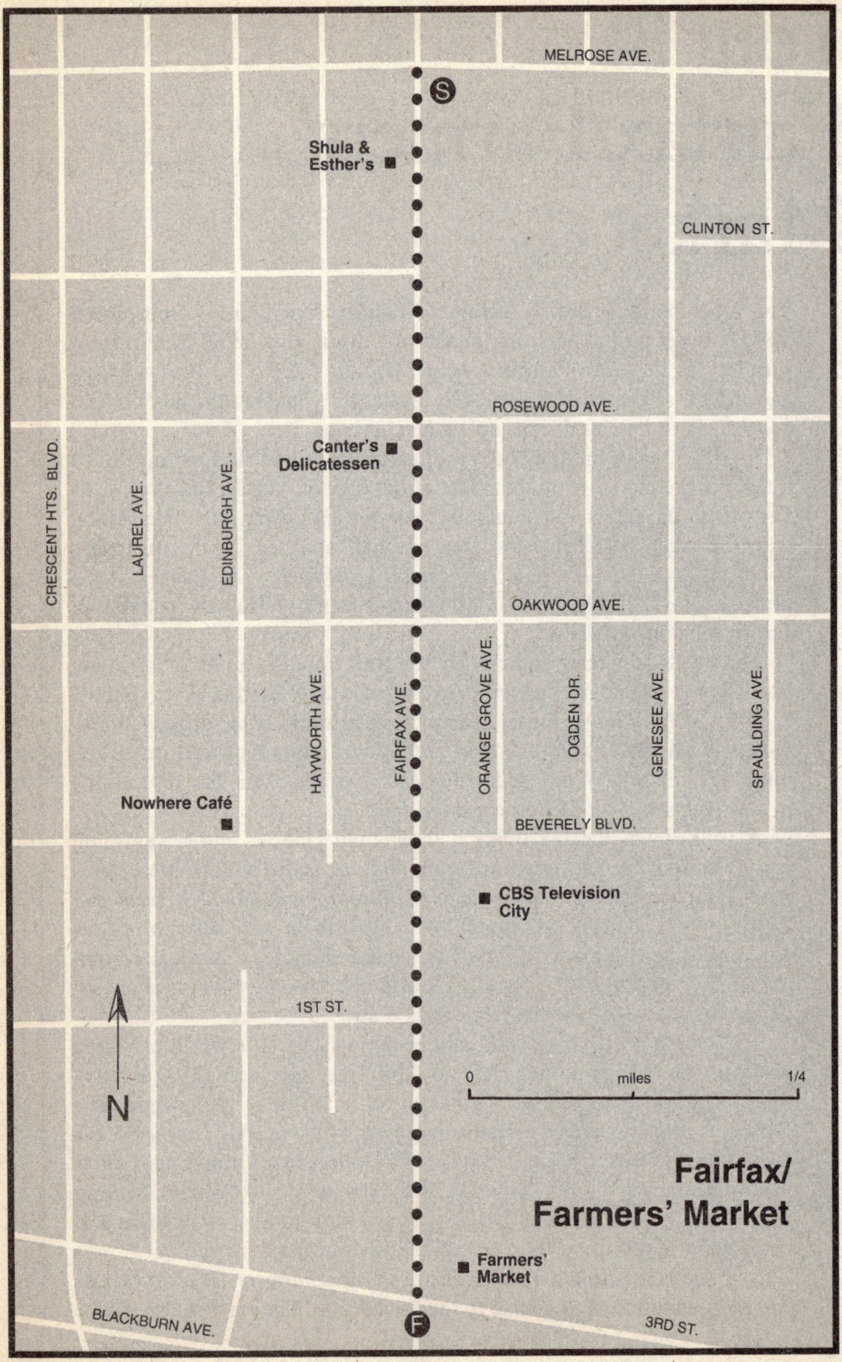
MELROSE AVE.
Shula &
Esther's
CLINTON ST.
ROSEWOOD AVE.
Canter's
Delicatessen
CRESCENT HTS. BLVD.
LAUREL AVE.
EDINBURGH AVE.
OAKWOOD AVE.
HAYWORTH AVE.
FAIRFAX AVE.
ORANGE GROVE AVE.
OGDEN DR.
GENESEE AVE.
SPAULDING AVE.
Nowhere Café
BEVERELY BLVD.
CBS Television
City
1ST ST.
0
miles
1/4
N
Fairfax/
Farmers' Market
Farmers'
Market
BLACKBURN AVE.
3RD ST.

reached from the Santa Monica Freeway No. 10. Just 3 miles north of the Fairfax Exit, you'll spot the market's distinctive, white clock tower with a weather vane on top. Summer hours are 9 AM to 7 PM Mondays through Saturdays, 10 AM to 6 PM Sundays. Winter hours are 9 AM to 6:30 PM Mondays through Saturdays, 10 AM to 5 PM Sundays; closed major holidays. Admission and 3-hour parking are free. 6333 W. Third Street; phone: 213-933-9211.

Started in a vacant lot on the corner of Third Street and Fairfax Avenue, the *Farmers' Market* has been a major Los Angeles tourist attraction for over 50 years. In July 1934, a number of local farmers formed a cooperative to sell fresh produce at bargain prices. The original market had 18 stalls. Today there are more than 160. (You can pick up a map at the *Farmers' Market* office, Gate 1.)

This lively, open-air market is normally swarming with activity, especially on weekends, when it's jam-packed. And although it's become a little too touristy, it's still a pleasant place to wander around. There are colorful shade awnings over the stalls, picnic tables hiding under umbrellas, tempting delicacies at the food stands, fresh produce galore, and shops selling everything from pet food to Lotto tickets — clothing, jewelry, souvenirs, you name it.

The *Farmers' Market* had fallen out of fashion during the 1970s; it came back to life in the late 1980s when new stalls opened and a number of the restaurants became in-spots. The *Gumbo Pot* (phone: 213-933-0358) became known for the best Cajun-creole food in town. *Kokomo* (phone: 213-933-0773), a new-age American café, won raves for great food (including the best BLT in town) dished up in a lively setting. And a wine and beer bar named *326* (after its location; phone: 213-937-2337) gained attention for serving fine California wines and beers made only at small West Coast breweries such as Anchor Steam and Sierra Nevada.

The *Farmers' Market* became a trendy spot when writers from nearby CBS Television City started coming by in the mornings. They'd stop at *Bob's* for a coffee refill and the city's most delicious donuts (try the glazed buttermilk variety), then sit at the outdoor tables, exchanging gripes about actors and producers, and thumb through the "trades." You can pick up copies of *Variety* and the *Hollywood Reporter* at *Al's News* (Oakwood and Fairfax Aves.), one of the best newsstands in Los Angeles. The writers gave the place an air of sophistication; soon the cast and crews from the TV shows started coming by as well, and the area was back in vogue.

Everyone has a favorite destination at the *Farmers' Market*. *Du-Par's* restaurant is known for scrumptious pies and brownies and delicious pancakes and French toast. *Tusquellas Fish & Oyster Bar* serves the best fresh fish and chowders, and also runs a seafood store at the market. Dozens of freshly squeezed fruit and vegetable juices can be had at *Paul's Juice and Salad Bar*. Actor Corbin Bernsen has been seen buying the chocolate-covered marshmallow caramels at *Littlejohns English Toffee*

House. (The store still is run the way it was back in the 1940s, when candy was made by hand.) And *Guns 'n' Roses* lead singer Axl Rose was spotted sipping a fresh-squeezed limeade at *Gill's Old-Fashioned Ice Cream* stand. (*Gill's* has been around since 1937, long before anyone ever heard of two guys named Ben and Jerry.)

Farmers still sell their wares here. Try *Farmers' Market Fruit & Produce, Stone's Farm Fresh Produce,* or *Lopez Produce* for fruit and vegetables grown on nearby farms. The corn still is picked and sold on the same day, but the prices are a little higher than they were in 1934.

Tour 4: Beverly Hills

Go to Rodeo Drive and shop till you drop. But don't stop there. Beverly Hills is a beautiful and historic area with stunning homes and parks. You would be remiss if you came here and left with nothing but bulging shopping bags.

Now one of the best-known neighborhoods in all the world, Beverly Hills had a tough time getting off the ground. Originally a Spanish land grant called Rodeo de las Aguas (the gathering of the waters), the 4,500-acre property was owned by Maria Rita Valdez. In 1852, after repeated Indian attacks, Maria Rita sold Rancho Rodeo to two neighbors who went bust trying to raise wheat on the land.

Several attempts to drill for oil on the property also were unsuccessful, so the land was used to grow lima beans. But at the turn of the century, the Amalgamated Oil Company struck another precious commodity — water. The firm changed its name to the Rodeo Land and Water Company and began an attempt at real-estate development in 1907. Burton E. Green, the president of the company, envisioned a planned community of beautiful homes, tree-lined streets, and spacious parks.

Green called his utopia Beverly Hills after Beverly Farms, Massachusetts, where President Taft was vacationing. Unfortunately, the world didn't beat a path to his door — until 1912, when the ultra-posh *Beverly Hills* hotel opened (see below) and people started coming. Beverly Hills was incorporated as a village in 1914.

But the association of Beverly Hills with luxury and Hollywood magic really began in 1920, when Mary Pickford and Douglas Fairbanks moved in. Pickfair, their private estate, a refurbished hunting lodge, came to symbolize the glamour of Hollywood to the outside world. Soon movie moguls and the cream of the Hollywood crop — Charlie Chaplin, Buster Keaton, Jeanette MacDonald, Gloria Swanson, and Rudolph Valentino — moved into this new playground for the rich, famous, and filmed.

Today, Beverly Hills is still home to movie stars and anyone with a high net worth — but it also has become one of the world's most conspicuous capitals of consumption. A stroll through the small commercial heart of the community will afford you many opportunities to dispose of your cash. Begin your walking (and spending) tour of Beverly Hills at Rodeo Drive, LA's gallant attempt to emulate the grand shopping boulevards of Europe. All you need is money — or a very high limit set on your credit cards (see *Shopping* in THE CITY).

When you're tired of shopping — and the potential for overdose is enormous in Beverly Hills — consider a stroll past some of the more interesting architectural and cultural attractions.

Start on the northeast corner of Beverly Drive and Wilshire Boulevard.

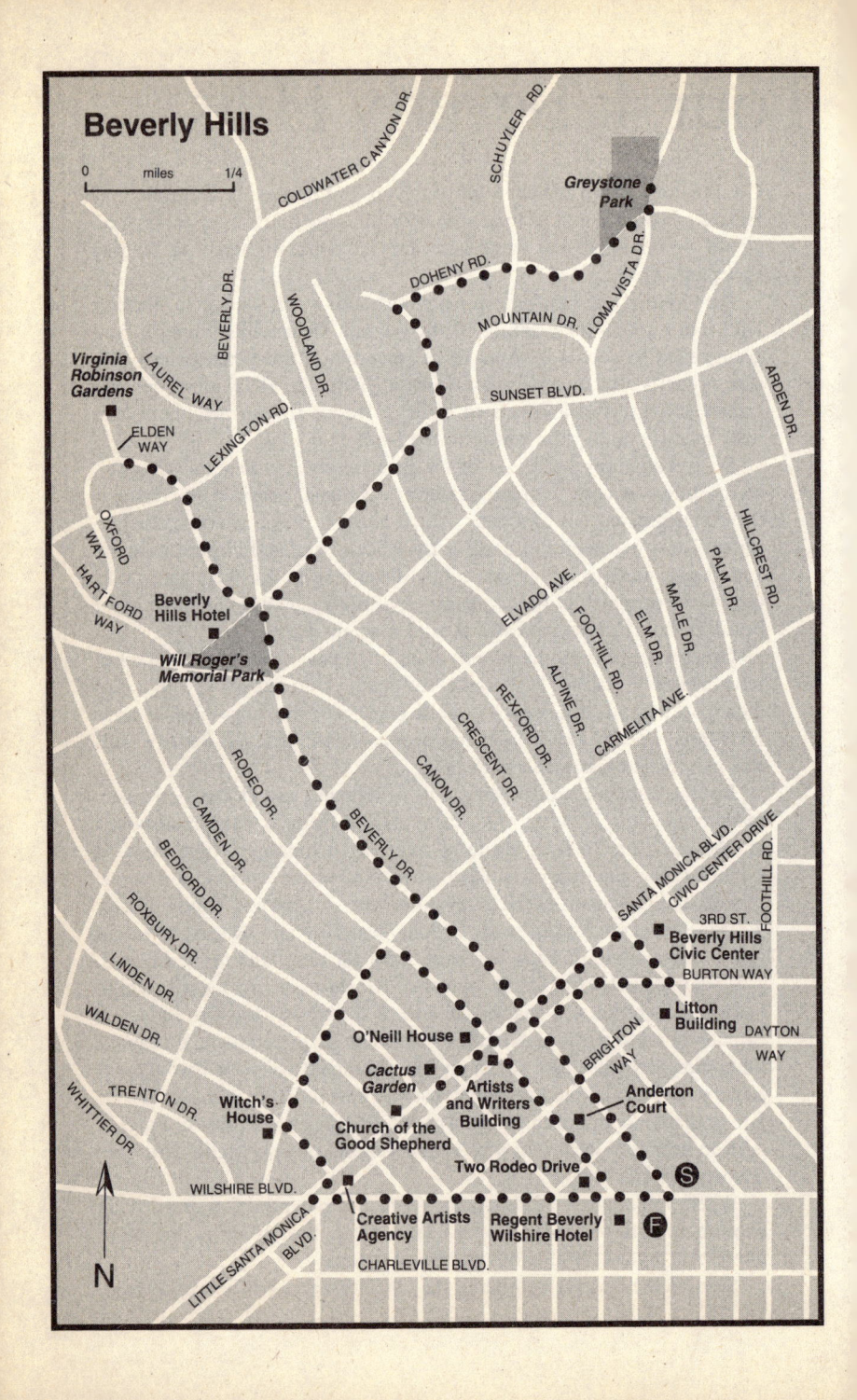

Beverly Hills

You can't miss the striking onion-shape dome of the Israeli Discount Bank (206 N. Beverly Dr.). Only in La-La Land would you find an Israeli bank inside a mosque. Actually, the Moorish-style building was built in 1925 as a movie theater. Called the *Beverly Theater*, it was known as the "theater of the stars," because so many world premieres were shown here from the 1920s to the 1940s. Right next door is Sterling Plaza, a handsome Art Deco office tower built in 1929 by Louis B. Mayer.

Go 1 block west (left) on Wilshire to Rodeo Drive. The magnificent Italian Renaissance–Beaux Arts structure is the *Regent Beverly Wilshire* hotel (9500 Wilshire Blvd.; phone: 310-275-5200), built in 1928. Stop in the *Lobby Lounge* for afternoon tea (see "Taking Tea" in *Eating Out*, THE CITY) and check out El Camino Real, the hotel's charming private street.

At this point, go north on Rodeo Drive and join the throng of determined shoppers swimming upstream. Saudi princes, Japanese tourists, and the monied international set will be sauntering along with you. On the north side of the intersection of Wilshire Boulevard and Rodeo Drive is *Two Rodeo Drive*, an upscale shopping complex featuring the Via Rodeo, a European-inspired, cobblestone shopping street. On Rodeo between Dayton Way and Brighton Way, stop and admire *Anderton Court* (332 N. Rodeo Dr.), an Art Deco–style shopping complex designed by Frank Lloyd Wright in 1953. Continuing north on Rodeo between Brighton and Little Santa Monica Boulevard, note the opulent *Rodeo Collection* shopping plaza (421 N. Rodeo Dr.) and its upscale shops including *Merletto* (425½ N. Rodeo; phone: 310-273-1038), *the* place for Italian lingerie.

On the northwest corner of the intersection of Rodeo Drive and Little Santa Monica Boulevard is the Artists and Writers Building (9507 Little Santa Monica Blvd.), a small Spanish colonial structure. Built in the early 1920s at the urging of humorist Will Rogers, it provides office space for creative artists. Billy Wilder, Jack Nicholson, Bill Bixby, and Ray Bradbury all have been tenants.

Turn right on Little Santa Monica Boulevard, and head 3 blocks east to Crescent Drive. On the corner is a very futuristic gas station, the Union 76 with its 1950s cantilevered canopy. Across the street is the Litton Building (360 N. Cresent Dr.), formerly the headquarters of the Music Corporation of America (MCA). This elegant American Federal Revival office building with a grand portico was built in 1937. (MCA is now located in Universàl City.)

Walk 1 more block east to Rexford Drive. Go north on Rexford and you can't miss the Beverly Hills Civic Center. This ambitious "Maya Deco"–style project links the fire station, police department, and library to the original 1931 Spanish-baroque Beverly Hills City Hall. The graceful arches, central rotunda, and landscaped courtyards make this a very civil civic center.

Continue north to Santa Monica Boulevard and head west. Between Crescent and Canon Drives, notice the Italian Renaissance–style US Post Office (469 N. Crescent Dr.), built in 1933. Inside, this terra cotta and brick landmark has impressive vaulted ceilings covered with mosaics and murals depicting scenes of city street life.

Along Santa Monica Boulevard is a 2-mile stretch of greenery planted with a wide variety of trees, flowers, and shrubs. Beverly Gardens was created in 1911 to relieve the stark, barren look of the developing city. In the park, between Beverly and Rodeo Drives, is *Hunter and Hounds,* a statue from the Château Thierry in France. The work of Henri Alfred Marie Jacquemart, it was donated by former Beverly Hills residents, the Longyears, as a memorial to their son, who was killed in World War I.

Stay on Rodeo Drive; half a block north of Santa Monica Boulevard is a private residence worth noting. Built in 1986, the O'Neill House (507 N. Rodeo Dr.) is a fine example of Gaudí-esque Art Nouveau architecture. The designer, Don Ramos, added elaborate mosaic tiles, art-glass windows, and skylights.

Walk back down to Santa Monica Boulevard and the park. Head west (right) 1 block to Camden Drive. Between Camden and Bedford Drives, the Cactus Garden has an incredible collection of cacti and succulents from around the world.

About 1 block south, between Bedford and Roxbury Drives, is the oldest church in Beverly Hills. Dedicated in 1925, the Church of the Good Shepherd (505 N. Bedford Dr.) has been the scene of some extravagant comings and goings. In 1950, Elizabeth Taylor said "till death do us part" for the first time here (to Conrad "Nicky" Hilton). In 1926, Rudolph Valentino got one of the world's greatest send-offs. Other spectacular funerals have been held here for Gary Cooper, Jimmy Durante, Peter Finch, Alfred Hitchcock, and Rosalind Russell.

Head northwest on Roxbury Drive to Carmelita Avenue. Walk south (left) for 2 blocks to Walden Drive and follow the bread crumbs to the Witch's House (516 N. Walden Dr.). The storybook-style cottage, designed by Henry Oliver, is entered by an arched bridge over a moat. It was built in 1920 as an office for a Culver City movie studio. It was moved to Beverly Hills in 1926, and has been a private residence ever since.

Go south back to Santa Monica Boulevard on Walden Drive. Walk west 1 block on Santa Monica, and you'll be at the intersection of Santa Monica Boulevard and Wilshire Boulevard. The Electric Fountain, built in 1930, represents the story of early California history; the statue on top symbolizes an Indian rain prayer.

If you're intrigued by modern architecture, stop by the Creative Artists Agency building (9830 Wilshire Blvd.), 1 block east of Little Santa Monica Blvd. There's a gigantic Lichtenstein in the lobby of this curved marble, glass, and steel I.M. Pei creation.

Walk back east on Wilshire Boulevard. Along with the palm trees, there's lively pedestrian traffic, a parade of snazzy cars, a mixture of new high-rises and older buildings, specialty shops, and some of Los Angeles's best department stores — *Neiman Marcus* (9700 Wilshire Blvd.) and *Saks Fifth Avenue* (9600 Wilshire Blvd.).

Back at Beverly Drive (where you started), you'll need your car for the second half of the tour. Before heading out, grab a bite at *Nate 'n' Al* (414 N. Beverly Dr.; phone: 310-274-0101), one of the best delis in LA, and a longtime favorite with big-name stars. For something a little more upscale, dine alfresco at the *Bistro Garden* (176 N. Canon Dr.; phone: 310-550-3900).

This half of the tour takes you to some splendid old Beverly Hills locations. (You might actually want to do this part first or save it for another day's adventure.) Go north on Beverly Drive to Sunset Boulevard. Park and visit the Will Rogers Memorial Park (9650 Sunset Blvd.). The Oklahoma humorist was sworn in as honorary Mayor of Beverly Hills at a 1926 ceremony held here.

Right behind the park is the renowned *Beverly Hills* hotel (9641 Sunset Blvd.; phone: 310-276-2251). Referred to as the "pink palace," this sprawling, Mission Revival hotel (now closed and undergoing extensive renovations) opened in 1912 and quickly became a symbol of the glamour of Hollywood. The *Polo Lounge,* world-famous watering hole for celebrities, was home of the power breakfast on the West Coast. At press time, the hotel and restaurant were set to reopen next year.

Because Rodeo Drive gets all the attention, there are two remarkable sites here that, unfortunately, are overlooked — but don't leave Beverly Hills without seeing them. The Virginia Robinson Gardens (1008 Elden Way; phone: 310-276-5367) are just behind the *Beverly Hills* hotel. This historic, 6-acre estate — the oldest in Beverly Hills — planted with tropical flowers, palms, and rarities was the former home of Mr. and Mrs. Harry Robinson (the department store heirs). Tours are given Tuesdays through Thursdays at 10 AM and 1 PM and Fridays at 10 AM only. Reservations necessary; admission charge. To get here from the *Beverly Hills* hotel, go east on Sunset Boulevard. Make a left onto Crescent Drive and make a right onto Elden Way.

From here, head over to Greystone Park (905 Loma Vista Dr.; phone: 310-550-4796). Although the mansion, built in 1928, is now closed to the public, the panoramic view of Beverly Hills and the greater Los Angeles area is worth the trip. The 18 acres of landscaped gardens are open 7 days a week from 10 AM to 5 PM. Classical music concerts and other cultural events are often held at this lovely park. Continue east on Sunset Boulevard. Turn north on Foothill Road which becomes Doheny. Go right on Doheny and continue east. Turn left on Loma Vista Drive.

If you really want the VIP treatment, hire an "Ambassadear" (phone: 310-271-8174). These lovely and informative guides, wearing designer uniforms, arrange private tours. Cost is $15 an hour, with a 4-hour minimum. Whether you decide to tour Beverly Hills on foot, in the trolley, or with a private escort, make sure you see more than the inside of a Rodeo Drive boutique.

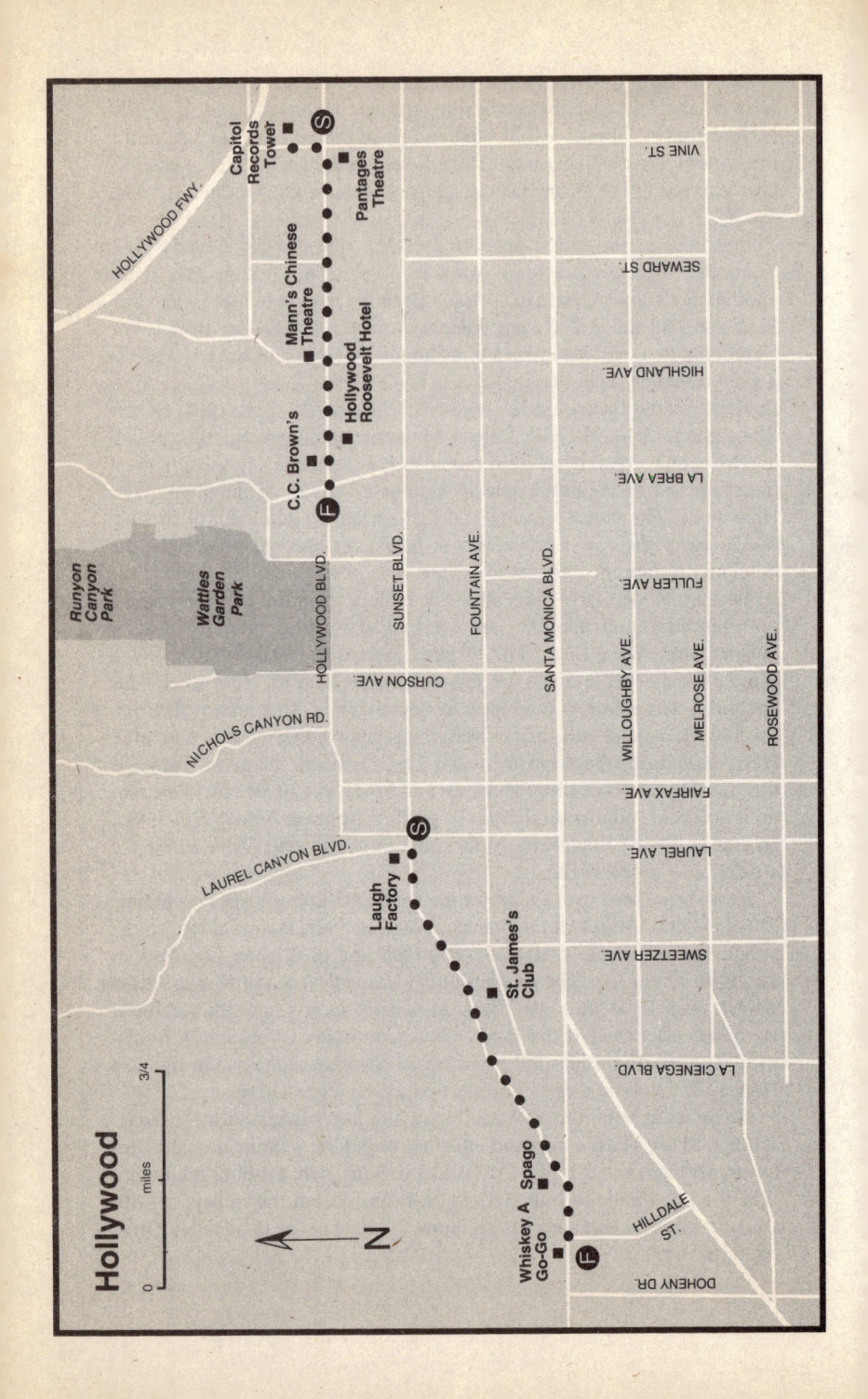

Hollywood

- Capitol Records Tower
- Pantages Theatre
- Mann's Chinese Theatre
- Hollywood Roosevelt Hotel
- C.C. Brown's
- Laugh Factory
- St. James's Club
- Spago
- Whiskey A Go-Go

Tour 5: Hollywood

To most people, Los Angeles is synonymous with Hollywood, and it's where "California Dreaming" really began. Taking in the sights on Hollywood Boulevard and Sunset Boulevard is something that's easy to do on your own. So this walk takes you past the circular *Capitol Records* tower and the luxurious *Pantages Theatre,* before ending at the *Hollywood Roosevelt* hotel, a total of 1½ miles and approximately 2 hours.

Those with a specific interest in Hollywood and the early architecture of the area should take a *Hollywood Heritage* tour. A nonprofit preservation organization, it provides tours of Sunset Boulevard and Hollywood Boulevard at noon on the second Sunday of every month (the tours alternate from month to month). Both tours are roughly 1 mile in length and last about 2 hours. The cost is $6 per person. To find out which tour will be offered during your visit and to make reservations, call 213-874-4005.

A good starting point for your own Sunset Boulevard walk is at the *Laugh Factory* (8001 W. Sunset Blvd.). This is where West Hollywood really starts. It's 100% LA. In fact, the farther west you stroll, the greater the number of toney shops, chic cafés, and lovely hotels you'll see (many of these are favorite celebrity haunts). Though most of the original sights are gone, this still is one of LA's trendiest and most attractive streets.

Across the boulevard from the *Laugh Factory* is the new 30,000-square-foot *8000 Sunset* mall (8000 Sunset Blvd.), housing numerous shops including *Virgin Megastore* (phone: 213-650-8666), the first US outlet of the international music store chain which carries everything from tapes and CDs to accessories and clothing; the *Westward Ho Market* (phone: 213-650-5591), a grocery with a coffee bar and one of the finest bakeries in town; and a five-screen *Laemmle Theatre* complex (phone: 213-848-3500). The *St. James's Club* (8358 Sunset Blvd.; phone: 213-654-7100) is one of the best examples of Art Deco architecture in town. Once an apartment building to the stars, it is now an upper-crust, swank hotel (see *Checking In,* THE CITY). The *Comedy Store* (8433 Sunset Blvd.; phone: 213-656-6225) is one of the hot comedy clubs.

Playboy (8560 Sunset Blvd.) is an average-looking building except for the black and white bunny on the side. Hugh Hefner used to live in a penthouse here. *Spago* (1114 Horn Ave.; phone: 310-652-4025) is *the* dining place for anyone who's anyone or who wants to see or be seen (see *Eating Out,* THE CITY).

Not far away, *Book Soup* not only has one of the widest selections of books and magazines, it also is another place to be seen (8818 Sunset Blvd.; phone: 310-659-3110). The likes of Madonna and other superstars catch up on their reading by browsing the aisles here. *Whiskey A Go-Go*

(8901 Sunset Blvd.; phone: 310-652-4202) has a place in music lore: In the 1960s and 1970s this club launched the careers of some of the country's best-known recording artists, including *The Doors*. Today, bands still pack the club hoping to be discovered.

To walk Hollywood Boulevard (east to west), start at the Capitol Records Tower (1750 N. Vine St.). It's a futuristic, lavender building resembling a stack of records with a stylus on top, and can be seen from the Hollywood Freeway. (You're in Hollywood now, kids!)

Walk south down Vine Street and turn right (west) at the legendary corner of Hollywood and Vine. Though a bit disappointing in real life, the Walk of Fame is at your feet and quite a few architectural gems are tucked among the tourist traps and crowds. Along the way, don't miss the beautiful window displays in many of the shops that line the boulevard. Dressed by the *Hollywood Entertainment Museum,* these changing exhibits, aptly called "Windows on Hollywood," re-create the legendary years of the entertainment industry.

The *Pantages Theatre* (6233 Hollywood Blvd.; phone: 213-468-1700) is a must-see example of Art Deco at its finest. It's one of LA's premier theaters, with an ornate exterior and a spectacular, plush interior. Opened in 1930, the theater hosted the Academy Awards from 1949 to 1959.

Hollywood's oldest restaurant, *Musso and Frank Grill* (6667 Hollywood Blvd.; phone: 213-467-7788) was opened in 1919 and remodeled in 1937. Many well-known wordsmiths — F. Scott Fitzgerald, Ernest Hemingway, William Faulkner, and Lowell Thomas — have drowned their sorrows at the mahogany bar here. Some say that the martinis served in this dark, wood-paneled refuge are the best in town.

Housed in a pink-on-pink building (you can't miss it), the *Fredericks of Hollywood Lingerie Museum* (6608 Hollywood Blvd.; phone: 213-466-8506) spotlights the "unmentionables" once worn by Madonna, Cher, Mae West, Judy Garland, Zsa Zsa Gabor, Tony Curtis — yes, Tony Curtis! — and others.

The *Hollywood Egyptian Theater* (6712 Hollywood Blvd.; phone: 213-467-6167) was once the quintessential expression of Hollywood glamour. The site of the first movie premiere in Tinseltown (*Robin Hood,* starring Douglas Fairbanks), the theater has suffered from years of neglect and is no longer open to the public — but its exterior is still quite a sight.

Another stunning Hollywood Boulevard landmark, the *El Capitan Theatre* (6835 Hollywood Blvd.), opened in 1926 as a hall for song-and-dance variety shows. In 1941, when Orson Welles was unable to find a movie theater willing to screen *Citizen Kane,* his first feature film, he held the world premiere at *El Capitan.* The theater was remodeled as a movie house in 1942 and became the *Paramount.* (Cecil B. De Mille's film, *Reap the Wild Wind,* was the feature presentation.) Today, first-run movies can be seen in this gilded, Old World setting.

Built in 1927, *Mann's Chinese Theatre* (formerly *Grauman's;* 6925 Hollywood Blvd.; phone: 213-464-8111) remains one of Hollywood's most exciting (and crowded) spots; its Chinese-temple façade still is breathtaking after all these years. Compare your hands and feet to the celebrities' prints immortalized in cement. You can even catch a movie here.

Also built in 1927, the *Hollywood Roosevelt* hotel (7000 Hollywood Blvd.; phone: 213-466-7000) was the site of the first Academy Awards presentation and a favorite gathering place for Hollywood royalty. Today, luxury and style are mostly absent, but in 1987, David Hockney painted a free-form artist's rendering in blue on the bottom of the pool. And the *Cinegrill* has gained a reputation as one of the hottest spots for jazz.

Now it's time for a treat. Stop into *C.C. Brown's* (7007 Hollywood Blvd.; phone: 213-462-9262), a turn-of-the-century ice-cream parlor. Originally opened downtown in 1906, it moved to this location in 1929. Indulge in one of the best hot-fudge sundaes you've ever had in this old-fashioned soda shop. (In the 1930s, Judy Garland waited on tables here.) Not too far away is the *Hollywood Galaxy* (7201 Hollywood Blvd.) — a high-tech, tri-level entertainment complex with a broad multileveled walkway circling a courtyard. It's fun just to walk around this 148,000-square-foot funhouse, take in a movie at the multiplex theater, enjoy ethnic food at the international food court, or simply shop in the many stores.

Westwood

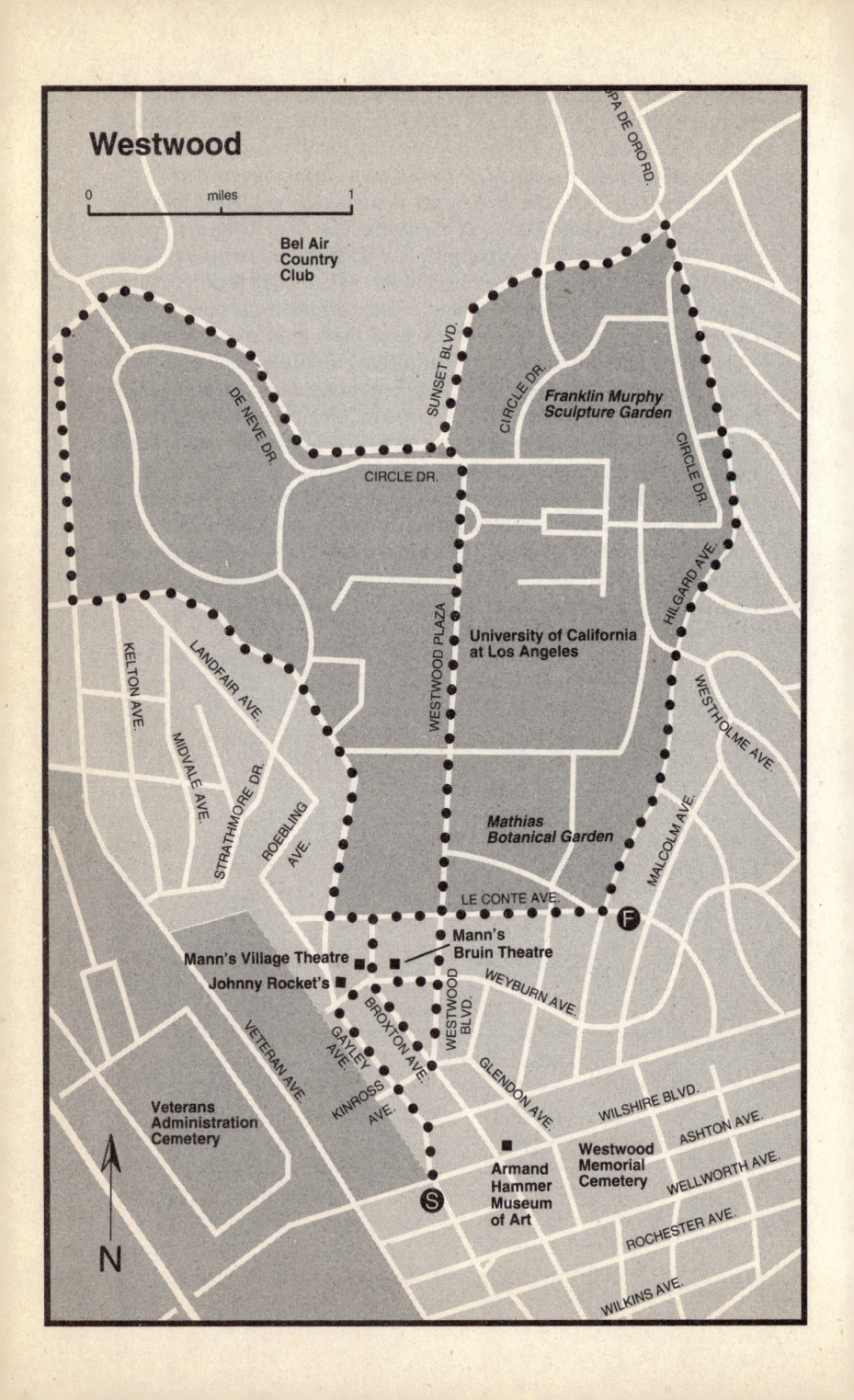

0 — miles — 1

- Bel Air Country Club
- PA DE ORO RD.
- DE NEVE DR.
- SUNSET BLVD.
- CIRCLE DR.
- Franklin Murphy Sculpture Garden
- CIRCLE DR.
- HILGARD AVE.
- WESTHOLME AVE.
- WESTWOOD PLAZA
- University of California at Los Angeles
- KELTON AVE.
- LANDFAIR AVE.
- MIDVALE AVE.
- STRATHMORE DR.
- ROEBLING AVE.
- Mathias Botanical Garden
- MALCOLM AVE.
- LE CONTE AVE.
- F
- Mann's Village Theatre
- Mann's Bruin Theatre
- Johnny Rocket's
- WEYBURN AVE.
- VETERAN AVE.
- GAYLEY AVE.
- BROXTON AVE.
- WESTWOOD BLVD.
- KINROSS AVE.
- GLENDON AVE.
- S
- Veterans Administration Cemetery
- Armand Hammer Museum of Art
- WILSHIRE BLVD.
- ASHTON AVE.
- Westwood Memorial Cemetery
- WELLWORTH AVE.
- ROCHESTER AVE.
- WILKINS AVE.

N

Tour 6: Westwood

The closest thing Los Angeles has to a college town, Westwood Village is an affluent, clean-cut version of New York City's Greenwich Village, bounded by the fashionable neighborhoods of Brentwood, Bel-Air, and Beverly Hills. Bustling with activity, it has nice movie theaters, appealing restaurants, lots of clothing stores catering to the college crowd, and the beautifully landscaped UCLA campus to explore.

Take the Santa Monica Freeway No. 10 west to the San Diego Freeway No. 405 north. Take the Wilshire Boulevard East exit. When you get off the freeway, continue east for a half mile and make a left (north) onto Gayley Ave. If this is your lucky day, you might find a parking spot. If not, there are parking lots all over the neighborhood ($4 to $6 for the day).

Developed in the 1920s as a Mediterranean-style shopping village, all the buildings — homes, shops, banks — in Westwood were to have a Spanish colonial look. Modern-day real-estate development has somewhat eroded the spirit of the place, but, happily, a few architectural reminders are still extant.

The heart of Westwood is between Wilshire Boulevard to the south (lined with skyscrapers and pricey high-rises), Le Conte Avenue to the north, Gayley Avenue to the west, and Westwood Boulevard to the east. It is fairly small and incredibly easy to get around. How you walk it is totally arbitrary (probably depending on where you find parking), but here's one way to get started.

From the corner of Wilshire Boulevard walk north on Gayley Avenue. Along the way you'll pass *Light & Healthy* (1115 Gayley Ave.; phone: 310-208-1767), a very inexpensive, but very good, sushi bar. Continue north on Gayley until you come to Weyburn Avenue. Turn right on Weyburn and stroll past the cafés and eateries such as *Johnny Rocket's* (10959 Weyburn Ave.; phone: 310-824-5656), the always-packed, 1950s diner famous for its burgers and shakes. If your thirst is more for knowledge, stop by *Alexandria II Bookstore* (10944 Weyburn Ave.; phone: 310-824-7575), an enchanting haunt for new age and metaphysical paraphernalia, books, and tapes.

Two of the most beautifully preserved movie theaters in Los Angeles are on the east and west corners of Weyburn and Broxton Avenues. *Mann's Village Theatre* (961 Broxton Ave.; phone: 310-208-5576), known as the "Fox," opened in 1931 as part of the Fox Studios' theater chain. Built in the Spanish colonial style of early Westwood, the theater's gleaming white tower still dominates the village. Its snazzy exterior and plush interior make it a popular choice for big Hollywood premieres. Across the street, on the eastern corner, is the less spectacular, but still striking, 1930s Moderne *Mann's Bruin Theatre* (948 Broxton Ave.; phone: 310-208-8998).

Walk west along Weyburn and turn right (south) down Broxton Avenue to *Stratton's Grill* (1037 Broxton Ave.; phone: 310-208-0488), one of Westwood's most popular watering holes. The outdoor plaza on the western side of the street at the end of Broxton Avenue is another big draw. Silver jewelry, leather goods, and a variety of offbeat knickknacks can be purchased from the street vendors.

Broxton ends at the intersection of Westwood Boulevard and Kinross Avenue. At the end of Broxton, note one of Westwood's first Spanish-style landmarks. This temple-like structure, built in 1929, now houses *Contempo Casuals* (1099 Westwood Blvd.), which carries a stylish collection of women's clothing. Turn left (north) up Westwood Boulevard. Mixed in among the very popular clothing store chains is *Butler/Gabriel Books* (919 Westwood Blvd.), one of LA's very best bookstores; also visit their *Sale Book Annex* (901 Westwood Blvd.) for a wonderful selection of offbeat tomes.

Make a left (west) at Le Conte Avenue. *Bonnie and Clyde* (10912 Le Conte Ave.) is a great little clothing shop with funky designs for men and women. Continue west on Le Conte for a block until you come to Broxton Avenue. Make a left (south) and stroll down the northern stretch of this shop-lined street until you come to Weyburn Avenue; make a left onto it. Wander into all the T-shirt shops and cafés. When you come to Westwood Boulevard, turn left (north) and follow it up into the UCLA campus. (Once you pass Le Conte Avenue, Westwood Boulevard becomes Westwood Plaza.)

On weekdays, don't even attempt to park at the UCLA campus — even students can't find a space here. Best bet is to park in Westwood and walk north up Westwood Boulevard to the campus. Or get on one of the free shuttle vans that stop at the parking lots in Westwood and go up to the campus. (For information on the shuttle, call 310-825-4321.) On-campus parking is possible on weekends; someone at the Visitors' Center or information booths can direct you.

Although quite beautiful, UCLA is a large and confusing campus. Begin by picking up a map at the Visitors' Center, in the Uberroth Building (phone: 310-206-8147). Even with a map, you might get all turned around, but this is an awfully pretty place in which to get lost.

UCLA moved to Westwood in 1929. Over the years, the beautifully landscaped, 411-acre campus has become a city within a city. Allow plenty of time to wander the shady, tree-lined walks and appreciate the views, grassy knolls, gardens, and architecture.

Generally, the landscaping is more impressive than the buildings, but the first four, built in 1929 around the original quadrangle, are stunning. Known as the Quad — Royce Hall, Haines Hall, Kinsey Hall, and Powell Library — are Italian Romanesque brick palazzi.

If you're dying for a UCLA sweatshirt — or haven't found a map yet — stop at the UCLA bookstore in the Ackerman Student Union by the

Bruin bear statue. There's also a cafeteria in the building with a full-menu selection at low prices.

Don't miss the Franklin Murphy Sculpture Garden at the northeast end of campus, where major works by Henry Moore, Joan Miró, Henri Matisse, Auguste Renoir, and others are displayed. This is a quiet spot to sit and contemplate the meaning of life — or just to decide where to have dinner.

The northwest part of campus is a lush green, hilly paradise, best explored on foot. Take your time and enjoy the pleasant views and wooded areas. Sunset Boulevard, lined with gorgeous estates, is the northern border of the campus.

Hilgard Avenue forms the eastern border and is lined with well-tended sorority houses from Le Conte Avenue up to about Westholme Ave. (James Dean, one of UCLA's most famous dropouts, lived in the Sigma Nu house at 601 Gayley Ave.) Stop at the Mathias Botanical Garden, a woodsy retreat with exotic plants, right off Hilgard in the southeast part of the campus. Afterward, walk north up Hilgard and admire the houses.

If you're interested in a walking tour of the campus, free tours are offered Mondays through Fridays at 10:30 AM and 1:30 PM. You need to make a reservation by calling 310-825-4321. Meet at the Morgan Center Hall of Fame in front of the Ackerman Student Union by the *Bruin* bear statue. Led by students, the 90-minute tours emphasize the history of UCLA and take visitors through its noteworthy buildings.

Before leaving Westwood, there are two other sites that might capture your fancy; the *Armand Hammer Museum of Art* (10899 Wilshire Blvd.), on the northeast corner of Westwood and Wilshire Boulevards, and the Westwood Memorial Park (1218 Glendon Ave.), where Marilyn Monroe, Natalie Wood, Armand Hammer, and other notables are buried (also see *Grave Matters* in DIVERSIONS).

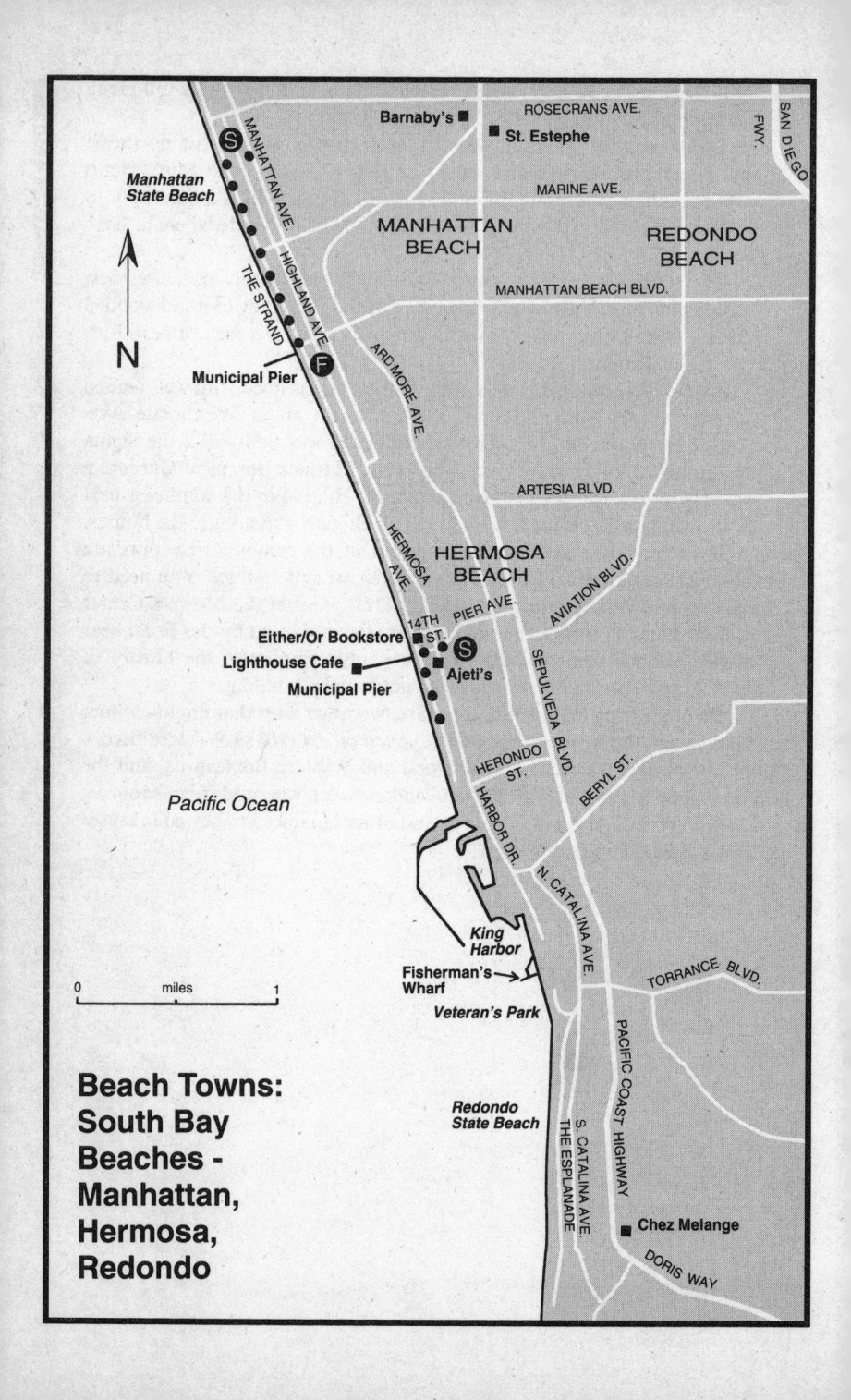

Beach Towns: South Bay Beaches - Manhattan, Hermosa, Redondo

Tour 7: Beach Towns: South Bay Beaches — Manhattan, Hermosa, Redondo

South of Venice, there is a trio of beach towns — Manhattan Beach, Hermosa Beach, and Redondo Beach — that epitomize the Southern California "life's a beach" lifestyle. Originally just summer resorts, these beachfront towns have become thriving, year-round communities.

In 1907, the owner of the *Redondo* hotel was looking for an advertising gimmick to attract guests and get visitors to buy homes in the area. While on vacation in Hawaii, he saw a surfer named George Freeth — half Hawaiian, half British — riding the waves. Back in California, with Freeth as his star attraction, he set up surfing exhibitions. Every Sunday, thousands flocked to the beach in front of the hotel to watch the new sport.

Over the years, the popularity of the area continued to grow. In the 1960s, a group of local blond-haired, blue-eyed surfers, who called themselves the *Beach Boys,* started singing and the rest, as they say, is history. If you hold a seashell to your ear, you can almost hear the strains of "Surfer Girl."

Although California has more spectacular beaches, these towns offer a special taste of beach life. Take the San Diego Freeway No. 405 south and exit on Rosecrans Avenue. Go west. In a few miles, Rosecrans ends at Highland Avenue in Manhattan Beach. Make a left (south) onto Highland Avenue and continue south. Park along the street.

Manhattan Beach is the trendiest of the beach towns — a yuppified, upscale community of commuters. Hermosa Beach is the quintessential laid-back beach town with run-down charm. Redondo Beach is more of a resort town, with big oceanfront hotels and restaurants. In each, the activity centers around the pier and in the shops and restaurants along the waterfront.

Manhattan Beach is the first town when traveling south from Los Angeles. A hotbed of funky chic, it's the place where arbitrageurs and the smart young producer set live before making the big step up to Malibu. The steep streets and pastel-colored bungalows are reminiscent of San Francisco (although these days, a lot of the bungalows are being torn down to make way for ultramodern glass and metal structures).

Walking along The Strand by the water in Manhattan Beach is a real treat; the magnificent homes (many costing upward of $3 million) are something out of the movies. The Municipal Pier is another good vantage point for gazing out to sea. Manhattan Avenue, 2 blocks up from The Strand, is a pretty street where the locals congregate at such trendy restaurants as *Sunsets* (117 Manhattan Beach Blvd.; phone: 310-545-2523), an ideal place to watch the day end. Or, if you prefer an Italian feast, try *Mangiamo* (128 Manhattan Beach Blvd.; phone: 310-536-0730) or *Lido Di Manhattan* (1550 Rosecrans Ave.; phone: 310-536-0730), two of the best restaurants in town, owned by Ron Guidone. Shop for beach gear in chic boutiques like *Pete's Place* (1100 Manhattan Ave.; phone: 310-372-0900), with its string bikinis and outrageous swimwear designs. And while you're at it, pick up some wild westernwear and accessories at *Howdy's* (1209 Highland; phone: 310-546-9989).

Start the day out right at *Bill's Pancake House* (1305 Highland Ave.; phone: 310-545-5177), where cheddar cheese–bacon waffles and Istanbul omelettes are the favorite of the day. But prepare to wait: This funky little place is the most popular spot around.

Farther inland near the *Manhattan Village Shopping Center,* on Sepulveda Boulevard between Rosecrans and Marine, is *Barnaby's* (3501 N. Sepulveda Blvd.; phone: 310-545-8466), a turn-of-the-century English hostelry that puts up guests in style. Or head over to the delightful *Manhattan Market Place* (1570 Rosecrans Ave.), where you can enjoy some of the best Chinese food this side of the Orient at *Monkee's* (phone: 310-643-6661). Also, be sure to stop in at *Bristol Farms,* stocked to the rafters with exotic foods, wines, cheeses, and other products.

Continue south from Manhattan to Hermosa Beach. This community is less affluent, and certainly less pretentious, than Manhattan Beach. There's a blue-collar feel about the place, but what Hermosa lacks in polish it makes up for in friendly, small-town atmosphere. The folks here are more concerned with welcoming visitors than impressing them.

There are several metered, municipal parking lots, so go armed with plenty of quarters; tourists are not exempt from parking fines. Hermosa features wonderful little eateries such as *Good Stuff* (at 13th St. and The Strand; phone: 310-374-2334), offering casual patio dining and healthy food; the *Bottle Inn* (26 22nd St.; phone: 310-376-9595), for solid Italian fare; and *Casablanca* (53 Pier Ave.; phone: 310-379-4177), one of the city's most romantic eateries, with cozy booths and lovely atmosphere.

In Hermosa, continue south on Hermosa Avenue until you come to 14th Street. You should have no trouble finding parking. The town is simple, shunning expensive boutiques and restaurants, and easy to get around. The shops cater to beachgoers and locals. As in Manhattan Beach, stroll along The Strand — there are a number of small restaurants and inexpensive shops in which to browse. Walk out on the pier and head up Pier Avenue for more activity.

The *Lighthouse Café* (30 Pier Ave.; phone: 310-376-98330) is a music club that's been going strong since the 1950s. Make a point of stopping in at the *Either/Or Bookstore* (124 Pier Ave.; phone: 310-374-2060), and if you're really adventuresome, have dinner at *Ajeti's* (425 Pier Ave.; phone: 310-379-9012), an authentic Albanian restaurant.

The third town south of LA is Redondo Beach. Although popular since the 1890s, this beach community has a newer feel than Hermosa and Manhattan; the large hotels and apartment buildings that line the coast make it more like a resort. Marinas dominate King Harbor — boats are everywhere, as are big-name restaurants and hotel chains. The area is family-oriented and caters to tourists in a big way.

When you enter Redondo Beach, Hermosa Avenue turns into Harbor Drive. Follow the signs to King Harbor. (There are several huge parking garages nearby.) Redondo Beach Marina, the International Boardwalk, and the pier (Fisherman's Wharf) are lined with seafood restaurants and souvenir shops — the restaurants stay open late on summer evenings. The charming *Portofino Inn* (260 Portofino Way; phone 310-379-8481) is a good bet for overnight accommodations.

Interesting dining choices include *Tony's on The Pier* (210 Fisherman's Wharf; phone: 310-374-9246), where the food is as good as the ocean view, or *Millie Riera's Seafood Grotto* (1700 Esplanade; phone: 310-375-0531). A throwback to the past with its retro-look, this is where locals and tourists alike flock to sample generous portions of home-style cooking (mostly seafood) and spectacular sunsets.

In Redondo, what was The Strand becomes The Esplanade. Go for a stroll, check out the beach activity, and enjoy great views of the ocean. Walk down to the water and kick off your shoes. For more browsing, wander over to Catalina Avenue. *Chez Mélange* (1716 Pacific Coast Hwy.; phone: 310-540-1222), one of the hottest restaurants in the South Bay area, has a vodka/champagne/caviar bar and a menu that ranges from Cajun to Oriental.

If you're interested in a good workout, an extremely popular bike path, the South Bay Bicycle Trail, runs along the water for 20 miles from the Santa Monica Pier all the way down through Manhattan, Hermosa, and Redondo to the city of Torrance. You can pick it up at any point, and it's a great way to experience these beach towns. Bike rental shops to try are *Fun Bunns* (1144 Highland Ave., Manhattan Beach; phone: 310-545-3300) and *Jeffers* (1338 The Strand, Hermosa Beach; phone: 310-372-9492).

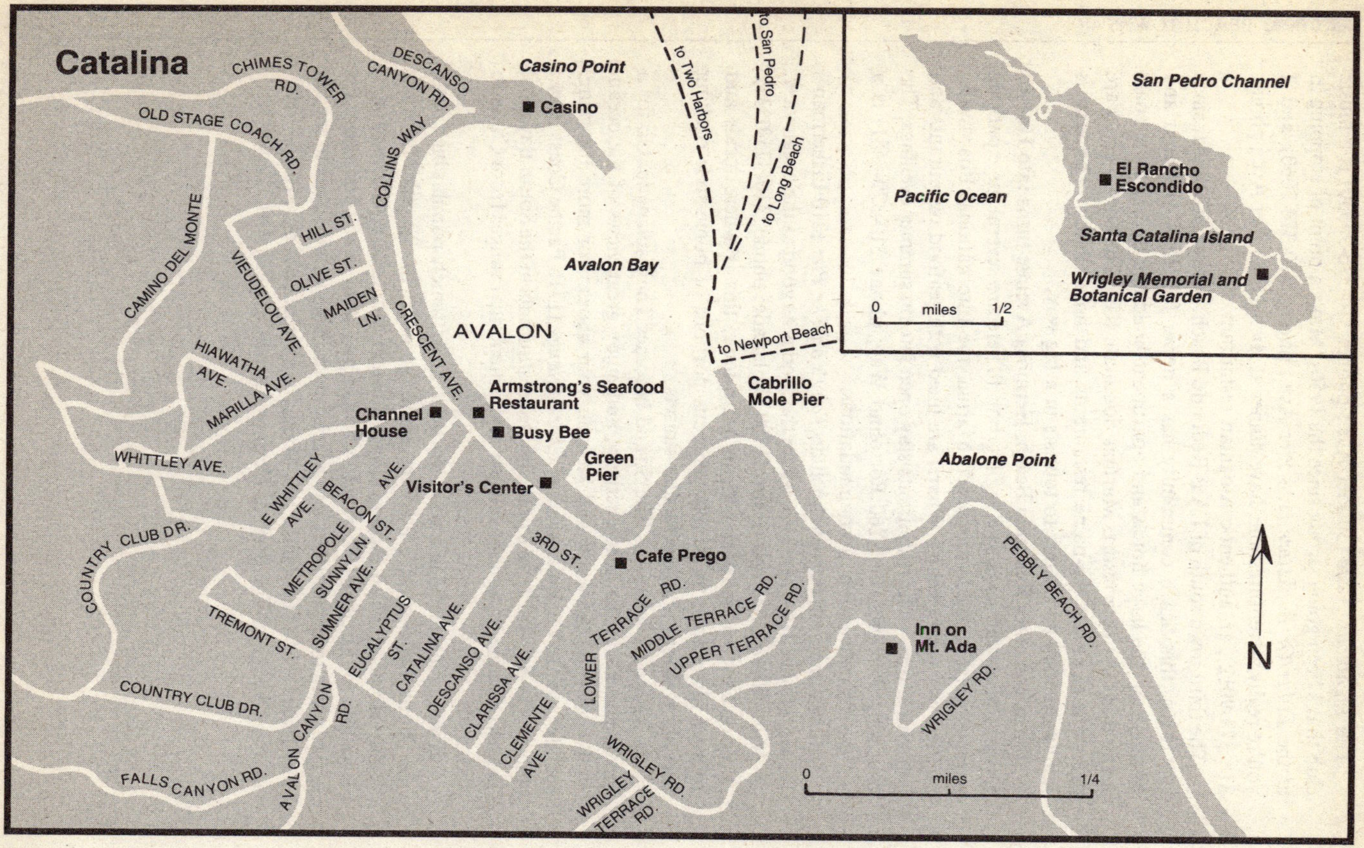
Catalina
Casino Point
Casino
Avalon Bay
AVALON
to Two Harbors
to San Pedro
to Long Beach
to Newport Beach
Cabrillo Mole Pier
Abalone Point
Armstrong's Seafood Restaurant
Channel House
Busy Bee
Green Pier
Visitor's Center
Cafe Prego
Inn on Mt. Ada
CHIMES TOWER RD.
DESCANSO CANYON RD.
OLD STAGE COACH RD.
COLLINS WAY
CAMINO DEL MONTE
HILL ST.
OLIVE ST.
MAIDEN LN.
VIEUDELOU AVE.
CRESCENT AVE.
HIAWATHA AVE.
MARILLA AVE.
WHITTLEY AVE.
E WHITTLEY AVE.
BEACON ST.
AVE.
METROPOLE
SUNNY LN.
SUMNER AVE.
COUNTRY CLUB DR.
TREMONT ST.
EUCALYPTUS ST.
CATALINA AVE.
DESCANSO AVE.
CLARISSA AVE.
CLEMENTE AVE.
3RD ST.
LOWER TERRACE RD.
MIDDLE TERRACE RD.
UPPER TERRACE RD.
COUNTRY CLUB DR.
AVALON CANYON RD.
FALLS CANYON RD.
WRIGLEY RD.
WRIGLEY TERRACE RD.
WRIGLEY RD.
PEBBLY BEACH RD.
0 miles 1/4
N
San Pedro Channel
Pacific Ocean
El Rancho Escondido
Santa Catalina Island
Wrigley Memorial and Botanical Garden
0 miles 1/2

Tour 8: Catalina

To experience what California was like before the freeways, land booms, overbuilding, and smog, take a slow boat to Santa Catalina Island — referred to by one and all as Catalina. Don't be surprised when the ferry captain calls out, "We're docking in the town of Avalon, on the island of Catalina. Passengers are advised to set their watches back 50 years."

Indeed, Catalina Island, 22 miles from Los Angeles Harbor across the San Pedro Channel, is what the whole California coast once was like. The sleepy little town of Avalon is a charming, old-fashioned beach community, and the rest of the island is wilderness. Wild goats, boars, and a herd of bison (left by the film crew of *The Vanishing American* in 1924) roam free.

You can make this trip back in time by boat, helicopter, or small plane (for further information, see below). Flying is faster, but arriving by boat is part of the charm. As you dock, the ocean fog lifts, revealing the picturesque harbor of Avalon Bay and the mountain peaks rising in the distance. Come for the day or stay awhile at one of the many lovely little hotels. There also are camping grounds for outdoors enthusiasts. Summertime is the high season here. Spring and fall actually are nicer and the hotel rates are lower, but many of the shops and restaurants close.

Today, the Santa Catalina Island Conservancy — a nonprofit foundation — has title to 86% of this 28-mile-long by 8-mile-wide island; its goal is to preserve its natural resourses. Until 1975, Catalina Island was the domain of the Wrigley Family — the chewing-gum tycoons and owners of the Chicago *Cubs*. In 1919, William Wrigley, Jr. purchased this piece of paradise for use as a combination tourist attraction, private estate, and spring training camp for the *Cubs*.

The town of Avalon already was there, built in the late 19th century by developer George Shatto. But it was Wrigley, Jr. who turned the village into a major tourist destination, building a wonderful casino at the end of the harbor.

The *Casino* (end of Cresent Ave.; phone: 310-510-2000), an eccentric bit of Spanish Moderne architecture, is really a combination 1,000-seat movie theater and 20,000-square-foot grand ballroom (boasting what is supposedly the largest circular dance floor in the world). During the 1930s, all the famous big bands played the *Casino Ballroom* — Glenn Miller, Benny Goodman, Tommy Dorsey — and all of Los Angeles dreamed of spending a weekend on Catalina Island. Today, you can still dance to big-band music on weekends, see first-run movies, and go on a guided tour of this fabulous place.

The ferry boats to Catalina disembark at Cabrillo Mole Pier. Everything is within easy walking distance, but most of the activity is centered on Crescent Avenue. Walk up Pebbly Beach Road to Crescent Avenue (Avalon's main drag) and stop at the Visitors' Center (phone: 310-510-2000) on the corner of Crescent and Catalina Avenues, across from Green Pier (it's easy to find; the boat's crew can direct you). Pick up a map and other useful information. Rental cars are not allowed on the island, so if you're not in the mood to walk, find out about golf cart and bicycle rental. The tourist office also has lots of information on organized tours.

From the moment you set foot in Avalon, you'll be caught up in the spirit of the place. The town, a delightful mix of Mediterranean and Victorian architecture, is small enough to find your way around easily. It takes about a half hour to walk from Cabrillo Mole to the other end of Crescent Avenue where the casino is. It's flat most of the way, although the side streets off Crescent Avenue are fairly steep. Along the waterfront, there are plenty of stores, food stands, restaurants, and curio shops to keep you busy.

There are many other things to do on a trip to Catalina besides strolling through Avalon. Visit the Wrigley Memorial and Botanical Garden (1400 Avalon Canyon Rd.; phone: 310-510-2288), go for a ride on a glass-bottom boat (the waters around Catalina are known for exquisite marine life), take a tour around the island to see the wildlife and the Arabian stallions at the Wrigley family's El Rancho Escondido on the west side of the island, or rent a golf cart and tootle around on your own.

If all that fresh air is making you hungry, the first restaurant you'll spot in Avalon is *Café Prego* (603 Crescent Ave.; phone: 310-510-1218); serving dinner only, it offers Old World charm with good pasta and fish dishes. Another good choice is *Armstrong's Seafood* restaurant (306-A Crescent Ave.; phone: 310-510-0113). Since this also is a fish market, you can be sure the seafood is fresh — mesquite-grilled dishes are their specialty. Right next door is the *Busy Bee* (306-B Crescent Ave.; phone: 310-510-1983); this popular local hangout is one of the few places open for breakfast, lunch, and dinner. Enjoy tasty salads, sandwiches, burgers, vegetable platters — and a great view. Both *Pirrone's* (417 Crescent Ave.; phone: 310-510-0333) and the *Channel House* (205 Crescent Ave.; phone: 310-510-1617) have good food and great harbor views. For a quick snack, try a delicious abalone burger from one of the food stands out on the pier.

Chances are you'll want to stay on Catalina for more than a day. There are a number of good hotels from which to choose. The gorgeous *Inn on Mt. Ada* (398 Wrigley Rd.; phone: 310-510-2030), built in 1921, is the former Wrigley mansion. There are 6 lavish rooms with spectacular views. The venerable *Zane Grey* hotel (199 Chimes Tower Rd.; phone: 310-510-0966) was originally built in 1926 as a summer home for the novelist. This 18-room Hopi-style pueblo sits high on a bluff above the harbor. (Even if you're just here on a day trip, these two places are worth checking out.)

Down on Crescent Avenue, the *Vista del Mar* hotel (417 Crescent Ave.; phone: 310-510-1452) is right in the center of town. There are 14 Mediterranean-style rooms with fireplaces. The 72-room *Pavilion Lodge* (513 Crescent Ave.; phone: 310-510-1788) also is in the heart of town. The *Catalina* hotel (129 Whittley Ave.; phone: 310-510-0027) is a renovated Victorian era building; built in 1892, the 32-unit facility offers rooms and cottages. And stop in at the *Chi-Chi Club* (107 Sumner Ave.; phone: 310-510-2828), where performances of jazz and bluegrass will liven up your evening.

GETTING TO AND AROUND CATALINA

BY BOAT This is the most popular and least expensive way to go. Boats leave from the Catalina Island Terminal at Long Beach Harbor and San Pedro Harbor. Reservations are advised. Arrive early, especially during the summer season. *Catalina Cruises* (phone: 800-888-5939) take about 2 hours. The boats are big (accommodating several hundred passengers) and comfortable, and serve snacks on board ($28 round trip). *Catalina Express*'s (phone: 310-519-1212) airline-style 60-seaters make the trip in 90 minutes. It's a faster but, some say, less enjoyable trip ($31 round trip).

BY AIR The helicopter ride from the Catalina Island Terminal at Long Beach or San Pedro takes about 15 minutes to the Pebbly Beach heliport. There also are several other departure points, so call for directions. Reservations must be made a week in advance. *Helitrans* (phone: 310-548-1314 or 800-262-1472) charges $100 round trip; $150 from LAX Airport. *Island Express* (phone: 310-491-5550) charges $100.

Santa Catalina Island Company (phone: 310-510-2000) and *Catalina Adventure Tours* (phone: 310-510-0409) also offer tours of the island. Book tours at the boat terminal ticket booths in Long Beach or San Pedro or at the Visitors' Center when you arrive on Catalina.

Index

ABC-TV, 99
Accommodations
  bed and breakfast, 60–61
  hotels, 40, 60–71
  on the Queen Mary, 38
  Relais & Châteaux, 62–63
  Santa Barbara, 40, 62–63
African Marketplace & Cultural Fair, 44
Ahmanson Theater, 35, 96, 124
Airplane travel, 9–12
  charter flights, 10
  consumer protection, 12
  discounts on scheduled flights, 10–12
    bartered travel sources, 12
    consolidators and bucket shops, 11
    courier travel, 10–11
    generic air travel, 12
    last-minute travel clubs, 11–12
  insurance, 15
  scheduled flights, 9–10
    baggage, 10
    fares, 9
    reservations, 9
    seating, 9
    smoking, 9
    special meals, 10

transportation from the airport to the city, 12
Armand Hammer Museum of Art, 45, 147
Audience participation shows (television stations), 98–100
Automated teller machines (ATMs), 20
Automobiles. *See* Car, traveling by

Banking hours. *See* Business hours
Baseball, 55
Basketball, 55
Beaches, 93–94, 95–96, 107–9, 113, 148–51
Beach towns (Manhattan, Hermosa, Redondo)
  map, 148
  walking tour, 149–51
Bed and breakfast establishments. *See* Accommodations
Beverly Hills, 33–34
  maps, 2, 136
  walking tour, 135–39
Bicycling, 55
Burke Williams Day Spa & Massage Centre (Santa Monica), 105
Bus, traveling by, 12, 41–42, 124
Business hours, 21

Cabrillo Beach, 108–9
Car, traveling by
   insurance, 13, 15
   maps, 41
   renting a car, 12–13
Cash machines. *See* Automated teller machines (ATMs)
Catalina Island, 38
   map, 152
   transportation to and around, 155
   walking tour, 153–55
CBS-TV, 99, 131
Cemeteries, 38, 102–4, 147
Charter flights, 10
Chinatown, 35, 121–22
Cinco de Mayo (festival), 43
City Hall Tower, 30, 34, 123
Climate, 9
Colleges and universities, 48, 146–47
Consumer protection, 12
Credit cards, 20
   telephone calls with, 21–22
Cruises. *See* Ship, traveling by

Disabled travelers, 15–18
Discounts on scheduled flights, 10–12
Disneyland, 29, 39, 91–92
Donut Hole, 101
Doolittle Theatre, 58
Dorothy Chandler Pavilion, 35, 58, 124
Downtown Los Angeles
   maps, 3, 120
   places of special interest, 34–36
   walking tour, 119–24
Driving. *See* Car, traveling by

El Capitan Theatre, 142
El Pueblo de Los Angeles, 113, 119–21

Emergencies
   medical assistance, 22
   telephone number, 22
Exotic Feline Breeding Compound, 101

Fairfax Avenue
   map, 132
   walking tour, 131–34
Family Feud, 100
Farmers' Market, 36, 92
   map, 132
   walking tour, 131–34
Ferries. *See* Ship, traveling by
Festival of the Arts and Pageant of the Masters, 44
Finley & Gibbons Fashion Flowers, 101
Fishing, 55–56
Fitness centers, 56
Fletcher Bowron Square, 124
Football, 28–29, 56
Forest Lawn Hollywood Hills, 103–4
Forest Lawn Memorial Park, 38, 103
FOX-TV, 99

Game shows, participating in, 100
Gene Autry Western Heritage Museum, 45–46
George C. Page Museum of La Brea Discoveries, 36–37
Glen Ivy Hot Springs (Corona), 105–6
Golf, 56, 110
Gower Street, 31–32
Graumann's Chinese Theatre. *See* Mann's Chinese Theatre
Greek Theatre, 59, 96
Greystone Park, 139
Griffith Park, 37

Handicapped travelers. *See* Disabled travelers
Health care
  emergency number for medical assistance, 22
  hospitals and pharmacies, 22
  insurance, 15
Hermosa Beach, 150–51
Hiking, 94–95
Hillside Memorial Park, 104
Hockey, 56
Holidays. *See* Special events
Hollywood
  maps, 2, 140
  places of special interest, 30–34
  walking tour, 141–43
Hollywood Bowl, 35, 59, 96–97
Hollywood Memorial Park, 103
Hollywood Movie Costume Museum, 46
Hollywood Studio Museum, 31
Hollywood Wax Museum, 30–31
Holy Cross Cemetery, 104
Horse racing, 56–57
Hospitals. *See* Health care
Hotels. *See* Accommodations

Insurance, 13, 15
International Festival of Masks, 45
International Surf Festival, 44

J. Paul Getty Museum, 38
Japanese American National Museum, 46, 123
Jeopardy, 100
Joffrey Ballet, 124
Jogging, 57

Knott's Berry Farm, 29, 39–40

La Brea Tar Pits, 36–37

La Costa (Carlsbad), 105
Laguna Beach, 109
Legal aid, 23
Leo Carillo State Beach, 108
Little Tokyo, 35, 122–23
Local services, 42–43
Local transportation. *See* Transportation
Long Beach, 109
Los Angeles Bach Festival, 45
Los Angeles Children's Museum, 46, 123, 124
Los Angeles Civic Center and Mall, 34
Los Angeles County Fair, 44–45
Los Angeles Master Chorale, 35
Los Angeles Museum of Art, 36–37
Los Angeles Opera Company, 35, 124
Los Angeles Philharmonic, 35, 59, 124
Los Angeles Times Building, 123
Lotus Festival, 44

Mail, 21
Malibu Beach, 95–96, 108
Malibu Creek State Park, hiking in, 94–95
Malls, 92
Manhattan Beach, 149–50
Mann's Chinese Theatre (Graumann's), 29, 30, 142–43
Maps
  in this guide
    beach towns (Manhattan, Hermosa, and Redondo), 148
    Beverly Hills, 2, 136
    Catalina Island, 152
    downtown Los Angeles, 3, 120

Maps (*cont.*)
    Fairfax Avenue/Farmers' Market, 132
    Hollywood, 2, 140
    Los Angeles, 2–3
    Melrose Avenue, 126
    Westwood, 144
   sources for, 41
Marina del Rey, 109
Marineland, 29
Mark Taper Forum, 35, 58, 97, 124
Marriott's Desert Springs (Palm Desert), 106
Max Factor Beauty Museum, 32
Medical assistance. *See* Health care
Medieval Times, 39
Melrose Avenue, 93
   map, 126
   shopping, 51, 93, 125–30
   walking tour, 125–30
Monarch Beach, 110
Money
   sending, 20
   See also Automated teller machines (ATMs); Credit cards; Traveler's checks
Montana Avenue, shopping, 51–52
Moreno Valley Ranch, 110
Mt. Olympus (in Laurel Canyon), 30
Movieland, 29
Movieland Wax Museum, 39
Mulholland Drive, 30
Museum of Contemporary Art (MOCA), 35–36, 123
Museum of Flying, 46
Museum of Neon Art, 46
Museum of Science and Industry, 46
Museums, 45–48. *See also specific museums*
Music, 58–59, 96–98
Music Center, 29, 35, 58–59, 124

Natural History Museum, 46–47
NBC-TV, 99
Newport Beach, 109–10
Nightclubs and nightlife, 59–60, 97–98
Nisei Japanese Festival, 44
Norton Simon Museum of Art, 47

The Oaks at Ojai (Ojai), 106
Odyssey Theatre Ensemble, 58
Ojai Valley Country Club, 110
Older travelers, 19–20
Olvera Street, 34, 119–21
Orange County, places of special interest, 39–40

Pacific Coastal Highway (to Santa Barbara), 40
Package tours, 13–15
   for disabled travelers, 17–18
   for older travelers, 19–20
   for single travelers, 18–19
Palace, 59
Palace Court, 59
Palomino Club, 59, 97
Pantages Theatre, 58, 142
Paradise Cove, 108
Paramount Pictures, 31, 127
Pasadena Playhouse, 58, 97
Petite Elite Miniature Museum & Gallery, 101
Pharmacies. *See* Health care
Photo Express, 100–101
Photographing Los Angeles, 110–14
Plane, traveling by. *See* Airplane travel
Plaza, the, 34, 119–21
Polo, 57
Ports o' Call Village, 37

Queen Mary, 38

Radio, 41
Redondo Beach, 37–38, 149, 151
Redondo Beach Marina, 37–38
Renting a car, 12–13
Restaurants, 71–88, 93
   afternoon tea, 87–88
   Santa Barbara, 40, 62–63
Richard Nixon Library & Birthplace, 47
Robert H. Meyer Memorial State Beaches, 108
Rodeo Drive, 137
   shopping, 48–50, 137
Rose Bowl, 28, 56
Roxy (night club/music hall), 59, 97–98
Roy Rogers & Dale Evans Museum, 47

Sailing, 109–10
Santa Barbara, 40, 62–63
Sending money, 20
Senior citizens. *See* Older travelers
Ship, traveling by
   Catalina Island, 38
   cruise lines, 37, 38
   day cruises, 109–10, 155
   ferry companies, 155
Shopping, 48–55, 101
   an afternoon at the mall, 92
   discount stores, 52–55
   Farmers' Market, 36, 92, 131–34
   Melrose Avenue, 51, 93, 125–30
   Montana Avenue, 51–52
   Rodeo Drive, 48–50, 137
   Universal CityWalk, 33
   vintage, 55
   West Third Street, 51
Shubert Theatre, 58, 98
Silent Movie, 102
Simon Weisenthal Center Beit Hashoah Museum of Tolerance, 47
Single travelers, 18–19
Six Flags Magic Mountain, 37
Soccer, 58
South Bay beaches
   map, 148
   walking tour, 149–51
Southwest Museum, 47–48
Spago, dining at, 93
Spas, 104–7
Special events, 43–45
Special-interest packages. *See* Package tours
Sports and fitness, 55–58, 107–10. *See also specific sports*
Sport Walk of Fame, 101–2
Strawberry Festival, 43–44
Subway, 42
Surfing, 57
Swimming, 57

Tax, sales, 41
Taxis, 42
Telephone, 21–22, 41
Television, 41
   audience participation shows, 98–99
   game shows, 100
Temperature. *See* Climate
Temporary Contemporary Art Museum, 35, 36, 123
Tennis, 57
Theaters, 35, 58, 96–98, 124
Third and Broadway, 34–35
Time zone, 20
Tourist information, 23, 29, 40–41
Tournament of Roses. *See* Rose Bowl
Tours
   day cruises, 37, 38, 109, 155

Tours (*cont.*)
  guided, 14–15, 42, 104, 121, 123, 141
  helicopter, 37, 155
  walking, 117–55
    beach towns (Manhattan, Hermosa, Redondo), 149–51
    Beverly Hills, 135–39
    Catalina Island, 153–55
    downtown Los Angeles, 119–24
    Fairfax/Farmers' Market, 131–34
    Hollywood, 141–43
    Melrose Avenue, 125–30
    Westwood, 145–47
  See also Package tours; *names of individual tours*
Train, traveling by, 29
Transportation
  from the airport to the city, 12
  getting to and around Catalina, 155
  local, 12, 29, 41–42
  See also Airplane travel; Bus, traveling by; Car, traveling by
Traveler's checks, 20
Two Bunch Palms (Desert Hot Springs), 107

Universal Amphitheatre, 59, 98
Universal CityWalk, 33
Universal Studios Hollywood, 29, 32–33

Venice Beach, 93–94, 113
Virginia Robinson Gardens, 139
Volleyball, 57–58

Walking tours. *See* Tours; *names of individual tours*
Walt Disney Concert Hall, 35
Warner Brothers Studios, 32, 33
Weather. *See* Climate
West Third Street, shopping, 51
Westwood
  map, 144
  walking tour, 145–47
Westwood Memorial Park, 102, 147
Westwood Playhouse, 98
Whales watching, 94, 114
Wheeler Hot Springs (Ojai), 107
Wheel of Fortune, 100
Will Rogers Memorial Park, 139
Will Rogers State Beach, 108
Wiltern Theatre, 98